THE GUINNESS BOOK OF

SPEED

FACTS & FEATS

Bill Gunston, David Taylor & Andy Ewart

The late Andy Ewart made a major contribution in the planning of this book but unfortunately did not live to see it in print.

Editor: Beatrice Frei
Design and layout: David Roberts
First published in 1984

© **Bill Gunston, David Taylor & Andy Ewart
and Guinness Superlatives Ltd, 1984**

Published in Great Britain by Guinness Superlatives Ltd,
2 Cecil Court, London Road, Enfield, Middlesex

Typeset in 10/11pt Garamond and 9/10pt Rockwell
Typeset, printed and bound in Great Britain by
Redwood Burn Limited, Trowbridge, Wiltshire.

'Guinness' is a registered trade mark of
Guinness Superlatives Ltd

British Library Cataloguing in Publication Data

Gunston, Bill
    The Guiness book of speed facts and feats.
    1. Speed records
    I. Title   II. Taylor, David, *19— –*
    III. Ewart, Andy
    032'.02   GV1019

ISBN 0–85112–267–1

Title page illustration: Apollo spacecraft (NASA)—see pages
154/55, and Jeff Thomson (Syndication International).

CONTENTS

PART 1   THE LIVING WORLD

PART 2   THE TECHNICAL WORLD

INTRODUCTION

Those familiar with the extremely successful Facts and Feats series of books may wonder why this particular title has taken so long to appear. The answer lies in the sheer breadth of the subject. By comparison, the companion volumes on such topics as cars, animals, railways, soccer and the weather seem relatively easy to handle.

The publisher spent years looking for an author. Eventually they agreed that it was a two-man job, one author handling the speeds associated with living things and sport, and the other those associated with vehicles, technology and science. Even then one half had to be again subdivided, because those readers having a general interest in speed might find it hard to understand numerical speed of a tennis ball, the wing beat frequency of a humming-bird, or the problems of winning a relay race—all of which come in that half of the book.

Many who pick up this book will already have other titles in this series, and at least one copy of the *Guinness Book of Records*. The one thing we did not wish to do was merely get out scissors and paste and compile all the 'speed' information we could find in such existing sources. Indeed, at the start it took quite a while sorting out just what is meant by the word itself.

In the strictest sense a speed is a velocity, a rate of travel of a point in a particular vector direction. Such a definition is far removed from Vincent Pilkington's record of killing and plucking 100 turkeys in 7 h 32 min. Yet Mr Pilkington is surely a holder of a speed record.

Speed is relative. A car travelling at 48 km/h (30 miles per hour) would not be thought very fast. A human being capable of this speed would be unique.

We can define speed as the rate at which it takes a human being or an animal to perform a particular action, the rate being measured by seconds, minutes, hours, a year, or—at the outside—a whole lifetime.

But there is no constant scale. For example, just look at the sort of feats that can be performed in a second:

The best sprinters can cover 10 m in one second, while in the same time Concorde travels some 600 m or 655 yards. A cheetah covers 30 m (100 ft) a second at top speed—just under Britain's motorway speed limit. But this book also includes an object seen from Earth which each second appears to move 2 398 000 km!

Obviously the amount of information that could reasonably be included is limitless. Moreover, the publisher wished to provide more than bare lists of figures, and to flesh out the statistics with background information. How long does a sprinter take to reach maximum speed? If he averages a higher speed over 100 m than over 200 m (as some do), would he go even faster over 50 m? (The answer is likely to be no.)

The authors would welcome comments from readers, on both the numerical information and the items selected for inclusion. They regret their inability to say whether by the year 2100 there will be a 3-minute mile, or whether anything can travel faster than light.

Units

Throughout this book, SI (Système International d'Unités) abbreviations and units have been used.

Thus, lengths are expressed mainly in m (metres) and multiples thereof, though Imperial figures appear in brackets. Times are given in years, months and days (not abbreviated), h (hours), min (minutes) and s (seconds). Shorter times are given in subdivisions of a second with the s prefaced by m (milli, one-thousandth), micro (one millionth), n or nano (one billionth, in all cases using the US interpretation meaning 10^{-9}), p (pico, 10^{-12}), f (femto, 10^{-15}) and a (atto, 10^{-18}). Likewise, large distances are expressed in the familiar km or in lightyears. Many other units are prefaced by M (mega, one million times), G (giga, x 10^9) or T (tera, x 10^{12}). Frequencies, whether of a bird's wing beats or the oscillations of an atom, are given in Hz (one Hertz is one complete cycle per second); thus 1 GHz is one thousand million cycles per second. Velocities are given in ft/s, m/s, mph, km/h, knots (for ships), Mach numbers (for aircraft) and as decimal fractions of c (the speed of light).

PART 1
THE LIVING WORLD
by David Taylor

HUMAN SPEED

Growth in the human being proceeds from conception onwards. Technically, the human body never ceases to grow. Until death (and in the case of hair growth, beyond) each cell is constantly renewing itself. Obviously, the fastest rates of growth occur in the early years of life. The head, for instance, grows rapidly during infancy, achieving a maximum growth some time in early adolescence. However, increases in body weight may take place at any time.

Robert Wadlow, the world's tallest ever human at 272 cm (8 ft 11.1 in). (Alton Telegraph, USA)

Overleaf:
Ostriches playing a speedy game of follow-my-leader on the Etosha Pan, Namibia. (Ardea London Ltd)

Infant development

The rate of development in the human baby varies considerably. Height and weight increase occurs, but the most noticeable rate is that of cognitive and locomotive development. Most children are able to stand at the age of 1 year, but Dr Spock (1959) records an ambitious infant who did so at the age of 7 months. Similarly, most babies are able to walk by the age of 12–15 months. The record—adduced by Spock—is 9 months.

The greatest rate of infant development ever recorded must be that sustained by James Weir (1819–21). According to his tombstone in the old parish cemetery, Wishaw, Strathclyde, Scotland he weighed 50.8 kg (8 stone), had attained a height of 1.01 m (3 ft 4 in) and was 99 cm (39 in) in girth at the age of 13 months.

On average a child enters accelerated growth just before pubescence. The fastest increase in height is at about 11 years 6 months for girls and approximately 14–15 according to varying estimates for boys. Larger children tend to enter the period of rapid growth earlier and the range of differences among individuals at a given age increases until the average ages are reached. Subsequently it decreases until the slower children catch up. These statistics confirm a common assumption: that girls grow faster, and are notably taller and more mature, than boys at this stage.

Abnormally fast growth rates, either in weight or height, are frequently the results of illness. The commonest form of gigantism (generally defined as the attainment of a height in excess of 200 cm (6 ft 5 in)), is brought about by hyper-activity of the pituitary gland, frequently as a result of a benign tumour of the pituitary. Because of such glandular activity in adolescents, longitudinal bone growth may continue long after the usual time of cessation. The pre-acromegalic giant Robert Pershing Wadlow (1918–40) only began to grow at a rapid rate after a double hernia operation at the age of two: he had been a relatively normal baby. Similarly, vast increases in weight have often been reported in persons suffering from the rare disease bulimia, defined medically as a morbid desire to eat.

Some idea of the abnormally fast rate at which

Robert Wadlow was growing can be gained from the following table:

AGE IN YEARS	HEIGHT		
	cm	ft	in
22	272	8	11
21	265	8	8.75
20	261	8	6.75
19	258	8	5.5
18	253	8	3.5
17	245	8	0.5
16	240	7	10.5
15	234	7	8
14	226	7	5
13	218	7	1.75
12	210	6	10.5
11	200	6	7
10	196	6	5
9	189	6	2.5
8	183	6	0
5	163	5	4

Curiously, Wadlow's *rate* of growth was in no way erratic and in fact considerably under the records (as much as 13 cm (5 in)) claimed by adolescents in a single year. He merely grew at a sustained rate, both as a young child and after the time in which adolescent growth usually ceases. Even more curious, he was still growing at a strong rate during his terminal illness: a time when cellular activity normally declines.

Another astonishing rate of growth was that undergone by Adam Rainer, born in Graz, Austria in 1899. At the age of 21 he measured only 118 cm (3 ft 10 in). Yet by 1931 he had reached a height of 218 cm (7 ft 1.75 in)—the only person in medical history classifiable both as a dwarf and a giant.

It is noticeable that individuals experiencing record 'speed growth' rates are rarely long-lived. Research has established that the ageing rate is, as a rule, directly proportionate to the maturation rate ie, the sooner one's cells cease to multiply the faster they get old. The maximum duration of life is approximately five times the period taken to achieve full height and body weight.

Similar findings emerge from studies of the nutritional relation between the rate of growth and the rate of ageing. An experiment was conducted in which one half of a colony of rats was richly-fed and the other half either underfed or starved. The maximum duration of life among the rapidly-maturing (ie well-fed) rats was 896 days and in slowly-maturing (ie inadequately fed) rats 1320.

These statistics may alarm mothers convinced of the wisdom of producing 'bouncing babies'. However, this does not mean that we should starve our children: it is merely a reminder that overfeeding (and by implication all forms of 'speed growth') does not tend to promote longevity.

The fastest speed achieved by any part of the internal mechanism of the body not surprisingly involves the nervous system. The results of experiments published in 1966 demonstrated that the fastest messages transmitted by the human nervous system travel at a rate of 290 km/h (180 mph). This, however, is by no means a constant rate. In one's declining years, impulses are carried up to 15 per cent more slowly.

In precise terms, this means that a nerve impulse takes only 0.001 s to cross a synapse—approximately the time taken for a soap bubble to explode.

Fastest weight loss

William J. Cobb (b 1926), a professional wrestler from Macon, Georgia, between 1962–65 reduced his body weight from 346 kg (57 st 4 lb) to 105 kg (16 st 8 lb) in 3 years. Unfortunately, by October 1973 he had regained his former weight.

Paul M. Limmelman of Pittsburgh, Pennsylvania, between 25 December 1966 and August 1967 reduced from 215.9 kg (34 st 11 lb) to 58.9 kg (9 st 4 lb)—a loss of 156.9 kg (25 st 7 lb) in only 8 months, ie at an average rate of 1.8 kg (4 lb) a day.

Professional boxers, compelled to achieve minimum weights for the purposes of competition, have been known to shed several pounds in 24 h.

It should be stressed that this type of speed slimming is, medically speaking, extremely inadvisable. The human system is notoriously reluctant to cope with any sustained weight loss. Similar speed-dieting is common in the racing world. At least one jockey is known to have died as the result of slimming excesses.

Fastest weight gain

Unnatural weight gain, as we have remarked, is often the result of illness. The probable record is held by Arthur Knorr (b 1914) who died in Reseda, California, on 7 July 1960. During the last 6 months of his life he gained 136 kg (21 st 6 lb), achieving a total weight of 408 kg (64 st 4 lb).

Miss Doris James of San Francisco, California is said to have gained 147 kg (23 st 3 lb) in the 12 months before her death in August 1965, when she weighed 306 kg (48 st).

Sex

A great deal of prurient research has gone into establishing a fastest time for the completion of the human sex act. Predictably, sexologists have failed to come up with any reliable figures, although it appears that human beings are poor performers when compared to other mammals. Bulls, rams and stags, it emerges, engage in congress for no more than a few seconds, although the record (possibly 3 s) appears to be held by the chimpanzee.

Many other alleged 'records' exist, though of doubtful veracity and debatable taste.

Fastest accumulation of descendants

Several instances are recorded of matriarchs accumulating six generations of descendants before the age of 90. Mrs Ann V. Weirich (1888–1978) of Paxtonville, Pennsylvania, received news of her great-great-great grandson at the comparatively youthful age of 88.

Theoretically, a great-great-great-great grandchild remains a possibility, although countries in which an early age for motherhood is traditional are usually also noted for their low life expectancy.

Body movements

Pulse-rate
The human heart generally beats at around 70–72 beats/min, though this can rise to 120 (when engaged in sexual activity) or 150 plus when engaged in violent sporting activity eg squash, so much so that the game is often forbidden by doctors to the middle aged. Such a rate can only be maintained for relatively brief periods of time. Boys running on a treadmill at an English prison early in the present century experienced a pulse rate of 208 beats/min. This appears to be the absolute record.

General movement of body parts

Generally speaking, the human body is not noted for the speedy movement of its external limbs. A sprinter, running at top speed, can only make contact with the ground approximately 40 times in the course of a 100-m race.

The heart is by no means the fastest muscular rhythm the human body can achieve. Finger-tapping can be faster but only for a limited time. It is possible to accomplish 100 'taps' in 15 s, but after this the rate slows drastically. The same is true of blinking. With difficulty a rate of 70 'blinks' can be achieved per 15 s. However, this is impossible to maintain.

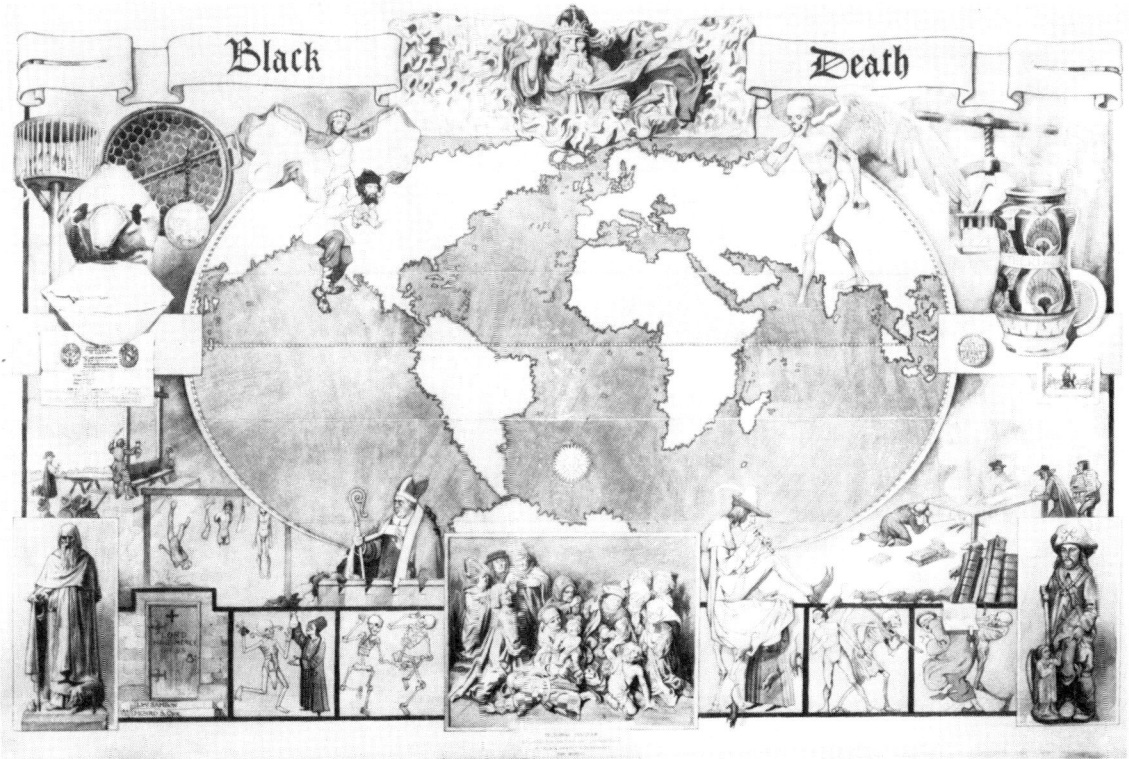

Orr and Sambon's grim 'Pictorial Diagram' illustrating the spread of the Black Death. (Wellcome Institute Library, London)

These speeds are outclassed by the wing beats of many insects. The wings of a beetle can oscillate at up to 175 Hz (cycles/s); bees reach 245 Hz and mosquitoes somewhere in the region of 585. The attainment, by a midge, of a wing beat of 1000 Hz has been recorded.

Fastest births

The fastest speed at which a woman has given birth to a single infant is impossible to estimate with any precision, the difficulty often being in determining the exact point at which labour begins.

However, a speed record exists for the natural birth of triplets: 2 min by Mrs James E. Duck of Memphis, Tennessee, on 21 March 1977, validation perhaps of the ancient joke in which rapid births were likened to the shelling of peas

Fastest mortality rate and spread of disease

It is difficult to estimate the speed at which a disease travels, largely as a result of varying incubation patterns and the prevalence in an area of other diseases similar to the epidemic. Mass hysteria has been known to affect large crowds in seconds, though possibly as a result of non disease-related factors. Developments in communications have meant that diseases can travel from continent to continent in a matter of hours, given an undetected 'carrier'.

Nevertheless, the fastest travelling disease via natural processes and that responsible for the fastest rate of mortality among a substantial population would appear to be 'The Black Death', the name given to the plague which ravaged Europe from 1347 to 1351 and which proved to be the greatest catastrophe experienced by the civilized world up to that time. The plague, in its bubonic, pneumonic and septicaemic forms, was caused by the bacillus *Pasteurella pestis*, transmitted by rat-fleas.

The Black Death was a source of constant, if morbid, inspiration to generations of artists. Here is an engraving of Holbein's conception of the Dance of Death. (Mary Evans Picture Library)

Originating in Asia, the infection spread to the Mediterranean by 1347, to North Africa, Spain and France by 1348 and to England (where it caused widespread social disruption) in February 1349.

A study of contemporary archives suggests a mortality varying in the different regions between one-eighth and two-thirds of the population. According to the French chronicler Jean Froissart (b 1337) nearly one-third of the world's population perished—that is, about 25 million people—in little over 3 years.

The Great Plague of London in 1664/5 resulted in more than 70 000 deaths (out of a population of 400 000) in a matter of months.

Why does plague travel so quickly?
The spread of infection among domestic rodents in the vicinity of human habitation creates conditions favourable for the outbreak of human plague, for when an epizootic outbreak reduces the rodent population, fleas from dead animals fail to find another rodent host and thus begin to infest man. Under suitable conditions large numbers of people may be included.

Fastest incubation period

Freak cycles and the impossibility of determining exactly when a sufferer has contracted the disease make this difficult to estimate. Septicaemic plague (see above)—marked by prostration and subsequent brain damage—may be fatal within 24 hours. Medieval chroniclers (whose evidence is not always reliable), the most notable being Froissart and Boccacio, record victims dying within hours of exposure to infection.

Mortality rates within individual countries

A combination of famine and epidemic influenza left 20 million people dead within a period of barely 10 years (1914–24) in Russia. However, this mortality rate may have been exceeded in northern China between 1876 and 1879, where 3 years of drought resulted in a famine that affected a total of 70 million Chinese. Conditions of anarchy prevailed in many towns and the populace resorted to slavery, murder and cannibalism. It was reported by Western visitors that children were being sold as food in market-places. Mass graves known as '10 000 man-holes' were created to accommodate carcasses.

Owing to the self-absorption of the ruling Manchu dynasty, news of the disaster failed to spread to the West until a year had passed: unfortunately, political and physical obstacles frustrated relief missions. It is estimated that between 10 and 13 million perished within a period of 2 years 6 months. This can be averaged out to achieve a figure of 10 000 deaths *per day*.

In a widespread famine (1333–37), the result of extensive drought and possibly exacerbated by the beginnings of the Black Death, as many as 6 million Chinese may have died.

THE ANIMAL WORLD

Animal growth

The rate at which animals grow, compared to human beings, may initially seem astounding. A caterpillar, for instance, turns into a butterfly after only 6 weeks. According to scientific estimates a human baby growing at the same rate would weigh 8 tonnes at the end of a corresponding period.

But development is relative. Although an insect or bird may appear to grow at a terrific rate, its life span is almost certainly extremely limited. Growth rates are also conditioned by circumstance. To put this bluntly, the survival of a species is ensured by the rate at which its young reach maturity. A number of species are capable of breeding only a short time after birth. This is not just an example of nature being capricious. It is often a vital part of the maintenance of the species' numbers.

The rate at which a species can reproduce should not surprise us either. Given natural conditions, only a small percentage of the young of any bird or insect can expect to survive. A Black Orpington hen once laid 361 eggs in 364 days. Though perhaps an extreme case, this is a *prima facie* instance of nature's ability to maintain a constant insurance policy, simply by having the *capacity* to produce large numbers of offspring. Thus, in the same way Victorian families tended to have a superfluity of children: not merely because parents were naturally philoprogenitive, or because of unreliable methods of contraception, but because there was a tendency of children not to survive.

Consequently, except in the most outsize or idiosyncratic species, accelerated growth rates can be observed. This often manifests itself in shortened gestation periods. For instance, the American opossum normally takes 8–13 days to produce offspring, although the young are exceedingly immature and immediately transferred to a mother's ventral pouch. However, the Syrian golden hamster can produce fully-developed young after an average gestation period of 15–16 days.

Animals live by their wits. The faster the growth towards maturity, the more chance the animal has of surviving in the wild. Ostrich chicks reach their full height at 5–6 weeks and at the age of a month can attain a speed of nearly 48 km/h (30 mph)—a skill that can probably mean the difference between life and death.

Amid all these 'speed' growths, the fastest rate in the animal kingdom is almost certainly that attained by the offspring of the blue whale (q.v.). *Balaenoptera musculus* develops from a barely visible ovum weighing a fraction of a milligram (0.000035 oz) to a weight of 26 tonnes in 22.5 months: that is, 10.5 months of gestation and 1 year of live growth.

Even these speeds, however, seem rudimentary when compared to those attained by microscopic organisms. The protozoan *Glaucoma*, which reproduces by the convenient method of binary fission, divides as frequently as once every 3 h. Thus, putatively, a single specimen could in the course of a day become the progenitor of 510 descendants.

Protozoa are also exceedingly fast-moving. *Monas stigmatica* covers 40 times its own length in a second. A human finds it difficult to cover seven times his length in this period.

Animal reproduction

The fastest production of litters by a mammal in the course of a single year is an astonishing 15 (average litter size: 4–9 mammals) by the meadow vole, a native of Canada and the northern parts of the USA. Females begin to breed at the age of 25 days; gestation occupies a period of approximately three weeks, and mating recurs soon after parturition.

Fastest rate of development

The fastest rate of growth to maturity, if not to actual corporeal size, is that undergone by the streaked tenrec (*Hermicentetus semispinosus*) a native of Madagascar. The animal is not often observed under scientific conditions, but two young born at Berlin zoo in July 1961 were observed to run almost immediately. At 6 days they were apparently fully-weaned and breakfasting off worms. It might be thought that this rapid rate of development would be the product of a swift gestation. However, unlike the meadow vole (q.v.), the tenrec has a gestation period of at least 50 days.

Fastest rate of extinction in a species

The disappearance of an animal species is usually a comparatively long drawn-out business, principally because total extinction is so difficult to verify. For instance, several authorities would deny that the Quagga or Steller's sea cow no longer exist—as a result of various unconfirmed, though plausible, reports of sightings during the last 50 years.

However, the evidence of verifiable data insists that the fastest rate of extinction suffered by any species was that undergone by the passenger pigeon (*Ectopistes migratorious*). In 1870 a conservative estimate put the number of passenger pigeons in the USA at over 2 billion. It was the bird's abundance which hastened its decline. In Petoskey, Michigan, in 1878 a flock nested in a forest 45 km (28 miles) long, the main body of birds—approximately 1000 million—occupying a compact mass 1.6 km wide and 8 km in length (1 mile–5 miles). Hunters dispatched 300 tons of birds in a month.

In the face of this onslaught the days of the passenger pigeon were numbered. The last of the

The great auk, which experienced a speedy demise in the 19th century, largely owing to the multifarious uses to which it could be put by human predators. (Mary Evans Picture Library)

species—a 29-year-old female called Martha—died on 1 September 1914. It seems reasonable to estimate that in the last years of the 19th century the birds were being exterminated at the rate of 30 million a year.

A similar, though less dramatic, decline was experienced by the great auk (*Pinguinus impennis*) which was reduced from a world population of several millions in 1730 to absolute zero in 1844, when the last specimen was killed by hunters on the island of St Kilda.

Animal speed—General

No two species of animal move in precisely the same way. But the most striking feature of the locomotory activities of vertebrates (ie animals with backbones) is the extent to which the same basic propulsive machinery is modified to meet the demands of environment.

In technical terms, the energy required for an animal to move is derived from the action of muscle fibres. These shorten in length when stimulated by impulses from the nervous system and develop tension when placed against some form of external resistance. Thus, when a cheetah, for instance, decides to pursue an antelope it takes the initial decision to move, picking up speed after the first bound when it meets with resistance (the ground, and to a lesser extent the air) which its muscles are stimulated to overcome. Then the animal will become faster and faster until a certain limit of endurance is reached.

This varies from species to species. A cheetah cannot run at top speed for much more than 550 m (600 yd). An antelope, in contrast, can keep going for several kilometres. A race horse can reach 69 km/h (43 mph) but only maintains this for 400 m (0.25 mile).

However, the relationship between animal speed and duration of effort is similar for a wide variety of muscular movements. It has been demonstrated that a fish 15 cm (6 in) long can keep up a speed of 160 cm/s (63 in/s) for possibly 1 s. However, it can maintain 70–80 cm/s (27–31 in/s) for very long periods.

Curiously, man's capacity for movement is about the same. For short periods of exercise a trained athlete develops 2–2.5 hp. For longer periods of effort (up to 2.5 h) output remains steady at about 0.5 hp. Yet for effort lasting all day (prolonged jogging, for instance) available power is not more than 0.2 hp. (See 'Running'.)

The speed at which an animal propels its body depends on the length of its legs and the frequency with which it can operate them. The longer the limb is in contact with the ground, the greater the impulse applied to the body and the faster the animal will move. Thus a race horse owes its speed to the length of its legs, as well as their comparative lightness in relation to the rest of the body, and the fact that as a result of this, forces operating both ways between the horse and the ground are reduced to a minimum.

Although from a biological point of view the speed performance of a mammal is related to the length of its limbs and to the pattern of movement, these figures have no significance unless they are related to the amount of time for which a given speed can be kept up. For brief periods, speed attained depends on the performance of the muscles, but for longer periods the 'speed' output depends on the rate at which the oxygen supply to the muscles prevents the onset of tiredness. Consequently, a race horse can maintain an *average* speed of

The fastest of all … *Acinonyx jubatus.* (Zoological Society of London)

64 km/h (40 mph) for approximately 45 s, but not more than 53 km/h (33 mph) for 5½ min. According to tests a highly-trained horse can trot at 19 km/h (12 mph) for 5 h.

Thus, for an animal to be fast it needs not merely long limbs relative to body weight, but well-developed bones and tendons. Figures show that the maximum speed of a greyhound, 58 km/h (36 mph), is not markedly different from that of a whippet, 53 km/h (33 mph), although the limbs of a greyhound can be as much as 50 per cent longer.

The record for the fastest burrower is probably held by the Eurasian mole rat (*Spalax microphthalmus*) which can shift 50 times its own weight in soil in 20 min.

Land mammals

There exists a superabundance of apparently 'extraordinary' mammal speed records. These should be viewed with extreme suspicion as they arise, largely, from faulty observation techniques. For instance there are frequent reports of a variety of the faster mammals outpacing cars or other forms of motorised transport. Yet it is difficult to maintain a constant speed in a car and rates may vary enormously. Thus the reports of (to take a common instance) antelopes running alongside cars maintaining a rate of 'about' 80 km/h (50 mph) usually indicate that the car was doing between 56–72 km/h (35–45 mph). Though the observation of amateurs may confirm or extend prognoses there is no substitute for detailed scientific observation—however ultimately disappointing, in terms of relatively inferior results, it may turn out to be.

A consensus of scientific opinion—supported by common observation—maintains that the fastest animal on Earth over short distances, by which we mean up to 550 m (600 yd), is the cheetah or hunting leopard (*Acinonyx jubatus*) with a probable maximum speed of 96–101 km/h (60–63 mph) and—perhaps even more remarkable—a gain in speed of 72 km/h (45 mph) in 2 s.

An explanation of the cheetah's speed can be found in its elegant streamlined shape and non-retractable claws. The only member of the cat family preserving this idiosyncrasy, it has pads resembling track shoe spikes.

It is not surprising that the animal is unable to maintain speeds in excess of 96 km/h (60 mph) in any chase exceeding 550 m (600 yd). It is not built for speed over a sustained distance: the slender hindquarters hide no very great reserves of strength. A distance acceptable to the hardier breeds of antelopes swiftly exhausts most cheetahs.

Detailed scientific observation of cheetah speeds was undertaken in September 1937 when eight specimens, brought to England by the naturalist K.C. Gandar Dower, were matched individually against greyhounds in a series of trials at Haringey dog track, London. Unfortunately, these tests proved nothing much more than the

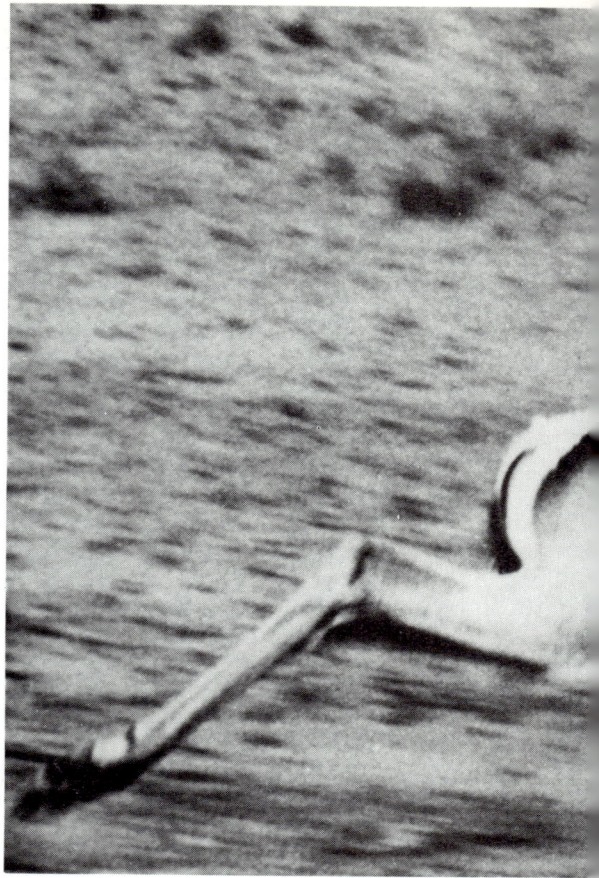

The American pronghorn—one of only two members of the animal kingdom capable of 96 km/h (60 mph). (Ardea London Ltd)

fact that the animal is loath to run at maximum speed under artificial conditions. The fastest times recorded in these trials were achieved by a female named Helen who managed an average speed of 70 km/h (43.4 mph)—equivalent to the speed of the fastest ever race horse.

What the trials did establish, however, was the animal's acceleration rate. Greyhounds given an 18-m (20-yd) start were frequently overhauled, though the rate of speed was not maintained.

It might be thought that reasonable results could be obtained by matching one cheetah against another in pursuit of an artificial bait. However, as well as remaining unimpressed by spurious 'chasers', both animals showed a complete absence of any competitive spirit. Earlier experiments at Romford stadium demonstrated that when two cheetahs raced each other and one

The springbok (*Antidorcas marsupialis*) in mid-flight. (Ardea London Ltd)

took the lead, its opponent would stop and decline to complete the course.

The use of artificial inducements as a means of obtaining high speeds was tried again by a researcher at the University of California, Los Angeles in 1960. In this instance a specimen was timed and photographed as it pursued a piece of meat attached to a cord pulled at speed. However, the animal, named Ocala did not exceed a speed of 60 km/h (37.5 mph). Probably, as Dr Milton Hildebrand observed, the cheetah 'regarded the exercises as a game'; which suggests that *Acinonyx jubatus* is not easily fooled.

Acceptable observation in the wild reveals the unreliability of these statistics as a guide to maximum performance. A film sequence of a running cheetah, obtained by Walt Disney Productions in 1959, demonstrated a top speed of 89.6 km/h (56 mph). At this velocity (which took 3 s to reach from a standing start) the animal completed a single stride in 0.28 s. Each stride covered approximately 7 m (23 ft), which is a respectable distance for a world class female long-jumper.

Col Richard Meinertzhagen in 1957 recorded racing a cheetah by car in Kenya at a speed of 81.6 km/h (51 mph).

If one thing has been established about mammalian speeds it is that best results are not obtained in staged conditions. It seems fairly clear that a cheetah will run appreciably faster when chasing game in the wild than while chasing a lump of meat round a racing track—if only because the former is a vital activity and the latter is not.

The roe deer (*Capreolus capreolus*), Britain's fastest mammal, speeds away from the camera. (Ardea London Ltd)

Over longer distances the fastest of all land mammals is the pronghorn antelope (*Bovidae antilocapra*) occasionally known as the prong-buck. It is the sole existing representative of the family *Antilocapridae*, intermediate between deer and cattle. The pronghorn survives only in the western half of North America from south-western Canada to north-western USA. Cruising speeds of 64 km/h (40 mph) over distances of several miles have been recorded.

Fortunately, for scientific observers, the prong-horn takes a peculiar delight in racing motor cars. A reasonable cruising speed would seem to be that recorded by Mr Donald Robins of the US Grazing Service who on 10 October 1941 paced four pronghorn bucks over a distance of nearly 4 miles in Malheur County, Oregon. The animals had already run approximately 180 m (200 yd) before they drew level with the car

which they continued to outdistance for the next 4 miles. The car recorded an average speed of 48 km/h (30 mph).

Yet pronghorns are capable of attaining even higher speeds when pressed. The naturalist Einarsen conducted a number of 'pacing' tests (racing pronghorns with cars travelling at fixed speeds) on 14 August 1939 on a dried-up lake bed in Oregon. At one stage Einarsen recorded the case of a buck which kept abreast of the car at 80 km/h (50 mph) for nearly half a mile and then increased his speed. According to the naturalist: '... he turned towards us at about a 45 degree angle and disappeared in front of the car to reappear on our left'. The animal appears to have gained enough speed to manage a dash across the front of a car whose speedometer registered 98 km/h (61 mph). If the speedometer was accurate (and there is no reason to suppose that it was not) the pronghorn must have been travelling at approximately 104 km/h (65 mph).

The pronghorn is also remarkable for its prolonged cruising speed: it can maintain 64 km/h (40 mph) for several miles, accompanied by leaps of 3–6 m (10–20 ft).

The cheetah and the pronghorn appear to be the only two mammals capable of exceeding 96 km/h (60 mph). Yet other species have been observed to travel at 67.2 km/h (42 mph) for a mile and 88 km/h (55 mph) in a half-mile dash. During the Asiatic expedition of the American Museum of Natural History in 1922–23 Dr Andrews, leader of the party, recorded that a herd of Mongolian gazelles described a semi-circle in front of his car, which was moving in a straight line across the Gobi desert at a rate of 64 km/h (40 mph). Andrews estimated their speed at undoubtedly 88 km/h (55 mph) and possibly as much as 96 km/h (60 mph).

Two other members of the antelope family, the springbok (*Antidorcas marsupialis*) of the African grasslands and the Indian blackbuck (*Antilope cervicapra*) are also exceptionally fast over short distances and can probably reach 80 km/h (50 mph) when pressed. Normal cruising speed, however, is some 32 km/h (20 mph) below this.

Fully-grown kangaroos are capable of maintaining cruising speeds of 32–48 km/h (20–30 mph). Their magnificent bounds give an

Cetacean speed

SPECIES	CRUISING				MAXIMUM			
	km/h	*m/s*	*mph*	*ft/s*	*km/h*	*m/s*	*mph*	*ft/s*
Grey whale } Humpback }	5.6	1.5	3.5	5	13.7	3.6	8.5	12
Sperm whale	9.6	2.4	5	8	25.7–32.2	7.3	16–20	24
Fin whale } Blue whale }	16–24	4.6–6.7	10–15	15–22	48–64	13.4–18	30–40	44–59
Dolphin	16–24	4.6–6.7	10–15	15–22	48	15.6	30	45

impression of great speed but scientists calculate that they probably do not exceed 64 km/h (40 mph) and then only over short distances.

The Californian jack rabbit (misleadingly named, as it is actually a true hare) has been timed at a speed of 64 km/h (40 mph).

The fastest-moving primates are almost certainly the smaller gibbons of the genus *Hylobatus*, resident in south-east Asia and Indonesia. The practical difficulties involved in recording the speeds of these creatures as they wing their way through the tree-tops are almost insurmountable, and no exact statistical information exists. Nevertheless, tree-top level 'flights' in excess of 32 km/h (20 mph) are probably quite feasible.

On the ground considerable speeds have been obtained by the langur (*Presbytis entellus*) of India and Sri Lanka, possibly as much as 37–42 km/h (23–26 mph).

The gorilla has been credited with speeds of up to 48 km/h (30 mph) by the credulous compilers of books on big-game hunting. However, an authority has commented that, even when pursued, a troop will move off at only 8 km/h (5 mph).

United Kingdom

The fastest wild animal found in the United Kingdom is almost definitely the roe deer (*Capreolus capreolus*) which maintains a cruising speed of 40–48 km/h (25–30 mph) for more than 32 km (20 miles), achieving short bursts of up to 64 km/h (40 mph). On 19 October 1970 a terrified red deer registered a speed of 68 km/h

(42 mph) as it careered through a street in Stalybridge, Cheshire.

Numerous records, however, attach themselves to the speeds allegedly attained by foxes, most of questionable veracity. Huntsmen, disappointed in the chase, are notoriously prone to exaggeration.

Water mammals

Cetacea

Mammalian adaptation to life in water reaches its most advanced level in Cetacea (whales and dolphins) where propulsion is effected by the axial muscles of the body and the large tail. Another reason for whale and dolphin speeds is the 'streamlined' body and the smooth skin, although some naturalists have pointed out that the shape of the whale's body varies considerably from species to species.

Assessment of Cetacean speeds rests on precise observational data. It is possible to distinguish between cruising speeds—which can be maintained for perhaps 10–15 min—and short dashes.

Interestingly, despite the enormous differences in size, the speeds reached by the blue whale (24 m, 80 ft; 100 tons) and the dolphin (2 m, 6 ft; 91 kg, 200 lb) are about the same. What counts is the ability of the heart to provide an adequate supply of oxygen to the muscles—in this case of relative proportion.

The fastest swimming whale over short distances is probably the Sei which, when harpooned, can dash off at a pace of 48 km/h (30 mph) for a third of a mile. Observers estimate that this species can attain 56 km/h (35 mph) on the surface during its initial rush.

Apart from travelling at very high speeds, Cetacea also experience extremely fast growth rates. A whale calf's growth from a microscopic ovum weighing a fraction of a milligram (0.000035 oz) to a weight of 26 tonnes in 22.5 months (10.5 months gestation, 1 year of live growth) is the most rapid rate in the animal kingdom.

During the 1947/48 whaling season British scientists carried out speed tests on the blue whale (*Balaenoptera musculus*) in Antarctic waters. Precise measurements established that specimens could maintain a speed of 37 km/h (23 mph) for 10 min when frightened, 26 km/h (16 mph) for 2 hours and keep ahead of a whaling ship travelling at 18.5 km/h (11.5 mph) all day.

This corresponds almost exactly with the endurance rates noted in other, land going mammals. Significantly, the majority of high speeds have been recorded when the animal is subject to the stimulus of fear: a response observable throughout the animal kingdom. This suggests that man has definite reserves of speed capacity, never realised in traditional athletic contests and is capable—beyond doubt—of exceeding present 'maximum' speeds.

Dolphins and whales
It is possible to measure the speed of dolphins with some accuracy, owing to their habit of riding the bow-waves of destroyers. Speeds of 56–59 km/h (35–37 mph) have been recorded, although zoologists have cautioned that in bow-wave riding the dolphin attains its propulsive power from the moving vessel while remaining almost motionless. Deprived of this benefit, the swimming speed is slightly slower: 37–46 km/h (23–29 mph).

These bow-riding performances are outwardly impressive but it should be realised that this is not strictly classifiable as true swimming. Something of a slipstream phenomenon is actually taking effect. Scientists have aptly characterised this as a form of surfing requiring negligible physical effort.

Trained leopard dolphins at the Sea Life Park in Hawaii have been timed at 47 km/h (29.9 mph). It seems probable that a speed in excess of 48 km/h (30 mph) can be assumed.

Another fast-swimming marine mammal is the minke or piked whale. A family group of three were timed at 46.3 km/h (28.77 mph) in South African waters in 1968. Both this specimen and the Sei (q.v.) possess a normal cruising speed of 16–24 km/h (10–15 mph) which they are able to sustain for several hours.

Probably the fastest marine mammal over short distances is the killer whale (which, despite its name, is actually classifiable as a species of dolphin). In October 1958 a bull was timed at 55.5 km/h (34.5 mph) as it approached the SS *Montgomery* in the east Pacific. Subsequently, the animal circled the ship whose speed was 38 km/h (23.7 mph) for nearly 20 min before reverting to its original course. Other observers believe that this extremely powerful predator can reach speeds of up to 64 km/h (40 mph) in pursuing fast-moving prey such as the minke whale.

A record also exists of a school of short-finned pilot whales (*Globicephala macrolynchus*) circling a US Navy ship travelling at 40.7 km/h (25.3 mph) through the tropical Pacific. This feat of circumnavigation was maintained for several days.

Pinnipeds (seals, sea-lions, walruses)
The seal is a curious example of an animal in which the forelimbs are essential for movement on land, but play only a secondary role in water. Thus the animal is not properly adapted for aquatic life. Most seals swim at relatively high speeds (16 km/h, 10 mph) but how long they can maintain this rate is uncertain.

The fastest of all pinnipeds is probably the Californian sea-lion, which has been recorded at speeds of 40 km/h (25 mph). This speed may be matched or even bettered by the leopard seal—large but slender, silver grey above and white below with light and dark spots—of the sub-Antarctic islands.

Along with most amphibians, the movements of pinnipeds on land are rudimentary.

Mammalian speed table

NAME	MAXIMUM SPEED	
	km/h	*mph*
Cheetah	101	63
Pronghorn	98	61
Mongolian gazelle	88	55
Springbok	84	52
Thomson's gazelle	80	50
Grant's gazelle	75	47
Red deer	68	42
Black-tailed deer	66	40.5
Mountain zebra	64	41
Californian jack rabbit	64	40
Cape hartebeest	64	40
Blue wildebeest	60	37
Guanaco	58	36
Mongolian wolf	58	36
Coyote	56	35
Indian jackal	56	35
European rabbit	56	35
Cape buffalo	56	35
Roan antelope	56	35
Bison	51	32
Giraffe	51	32
Reindeer	51	32
Indian wild ass	51	32
Bat	51	32
Snowshoe hare	50	31

At the other end of the scale, it is revealing to learn that the common mole has a running speed of 4 km/h (2.5 mph) and the three-toed sloth a sedentary 0.2 km/h (0.1 mph).

It should be noted that the maximum speeds recorded here do not correspond with various speculative speeds suggested in the text. Monitoring animal speed in the wild is extremely difficult. If one is to err, it seems advisable to err on the side of caution.

The fastest-moving pinniped on a surface of ice or snow is allegedly the crab-eater seal (said by scientists to resemble a small torpedo when in flight) of the Antarctic regions. A specimen chased across tightly-packed snow on Signy Island, South Orkney, registered 18.9 km/h (11.8 mph) before it was brought down. Most of the creature's propulsive power comes from its hind-flippers which are held together, as in swimming, and thumped down with tremendous vigour while the front flippers are used to strike strong, backward strokes.

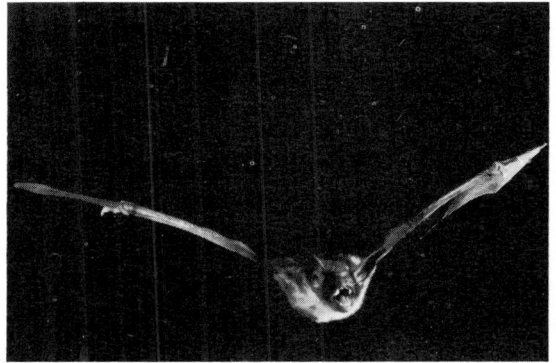

A mouse-eared bat in nocturnal flight. (Ardea London Ltd)

According to O'Gorman: 'When disturbed suddenly, the crab-eater can escape rapidly. This remarkably quick escape reaction from sleeping to approximately 19 km/h (12 mph) within seconds suggests that this more rapid locomotory pattern might be of considerable value to the crab-eater seal when attacked by its hereditary enemy, the killer whale, which is probably quite capable of upsetting ice-floes in its pursuit of prey.'

Flying mammals

Active mammalian flight is entirely restricted to bats. Flying mammals (*Phalangeridae*), such as the flying squirrel, glide rather than propel themselves. The bat, alternatively, finds it exceedingly difficult to move on land. Speed of flight varies according to size and species. The speed of the small brown bat (*Myotis myotis*) is about 4–5 m/s (13–16 ft/s) with a wing beat frequency of 11–12 Hz .

The highest measured flying speed recorded for a bat is 51.2 km/h (32 mph) for a free-tailed or Guano bat in New Mexico which logged 50 km (31 miles) in only 58 min. This speed is probably rivalled by the Noctule and long-winged varieties, both of which have been timed at 50 km/h (31 mph).

Fish

Although the movements of a fish's body appear to vary considerably from one species to another, fish move in two distinct ways: by oscillation of their tails from side to side, and by the movement of fins. Of these, the movement of the tail is the more significant.

Observation of fish speeds falls into two clearly-defined categories: their natural environment and laboratory conditions. In practice, reliable information is usually restricted to fish of a small or medium size whose performance can be judged by their ability to make headway against currents of estimated speed.

The maximum speed attained by any one species increases with the length of the body, whereas fish of the same length but of different species record substantial differences. Very few fish reach speeds as high as ten times their length per second. The maximum speed any fish can attain depends on the maximum frequency with which they can move their tails from side to side.

Endurance speeds vary wildly. The herring (*Culpea harengus*) is able to swim more than 1000 times its own length before it becomes exhausted, whereas the cod can cover only 40 times.

Speeds greater than body lengths have been recorded in the case of the tunny fish and the wahoo when running on a line in open water, although these fell rapidly after 10–20 s. Velocities were as follows:

SPECIES	LENGTH		VELOCITY		BODY LENGTHS/S
	cm	*ft*	*km/h*	*mph*	
Tunny	530–980	17.4–32.1	74.59	46.35	2.111
Wahoo	1121	37.36	77.05	47.88	1.893

Fish produce their most astonishing power when accelerating. Photographic records of small trout demonstrate that they can cover a distance of 5 cm (2 in) within 0.05 s starting from rest.

Alternative estimates of speeds reached as the result of a sudden intensive effort can be ascertained from measuring the height to which a fish—a salmon, for instance—can jump out of water. A 39 cm (3 ft) long salmon is capable of doing this at a rate of 9 m/s (29 ft/s).

Generally, ichthyologists agree that the fastest fish in the world over a comparatively short

distance is the sailfish (*Istiophorus*), found in tropical waters. Maximum speed has not been precisely estimated but in a series of trials carried out, using a stopwatch at the Long Key Fishing Camp, Florida, one sailfish took out 91 m (100 yd) of line in 3 s, which is equivalent to a speed of 110 km/h (68.18 mph).

The sailfish's high speed is attributable to 'streamlining': according to one naturalist it most properly resembles a small torpedo. When travelling at high speed, the long dorsal fin folds into a slot in its back and the pectoral and ventral fins are pressed against the body to reduce drag to an absolute minimum.

Phenomenal bursts of speed have also been credited to a distant relative, the swordfish. However, these estimates have usually been based on the depth of penetration achieved by the fish's bill into ship's timbers. A speed of 93 km/h (57.6 mph) has been calculated from the penetration of a bill 56 cm (22 in) into a piece of timber. Some authorities regard this type of calculation as questionable.

More recent calculations estimate that a 272 kg (600 lb) swordfish moving at a leisurely 16 km/h (10 mph) would hit a wooden vessel travelling at the same speed in the opposite direction with a force of about half a ton, all of it concentrated in the 2.5 cm (1 in) tip of the bill.

Experts put the maximum speed of the swordfish at about 56–64 km/h (35–40 mph).

In contrast, speeds of up to 105 km/h (65 mph) have been claimed for the American bluefin tuna. In 1938 a young bluefin weighing 27 kg (59.5 lb) was tested on an ingenious speedometer device, but registered only 70 km/h (43.4 mph) in a 20 s dash.

Fast speeds have also been recorded by some of the more lithe members of the shark species, principally the mako. A 4 m (12 ft) specimen pursued off Florida Keys in 1961 outpaced a speedboat travelling at 50 km/h (31 mph) for half a mile. Mako sharks have been observed to leap nearly 9 m (30 ft) out of the water. This presupposes a starting speed of at least 35 km/h (22 mph) merely to clear the surface. It means that the fish was in all probability moving at nearly 64 km/h (40 mph).

Similar velocities are achieved by the great blue

shark (*Prionace*), one of the few species known to attack man. A great blue tethered to a tachometer in 1928 registered a speed of 39 km/h (24.5 mph). In a further experiment involving water, an immature specimen held its own against a current running at 39 km/h (24.5 mph) and in short bursts of speed reached 69 km/h (43 mph).

The table on page 22 lists the record for wahoo acceleration—77.05 km/h (47.88 mph) on a light line.

Fish speed table

SPECIES	MAXIMUM RECORDED SPEED	
	km/h	mph
Sailfish	110	68.18
Marlin	80	50.00
Wahoo	78	47.88
Tunny	74	46.35
Bluefin tuna	70	43.40
Great blue shark	69	43.00
Bonefish	64	40.00
Swordfish	64	40.00
Four-winged flying fish	56	35.00
Tarpon	56	35.00
Mako	50	31.00
Needlefish	48	30.00

Domestic fish

An Atlantic salmon which made a leap of 3.45 m (11.4 ft) over a waterfall in Ross-shire, Scotland was calculated to have achieved an initial velocity of 32 km/h (20 mph) as it left the water at the floor of the fall.

The pike is also capable of rapid acceleration, but only for very modest distances. Lunging at prey it can achieve a speed of 24.6–41 km/h (15–25 mph).

Birds

In order that a bird shall be able to propel itself along a horizontal course, its body must be subjected to a force equal but opposite to its own weight and to a propulsive force sufficient to overcome the backward drag of the air moving past its body. Thus propulsive energy for flight can be produced from four main sources: the bird's own gravitational energy, its kinetic energy, the air and muscular effort.

Consequently, for a bird to achieve substantial speeds, it must satisfy a number of criteria. The fastest birds possess compact bodies, long and pointed wings, and truncated or very forked tails.

The changes which occur in the movement of wings as the speed of the bird rises can perhaps be regarded as a change from low to high gear. Certainly, when a large bird reduces its speed on landing, at least one naturalist has suggested that the bird is using its 'engine' as a 'brake'.

One must not assume that each part of the bird moves at the same speed. Variations exist in wing movements associated with different speeds of flight. Research in this field has focussed on pigeons. Scientists concluded that the frequency of beat shortly after take-off was 6–8 Hz and in full flight 4–6 Hz. As the speed of horizontal flight increased, the frequency of movements decreased. When flying at 16 m/s (52 ft/s) frequency had fallen to 5 Hz.

A swift—the world's fastest bird in level flight—approaching its nest. Note the grotesquely expanded food pouch. (Ardea London Ltd)

Starlings on the ascent: maximum airspeed can touch 80 km/h (50 mph). (Ardea London Ltd)

Subsequently, the observers demonstrated the complexity of wing movements. When a pigeon is flying at 21.06 km/h (13.09 mph) the speed of the wing tips might reach 80 km/h (50 mph) and develop the very large acceleration of 220 m/s^2 (722 ft/s^2).

Gliding

A bird can still move at speed when the wing-movements are extremely relaxed. Using optical methods of recording ground speed and taking into account the speed of the air relative to the ground along the line of flight, scientists discovered the average gliding air speed attained by the fulmar petrel was 12 m/s (40 ft/s), estimated stalling speed 7 m/s (23 ft/s).

Radar is now capable of measuring bird speeds at all altitudes over 304 m (1000 ft) with high accuracy. It can also track birds for long distances and thus establish speeds which are a correct measure of the average performance of a bird over a substantial length of time. This compares favourably with the old method of timing short, visible flights with a stop watch.

The fastest reliably measured air speed is 171 km/h (106.25 mph) by a spine-tailed swift in the USSR in 1942. Eight years before this, ground speeds ranging from 276–353 km/h (171–219 mph) were recorded by stopwatch for spine-tailed swifts over a 3 km (2 mile) course in the Cachar Hills, north eastern India.

This record appears rather less impressive in the light of recent radar findings, establishing that this bird cannot actually be seen at a distance of 1.6 km (1 mile), even with standard binoculars.

On 29 May 1960 a red-breasted merganser, flushed from the Kukpuk river, Cape Thomson, northern Alaska, by a light aircraft travelled at 127 km/h (80 mph) in level flight for nearly 13 s before turning aside.

Climbing

Angled flights obviously require greater muscle power.

Observation of starling flocks under carefully regulated test conditions produced average air speeds of 53–80 km/h (33–50 mph).

A number of useful experiments on bird air speeds were made by radar on the Isle of Lewis in the Hebrides by scientists from the field ornithology institute, Oxford, involving the timing of flocks of birds crossing from Iceland. Redwings achieved an air speed of 55.5–64 km/h (34.5–40 mph). Much higher speeds were obtained from studies of greyling geese. When direct visual association of these birds with radar echoes was possible, measured air speeds reached 98–101 km/h (61–63 mph).

A racing pigeon returning to its loft. Wing-tip speeds in this near-hovering condition are still as much as 80 km/h (50 mph). (Ardea London Ltd)

Pigeons

At first sight the highest speed ever recorded by a racing pigeon may appear to exceed that of the swift. A specimen owned by A. Vidgeon and son, Wickford, Essex taking part in the East Anglian Federation race from East Croydon on 8 May 1965 recorded a speed of 177.14 km/h (110.07 mph). However, the birds taking part in the race were backed by a strong following wind—a factor that always has to be taken into account in the estimation of avian flight.

More usual speeds average around 64 km/h (40 mph). It is doubtful whether any pigeon can achieve 96 km/h (60 mph) in level flight during windless conditions.

Significantly, the highest race speed recorded over a distance in excess of 1000 km (621 miles) bears out previous warnings about following winds. A hen pigeon flying from Murray Bridge, South Australia in the Central Cumberland Combine race recorded 133.46 km/h (82.93 mph). Wind conditions—doubtless exceptional—are not recorded.

Even in slow flight, however, the pigeon can move its wing from the up to the down stroke in 0.06 s.

Sea birds

The fastest flying sea birds are undoubtedly frigates, large representatives of the genus *Fregata*, often known as man of war birds, owing to their aggressive behaviour. Frigates exhibit all the classic characteristics required for avian speed: extremely long, slender wings, the span of which may exceed 2.3 m (7.5 ft), and scissorlike tails. The maximum scientifically-observed speed is 152 km/h (95 mph) but rates of 320 km/h (200 mph)—albeit rather fanciful ones—have been claimed by amateur observers.

The humming-bird

No investigation of avian speed would be complete without an examination of the humming-bird, for which air-speeds of up to 112 km/h (70 mph) have been claimed. However, wind tunnel tests suggested a maximum speed of only 48 km/h (30 mph).

Even this speed is somewhat surprising, given the fact that the humming-bird's wings are of average size in proportion to its body. However, the entire wing is nothing but a variable pitch propeller. In hovering flight—the subject of innumerable nature documentaries—the bird slants its body upwards at an angle of about 45°, in order that the plane of the wing beat remains horizontal. Owing to an extraordinary amount of rotation in the humerus, the wing—acting as an oscillating helicopter blade—forces the air rearwards with both up and down strokes. Thus each stroke is a power stroke. The fastest wing-beat frequency has been achieved by the horned sungem of tropical South America. One specimen measured with a stroboscope recorded 90 beats/s. Two hundred Hz has been reported for the narrow tip of the wing.

Thorntail humming-birds. (Ardea London Ltd)

Aquatic birds

The fastest swimming bird is the Gentoo penguin; its natural habitat is the Antarctic wastes. Naturalists on South Georgia, near the Falkland Islands, reported an underwater velocity of approximately 10 m/s, that is about 35 km/h (22.3 mph). When in haste, however, the bird probably attains a rate of 40 km/h (25 mph).

Speeds in excess of 29.44 km/h (18.4 mph) have been recorded for the Adelie penguin.

Ratites (flightless birds)

The concept of a 'flightless' bird may initially appear to be nothing more than an ungainly paradox. Yet these creatures are capable of astonishing speeds, which is the result of powerful hind legs. The emu of Australia has been credited with speeds approaching 64 km/h (40 mph). However, the speed champion of the ratites is the ostrich (*Struthio camelus*), whose powers of locomotion are worth examining in some detail.

Fully grown ostriches can certainly travel at speeds of 72 km/h (45 mph) for nearly 20 min without exhibiting signs of fatigue, although their habit of running in wide circles is not calculated to shake off pursuers.

A number of instances have been recorded in which ostriches overtook herds of hartebeest, the latter entirely capable of speeds of 64 km/h (40 mph).

After reports of ostrich speeds observed in the wild, there emerged a vogue in the early years of the present century—largely confined to the USA—for exhibiting them at race meetings. In 1907 a racing ostrich named Black Diamond was timed at 45.7 km/h (28.4 mph) over a half-mile course—this with a jockey strapped to his back.

Immature ostriches are also notorious for their speed rates. Month-old chicks have been timed at 48 km/h (30 mph).

Bird air speed table

SPECIES	SPEED	
	km/h	mph
Spine-tailed swift	170.58	106
Frigate bird	152.88	95
Spur-winged goose	141.61	88

Red-breasted merganser	128.74	80
White-rumped swift	123.91	77
Canvasback duck	115.86	72
Eider duck	112.65	70
Teal	109.43	68
Pintail	104.60	65
Mallard	104.60	65
Golden plover	96.55	60
Peregrine falcon	96.55	60
Canada goose	96.55	60
Racing pigeon	96.55	60
Quail	91.73	57
Sandgrouse	88.51	55
Merlin	88.51	55
Whooper swan	88.51	55
Lapwing	80.46	50
Snowgoose	80.46	50
Gannet	77.24	48

Insectivora

There exists very little reliable evidence pertaining to the flight speeds of insects. Much of what we know stems from the investigations of the French authority Professor Magnan who estimated insect velocities in a variety of ingenious ways.

In one series of experiments he tethered specimens to a thread wound round a small drum mounted on ball-bearings, the revolutions of which were recorded on a kymograph as the creature was in flight. In another series he reverted to the more conventional stratagem of timing the insect with a chronometer, aided by cinephotography, as it flew between two markers.

The fastest insect observed under these methods was the dragon fly which travelled at 28.7 km/h (17.86 mph). A hornet clocked 21.5 km/h (13.39 mph) and the fastest of five species of flies, a horse fly achieved 14.3 km/h (8.93 mph).

However, it seems highly unlikely that such artificial tests represent the maximum velocity of these insects in natural flying conditions. It appears that the sphinx moth, the horse fly and certain species of dragon fly can exceed 32 km/h (20 mph) over short distances in level flight.

An Australian entomologist reported that he timed a large dragon fly at 98 km/h (61.3 mph) along an 83 m (90 yd) stretch of stream, but

methods of estimation appear to have been imprecise.

Several butterfly species have remarkable flight powers. However, although they migrate several thousand miles (as much as 4828 km, 3000 miles) this is not a reliable guide to the speed of flight.

However in tests carried out by the BBC Natural History Unit at Bristol in 1966, during which 50 marked monarch butterflies were released near the city, one specimen reached Alvechurch, 129 km (80 miles) away in under 5 h. This represents an average speed of 27 km/h (17 mph).

According to the latest experiments the fastest airspeed which can be maintained by any insect is 39 km/h (24 mph) rising to a maximum of 58 km/h (36 mph) in short bursts. This disproves the fanciful claim of an American entomologist who claimed in 1926 to have observed a deer-bot fly travelling at 1316 km/h (818 mph).

Bees

Though the bee has been credited with remarkable speeds over short distances, its aerial progress is deceptive. Maximum estimated speed is 18 km/h (11 mph). It has been calculated that a relay of bees would utilise only a single gallon of nectar in cruising 4 million miles at an average speed of 11 km/h (7 mph).

Wing beats

Though insects maintain incredibly high wing beat speeds, this is only indirectly related to the rate of propulsion: a useful analogy can be drawn with the humming-bird, whose comparatively modest speeds we have already noted.

The wing beat of mosquitoes has been reliably gauged at 500 Hz, although observers claim that the creature is capable of much higher rates when it launches into sudden overdrive.

Yet the fastest wing beat of any insect under natural conditions is 1046 Hz by a tiny midge of the genus *Forcipomyia*. In experiments with truncated wings the rate increased to 2218 Hz. The muscular expansion/contraction cycle in 0.00045 s represents the fastest muscle movement ever recorded.

In contrast, the wings of the swallowtail butterfly beat at only 5 Hz.

Reptiles

The fastest speed at which a reptile has been recorded on land is 29 km/h (18 mph) by a six-lined racerunner lizard tracked by a car near McCormick, South Carolina. The lizard maintained this speed for over a minute before disappearing into the undergrowth.

The remarkable speed achievements of the lizard depend on a mechanism whereby the front limbs are anchored to the body. The pectoral girdle is extremely sturdy and can be rotated relative to the vertical column with considerable precision.

The above lizard's 29 km/h (18 mph) is probably a cautious estimate. The desert iguana and the gridiron tailed lizard are almost certainly as swift. The Komodo monitor, a dragon-like reptile found only on four small Indonesian islands, has been estimated to reach speeds in excess of 32 km/h (20 mph).

Tortoises
Famed proverbially for its want of haste, tests have tended to confirm the sloth of the tortoise. A starving specimen in Mauritius, lured by a cabbage, could not raise its speed to more than 0.27 km/h (0.17 mph). A desert tortoise timed in Utah, walked at a rate of 0.21 km/h (0.13 mph).

Tetrapods—fastest swimming
Powerful marine turtles—predominantly the streamlined leatherback—maintain impressive cruising speeds, but these can probably be increased four-fold in an emergency, possibly to 36 km/h (22 mph). These creatures are also capable of surprising sustained speeds; a female *Chelonia ryda* tagged at Tartugnero, Costa Rica was recovered near Campeche, Mexico having travelled 1960 km (1219 miles) in 275 days.

A female loggerhead, tagged in Australia; was recovered 63 days later off the coast of New Guinea. This represents a distance (supposing that the route taken was the shortest imaginable) of at least 3200 km (2000 miles).

Snakes
Innumerable legends exist in the African bush of fast-moving snakes, able to pursue and capture small animals. However, the black mamba— which has the reputation of being the fastest moving—has only achieved an official timing of 11 km/h (7 mph) over a measured distance of 43 m (47.5 yd) in Kenya in 1906. This specimen measured 1.6 m (5 ft 5 in). It is probable that a 3.6 m (12-ft) mamba could reach 16 km/h (10 mph) on level ground.

Stimulated by fear (ie when escaping from forest fires) the species is said to touch 32 km/h (20 mph) over short downhill distances. Maximum speed over level ground seems in the region of 24 km/h (15 mph).

Of snakes indigenous to Britain, the grass snake has a maximum speed of 6.75 km/h (4.2 mph).

Invertebrates

Among soft-bodied and hard-shelled animals, the fastest is usually agreed to be the squid, most probably one of the surface-dwelling species. It has been estimated from flight trajectories that flying squid leave the water at speeds in excess of 55 km/h (34 mph) when escaping from marine predators. In the early 1930s a giant squid was observed to overtake rapidly a tanker travelling at 21.6 km/h (13 mph) before attacking it—a futile, but adventurous manoeuvre. Observers on the ship estimated a speed of 32 km/h (20 mph).

Snails
The fastest-moving species of land snail is probably the common snail. A specimen in 1970 was observed to cover a distance of 0.6 m (2 ft) across glass in 3.0 min, equivalent to 132 h per mile. Absolute maximum speed is the 0.05 km/h (0.0313 mph) recorded by a specimen in the USA.

Echinoderms (sunstars, starfish)
Marine invertebrates are not known for their powers of rapid locomotion. A 19-armed sunstar has been observed to cover 1.15 m in 1 min—a speed of 0.0356 mph. However, detractors maintain that this rate of movement was measured down an incline.

Starfish are alleged to scuttle 75 cm/min thus achieving a rate of 0.043 km/h (0.027 mph). The species *Luidia Sarsi* has been designated the fastest.

Crustacea (crabs, lobsters)
Observers have estimated that the American

lobster can cover 7.6 m (25 ft) in less than 1 s at 25 km/h (17 mph).

The tagging of crabs has produced less remarkable results. In 1962 a female specimen covered 21 km (13 miles) in 23 days—an average of 909 m/day (995 yd/day), though greater rapidity has been observed over short scuttles.

Interesting locomotive differences are observable between the sexes. Female crabs are much more prone to travel than males.

Arachnids
The highest speed recorded for a spider on a level surface is 0.52 m/s (1.73 ft/s) but it cannot maintain this for more than 15 s.

Millipedes
The fastest-moving millipedes are extraordinary specimens of the order *Stemmiulida*. Researchers demonstrated that 20–30 mm (0.8–1.2 in) examples of the West African species *Diopsilius regressus* recorded take-off speeds of 1.73 km/h (1.07 mph) when effecting a typical jump.

Cultivated bamboo. A plantation at Nankin, China. (BBC Hulton Picture Library)

PLANT GROWTH

The speed of plant growth depends largely on the suitability of the environment, although various species—among trees the box and the yew—infallibly achieve slow rates of growth.

Plant growths are in no way constant or indeed predictable. The New Zealand small-leaved kowkai (*Sophora microphylla*), ultimately classifiable as a tree, begins as a slight shrub which forks again and again until it makes an impenetrable hummock 2 m (7 ft) tall. Subsequently, it remains dormant for a number of years until, without warning, a straight shoot springs out of the centre and eventually grows into a trunk 10 m (33 ft) high.

The fastest *constant* rate of growth is that achieved by the bamboo—botanically classifiable as a woody grass. Some 45 species of the genera have attained rates of up to 91 cm/day (36 in/day). This represents a speed rate of 0.00002 mph. Specimens go on to reach a height of 30 m (100 ft) in less than three months.

Tree growth is, of necessity—given the nature of the mineral transfer from soil to cellular tissue—more restrained. Yet an *Albizzia falcataria* planted in 1974 in Malaysia grew 11 m (35 ft) in 13 months. The fastest time in which a tree has reached 30 m (100 ft) in height is 7 years, achieved by a specimen of *Eucalyptus regnans* in Zimbabwe.

Plant growth rates towards maturity are capable of generating remarkable statistics. The seed, for instance, of the California redwood named 'General Sherman' (85 m, 280 ft) which stands in the Sequoia National Park, California probably weighed only 0.0047 g (1/6000 of an ounce). Its growth to maturity therefore represents an increase in weight of over 250 000 million fold.

The case of a *Liliacea hesperogucca whipplei* growing 3.6 m (12 ft) in 14 days was reported from the Scilly Islands in July 1978.

The world's most common grass, the Callie

hybrid of *Cynodon dactylon*, also known as Bermuda grass, can grow as much as 15 cm (6 in) in a day. Stolons reach 5.5 m (18 ft) in length.

The most obvious means of increasing plant growth is via the application of fertilizer— natural and artificial substances that increase the productiveness of plants. The Romans knew enough about soil fertility to recommend crop rotations, limiting acid soils, adding manure and growing legumes which fix atmospheric nitrogen. The essential problem was, however, to find the principle underlying plant growth. Van Helmont (1577–1644) conducted a significant experiment with a willow tree, planting a 2 kg (5 lb) tree in 90 kg (200 lb) of soil. Five years later the tree had grown to 169 lb, with the loss of only 2 oz of soil. Helmont concluded that water was the sole nutrient in use.

However, other early agriculturalists discovered different ways of increasing plant growth. The German agronomist J.R. Glauber achieved large growth rates via recourse to saltpetre. In 1699 John Woodward grew plants in a) rainwater, b) water from the Thames, c) effluent from Hyde Park and d) the effluent plus garden mould. The amount of growth increased with greater sediment in the water. An obvious conclusion was the value of soil. Thereafter, trained chemists were encouraged to study the problems of plant nutrition.

Plant growth cannot be sustained without the presence of a number of essential elements. These include:

LARGE AMOUNTS	SOURCE
Carbon	From air
Hydrogen	From air
Oxygen	From air
Nitrogen	Soil solids
Phosphorus	Soil solids
Calcium	Soil solids
Magnesium	Soil solids
Sulphur	Soil solids
SMALL AMOUNTS	
Boron	Soil solids
Copper	Soil solids
Iron	Soil solids
Manganese	Soil solids
Zinc	Soil solids
Molybdenum	Soil solids
Chlorine	Soil solids

THE ARTS AND ENTERTAINMENTS

Painting

The fastest-working artist—if judged only by his output—must be the Spanish master Pablo Picasso. In a 78-year career—by no means exclusively devoted to his profession—Picasso produced nearly 13 500 paintings, 100 000 prints and engravings, 34 000 book illustrations and 300 sculptures and ceramics.

Composing

The most speedy feat of musical composition is probably that accomplished by Georg Philipp Telemann (1681–1767) of Germany, who is reported in a single year to have composed 12 complete sets of services, this including a cantata every Sunday. Other highlights of a voluminous output were 78 services celebrating special occasions, 40 operas, between 600 and 700 orchestral suites, 44 passions and a host of minor compositions.

More exact details are available as a means of illustrating the career of Wolfgang Amadeus Mozart (1756–91) who composed over 1000 operas, sonatas, concertos and other pieces of music in a variety of forms; a remarkable achievement in such a brief career. His opera *The Clemency of Titus*, first performed in 1791, was written in 18 days. His last three major symphonic works—the Symphony No 39 in E flat major, the Symphony in G minor and the 'Jupiter' Symphony in C, were written in six weeks flat in 1788. Most remarkable of all was the composition of the overture to the opera *Don Giovanni*. This was written in full score at a single sitting in Prague in 1787, and completed on the day of its opening performance.

Hymnists

Mrs Frances Jan van Alstyre (1820–1915), the blind hymnist—or hymnologist—whose total output exceeded 8500 hymns, is alleged to have completed a single hymn in 15 min.

Language and literature

Authorship

The problem of determining the speed at which an author writes is an awesome one. Frequently, claims have had to be rejected as unverifiable. It is not enough, for instance, to adduce speed from the voluminous output of a lifetime. What is needed is evidence of sustained output over a measured period.

General

The English writer Charles Hamilton (1875–1961) certainly fulfils this criterion. Writing under the pen-names of Frank Richards, Hilda Richards and Martin Clifford (among others) he wrote the whole of the boys' weekly papers *The Gem* and *The Magnet* for over 40 years; this representing a weekly total of approximately 80 000 words.

Fiction

As we have remarked, precise data are often obscured by unwarrantable assertion. For instance the American writer Philip Wylie is alleged to have written a full-length Crunch and Des novel for the New York *Saturday Evening Post* in less than 24 h.

More obviously sustained and verifiable feats are these: Sir Walter Scott (1770–1832) dictated so fast that his secretaries could barely keep up with him, and finished two of the Waverley novels in three weeks. The elder Dumas in 1845 won a bet by completing the first volume of *Le Chevalier de Maison Rouge* in 72 h, writing with a quill pen on irregular hand-made paper.

Samuel Johnson (1709–84) is alleged to have written *Rasselas* in a single week as a means of defraying the expenses of his mother's funeral.

Among contemporary writers, John Fowles (b 1926) is estimated to have written the first draft of *The Collector* (1963) at the rate of 10 000 words a day. The English writer Anthony Burgess (b 1918), author of *A Clockwork Orange*, wrote five novels in a year when told

The prolific Pablo Picasso at work on another lightning sketch. (Black Star London)

Sir Walter Scott, whose breathless dictation outpaced amanuenses. (BBC Hulton Picture Library)

(erroneously) that he was suffering from terminal illness. The romantic novelist Charlotte Lamb has been known to write at the rate of a volume a week.

Drama

The Spanish playwright Lope De Vega (1562–1635) (whom Cervantes called 'the monster of nature') and author, allegedly, of 2200 plays, is reputed to have written several of his productions overnight. Certainly, he claimed that over 100 had been written in the space of a single day.

Samuel Johnson, lexicographer and wit, whose *Rasselas* was written in a week to pay for his mother's funeral. (BBC Hulton Picture Library)

John Keats—whose approaching death spurred him on to write some of the most memorable poems in the English language. (BBC Hulton Picture Library)

Among modern dramatists Edgar Wallace (1875–1932) wrote *On The Spot* in $2\frac{1}{2}$ days.

Poetry

Poets are preternaturally coy about the stamina of their inspiration. However, according to his biographer, W. Jackson Bate, the poet John Keats (1795–1821) wrote an average of 50 lines of poetry a day at the age of 18. This increased as he neared death. For instance, in April 1819 he wrote (among other poems) the Hermes sonnets, *La Belle Dame Sans Merci*, the sonnet to sleep and the *Ode To Psyche*.

The greatest individual feat must be that of Alfred (Lord) Tennyson who wrote *Crossing The Bar* while crossing to Yarmouth, Isle of Wight, from Lymington, Dorset, jotting down the 16 lines (almost unchanged in the final version) on an old envelope.

Dictation

The American author Erle Stanley Gardner (1889–1930) dictated his numerous novels to harassed amanuenses at the rate of 10 000 words a day.

Book publication

The fastest time in which a book has been published is 46.5 h from receipt of manuscript to finished copies. The title in question was *Miracle On Ice* by the staff of the *New York Times* from 27 to 29 February 1980. The 96-page story of the United States Olympic gold medal ice-hockey team was published by Bantam Books.

It is possible that this figure may have been beaten by the English publishing house Sidgwick and Jackson with their edition of *Campaign Diary* by Carole Thatcher which appeared at lightning speed after the close of the June 1983 British Election campaign.

Fastest selling book

Opinions differ. The Oxford University Press 'World's Classics' series, produced in runs of 10 000–20 000 copies during World War II, when there was a pronounced shortage of books, often sold out after barely an hour on the morning of publication, with queues forming in bookshops and department stores.

Alfred Lord Tennyson. 'Crossing The Bar' ranks as one of the fastest-ever feats of poetic composition.

The inscrutable Edgar Wallace, possibly the most fluent of modern dramatists. (BBC Hulton Picture Library)

Latterly, the greatest selling feat appears to have been accomplished by the first paperback edition of D.H. Lawrence's novel *Lady Chatterley's Lover*, published by Penguin Books in 1963 after a celebrated court case which was held, subsequently, to have destroyed the concept of literary censorship in Great Britain. The reading public, encouraged it was said by motives of prurience rather than literary curiosity, purchased 'in excess of 200 000 copies' within a few days.

Growth in magazine readership

A French literary paper *Le Constitutionel* managed in 1844/5 to increase its readership from 3000 to 40 000—a rise that seems to have been brought out by the serialisation of Eugene Sue's novel *Juif Errant*.

Gramophone records and recording artists

Fastest-selling long playing records

John Kennedy: A Memorial Album recorded on 22 November 1963, the day of the US President's assassination, sold 4 million copies at 99 cents in six days (7–12 December 1963).

The British record is held by the Beatles' double album *The Beatles* (also known as *The White Album*) with sales of 'nearly 2 million' during the first week of November 1968.

Fastest completion of stage repertoire

This accolade is probably held by the US recording group The Ramones who announced in mid-1977 that it now took them only 28 min to play their set of (approximately) 14 songs.

Recording session/LPs

Almost certainly this was the Beatles' first album *Please Please Me*, recorded on 11 February 1963 at the Abbey Road Studios, London. Producer George Martin pushed the group (John Winston Lennon b 1940, k 1980, James Paul McCartney b 1942, George Harrison b 1943, Richard Starkey alias Ringo Starr b 1940) through enough songs to complete the 14-track LP in 13 h.

Recording session/singles

The Beatles' second single *Please Please Me*,

The Jam: Paul Weller, Bruce Foxton and Rick Buckler. Some speedy recording sessions saw the emergence of *In The City* in 1977.

recorded on 26 November 1962, also at Abbey Road, was found acceptable on its first take: thus taking up only 3 min of studio time. George Martin recalls: 'At the end I pressed the intercom button and said 'Gentlemen, you have just made your first Number One'. They had.

Although exact times are unknown, a similar feat seems to have been achieved by the English recording group The Jam (Paul Weller b 1958, Bruce Foxton b 1955, Richard Buckler b 1955) in the completion of their first album *In The City* (April 1977). Certainly, according to the lead-singer Paul Weller, schedules were so tight that backing vocals for at least one track were recorded in the lift between floors of the recording studio.

Fastest pressing of record
A live album by the Jamaican vocal group Toots and the Maytals (Fred 'Toots' Hibbert, Raleigh Gardner, Jerry Matthews) was released by Island Records in September 1980, barely 24 h after recording at the Hammersmith Palais, London.

Fastest rise to number one

No fewer than eight single records have risen to the top of the BBC charts after only one previous week in the listing—ie in seven days.

LOVE GROWS	Edison Lighthouse	(1968)
BABY JUMP	Mungo Jerry	(1970)
BABY I LOVE YOU	Dave Edmunds	(1971)
MY SWEET LORD	George Harrison	(1971)
UNDER PRESSURE	Queen/David Bowie	(1982)
A LITTLE PEACE	Nicole	(1982)
HAPPY TALK	Captain Sensible	(1982)
PASS THE DUTCHIE	Musical Youth	(1982)

This is perhaps a less exacting feat than that performed by the (to date) 15 records which have entered the chart at No 1 as a result of accumulated advance sales.

14 Nov 52	HERE IN MY HEART	Al Martino*
24 Jan 58	JAILHOUSE ROCK	Elvis Presley
3 Nov 60	IT'S NOW OR NEVER	Elvis Presley
11 Jan 62	THE YOUNG ONES	Cliff Richard & The Shadows
23 Apr 69	GET BACK	The Beatles
3 Mar 73	CUM ON FEEL THE NOIZE	Slade
30 Jun 73	SKWEEZE ME PLEEZE ME	Slade
17 Nov 73	I LOVE YOU LOVE ME LOVE	Gary Glitter
15 Dec 73	MERRY XMAS EVERYBODY	Slade
22 Mar 80	GOING UNDERGROUND/ DREAMS OF CHILDREN	The Jam
27 Sep 80	DON'T STAND SO CLOSE TO ME	Police
9 May 81	STAND AND DELIVER	Adam & The Ants
13 Feb 82	A TOWN CALLED MALICE/PRECIOUS	The Jam
2 Dec 82	BEAT SURRENDER/ SHOPPING	The Jam
26 Mar 83	IS THERE SOMETHING I SHOULD KNOW?	Duran Duran

*First ever chart listing.

The theatre

Fastest theatrical disaster
Several dramatic works share the invidious distinction of being opened and closed on the same evening. However, perhaps the fastest demise of a professional piece was that sustained by Lord Lytton's play *The Lady of Lyons* which enjoyed its first and last night at London's Shaftesbury Theatre on Boxing Day 1888. More properly, the play never began. After waiting for an hour, with increasing impatience, the audience was invited to go home because no one could raise the safety curtain.

Fastest signs of audience disapproval
Numerous accounts exist of dramatic performances being given the bird almost simultaneously with the raising of the curtain. Yet the record would appear to be the speed of the disapprobation attracted by J. Hartley Manners' play *One Night in Rome* brought to the Garrick on 29 April 1920 by the impresario C.B. Cochran. Trouble began as the curtain went up—presumably owing to the fact that it failed to achieve one third of its normal height.

Lord Lytton (1831–91), whose *Lady of Lyons* inspired the fastest disaster in theatrical history. (Mary Evans Picture Library)

Samuel Beckett, the Irish playwright, novelist and poet: Nobel prize-winner in 1969. 'Breath' took only 35 s to perform. (Jerry Bauer)

The set, which was supposed to resemble an elegant drawing room, was compared by critics to an undertaker's parlour. Almost immediately the gallery began to express disapproval. Unfortunately, the script played into the audience's hands. Lines such as 'She makes it difficult to see her' brought jeers and cat-calls, and the play closed in uproar as stink bombs and handfuls of snuff were thrown at the stage (evidence perhaps that the reaction was premeditated).

Fastest performance
Dramatists and producers have vied for the distinction of staging the theatre's speediest performance. *Breath* by the Nobel Prize winning Irish writer Samuel Beckett (b 1907), a skit centring on the dramatic representation of breathing and light, was offered to the impresario Ken Tynan by the author in 1969. At its first showing—in an 'erotic review' staged by Tynan—it took only 35 s to perform.

This record may, however, be surpassed should

Members of the Monty Python's Flying Circus comedy team, responsible for the fastest completion of a TV programme. (BBC)

Fifty One Page Plays (or a part thereof) by the British *avant-garde* playwrights Nick Cave and Lydia Lunch [*sic*] ever receive a public performance. According to one of the authors, such a performance would entail 'having four stages. The audience would be herded like cattle to the centre, where they would be hit over the head with these vile little ditties about truth, beauty, love, each lasting from 10 seconds to a minute.'

Television

Fastest demise of a national TV series
The ABC network series *Turn On* first screened on 5 February 1969 lasted only a single day. The programme—a fast-moving comedy with computerised music and imaginative photography techniques—was cancelled forthwith when executives discovered that it contained a superfluity of double entendres. The following example has been quoted: 'A beautiful woman is about to be executed by firing squad. The squad leader, instead of enquiring 'Do you have a last request?' observes 'I know this may seem a little unusual, miss, but in this case the firing squad has one last request.'

Fastest completion of a TV programme
Owing to the universal practice of screening credits and acknowledgements, the official 'ending' of a TV programme usually occurs some minutes after the completion of the action. However, a record was established by the members of the Monty Python's Flying Circus comedy team (John Cleese, Eric Idle, Graham Chapman, Terry Jones, Terry Gilliam, Michael Palin) in a programme screened in November 1972. After 30 min one character asks 'What sort of an ending shall we have?' The reply is: 'an instant one'. The programme stops immediately.

THE HUMAN INTELLIGENCE
Political and social

Population explosions
The world's population continues to increase at a phenomenal rate. Significantly, the rate of increase has remained constant (while rising dramatically in selected areas) throughout the present century. Although estimates before 1900 are tentative and based on a variety of historical evidence, the following is an adequate representation of the rate of world population increase over the last 400 years:

YEAR	WORLD POPULATION	INCREASE OVER PREVIOUS POPULATION	TIME REQUIRED
AD	millions	millions	years
1600	400	–	1600
1750	700	300	150
1830	1000	300	80
1900	1550	550	70
1925	1907	357	25
1950	2497	590	25
1975	3828	1331	25
2000	7267	3439	25

Whereas in the early years of the century, world population increased by perhaps one third in a period of 25 years, it now looks set to double in the same time-span.

Comparative statistics are of peculiar interest. The annual world population increase is greater than the total population of Great Britain, ie 60 million. This means that the total number of births in the world each month is equivalent to half the population of Greater London or about one third the population of New York.

Between 1951 and 1961 the city of Lincoln,

England increased its population by some 7000. The human race is experiencing a similar increase every hour. To reduce the statistics even further, the current average birth-rate is 120 babies a minute or two a second.

Individual nations

The population of the Indian sub-continent increases at an abnormal rate. However, this increase is almost impossible to quantify exactly. It is estimated that the figure rose from 431 million in 1950 to 745 million in 1975. If the next quarter of a century sees the same rate of growth as the last—and the evidence suggests that it will—the figure in AD 2000 will certainly reach 1200 million.

Birth-rate

According to current estimates 1 million births occur in China each month.

In Western Europe, where precise data exists (in the form of a controlled register of births), the current fastest birth-rate is that of Kenya which in 1980 was recording a rate of 54.6 births per 1000 inhabitants.

The rate at which an area's population growth-rate rises can fluctuate wildly. Current 'speed' growths are being achieved by the following areas:

	ANNUAL GROWTH RATE[1]
1. Western Sahara	10.4
2. US Virgin Islands	9.6
3. Kuwait	5.9
4. Guam	5.0
5. Bahamas	4.1
6. Libya	4.05
7. Pacific Islands	3.8

[1] expressed as percentage of population

It may be argued that a number of these rates are in some measure artificial—the areas in question being the focus of redevelopment and expansion programmes.

Fastest growing urban areas

It is likely that the fastest rate of expansion is that currently being experienced by Mexico City, Tokyo-Yokohama, São Paulo, New York and Calcutta. Projected expansion figures are as follows:

	Now (millions)	AD 2000 (millions)
Mexico City	10 942 000	31 616 000
Tokyo-Yokohama	17 317 000	26 128 000
São Paulo	9 965 000	26 045 000
New York/New Jersey	17 013 000	22 212 000
Calcutta	8 077 000	19 663 000

Given the urban focus of economic development, it must be stressed that these figures are exceptional. By contrast many rural areas will suffer massive depopulation in the next quarter of a century.

Fastest arms importation

A record probably held by Iran which in a single year (1975) imported the equivalent of 1100 million US dollars' worth of arms. Vietnam was not far behind with 1001 million. Inflation rates—and the prevalence of civil and international warfare—make it appear probable that this record will shortly be exceeded.

Fastest rates of inflation

Inflation is generally defined as an abnormal increase in the supply of money, without a concurrent increase in goods and services available for purchase. This results in a rapid rise in the price level and a fall in the purchasing power of the monetary unit. Latterly, economists have placed less emphasis on the quantity of money as the major determinant of total spending and prices. Instead, current consumer and business spending is considered to be largely a function of income received.

The usual means of measuring increases in the rate of inflation is by a price index. However, the reliability of this is suspect—as different prices change at different rates. Thus any price index provides only a central tendency of many individual price changes in an inflation.

Inflation is nearly always associated with large increases in the quantity of money, usually created to finance ambitious schemes of government expenditure or in the wake of warfare.

The prevalence of all these economic factors to an abnormal degree leads to *hyperinflation*. The fastest rate of hyperinflation ever recorded was in Hungary in June 1946, where the 1931 gold

Scenes such as this—the use of tea-chests instead of cash registers—were common at the height of the German inflation. (BBC Hulton Picture Library)

pengo was valued at 130 trillion (1.3×10^{20}) paper pengos. Notes issued for szazmillio billion (100 trillion or 10^{20}) pengos on 3 June were withdrawn on 11 July 1946. Notes for 1000 trillion were printed but never circulated.

In Germany in 1923 inflation had increased 755 700 million fold on pre-war (1913) levels. Postage for a local letter cost 100 000 000 000 marks. Prices rose so rapidly in late 1923 that paper money lost half or more of its value in an hour and wages and salaries were paid daily, or at even shorter periods, to facilitate the quick spending of earnings.

Today inflation is recognised as a major international problem. The following countries are the more unfortunate ones:

	ANNUAL INFLATION RATE (PER CENT)	
	1980	*1981*
Argentina	87.6	131
Brazil	110	95.2
Ghana	88	130
Israel	135	101
Peru	60.8	72.7
Turkey	86.2	30.3

Great Britain

The fastest rate at which inflation has ever risen in the UK was between August 1974 and August 1975 when the prices index recorded an increase of 26.9 per cent. The Pearl tax and price index (taking into account tax relief) stood at 31.9 per cent in August 1975.

Immigration

The record for the rate at which migrants have flocked from one country to another is difficult to estimate, owing to the absence of precise statistics. Migration is an age-old phenomenon. People in flight from famine and plague were a common feature of existence in medieval Europe. In China repeated crop failure and flooding were still forcing large numbers of people to abandon their homes and resort to vagrancy in the mid-20th century. Russian famines which followed the Revolution and Civil War (1921–22) and the period of Collectivisation (1932) rivalled the great catastrophes of former times such as the Black Death (q.v.) with millions of peasants fleeing their fields and dying in thousands by the wayside.

Artists' impressions of the great 19th-century exodus from Ireland to America. In 1852, 352 000 Irish citizens were admitted to the USA. (Both BBC Hulton Picture Library)

Migration within an individual country

Migration from the rural areas of the USSR to urban areas reached approximately 23 000 000 in only 13 years (1926–39).

The 14 000 000 migrants who (often involuntarily) crossed the Urals in the few years before World War II represent one of the greatest population streams of all time.

America

One of the great emigrations of former times, the opening up of the USA in the early years of the last century is, fortunately, adequately documented. Undoubtedly, some of the fastest annual rates of immigration date from this period.

During the decade 1830–40 the annual figure was in the region of 60 000 immigrants. From 1840 to 1846 the average rose to about 90 000. However, in 1847 the great tide of immigration began with an enormous influx from Ireland following the potato famine, and in 1849 political instability led to substantial immigration from Germany. From 1847 to 1854 immigration was running at a rate of 250 000–400 000 people a year. It was at this period that the highest rate of immigration from one individual country to another was obtained. During 1852, 352 000 Irish citizens were admitted to the country.

This emigration led to one of the fastest depopulations in history. Over a corresponding period the population of Ireland fell from seven million to two million.

Yet the fastest rate of immigration in any one year was not achieved until 1907, with a total of 1 285 000 migrants. However, these figures include numbers of people who did not remain permanently in the United States. These 're-emigrants' are believed to have amounted to 30 per cent of the total.

Rate of increase of immigration into US 1820–1910

YEAR	NUMBER OF IMMIGRANTS
1820–1830	151 825
1831–1840	599 125
1841–1850	1 713 251
1851–1860	2 598 000
1861–1870	2 314 000
1871–1880	2 812 191
1881–1890	5 246 613
1891–1900	3 157 564
1901–1910	8 795 386

The most remarkable increase came in the period 1901–10 when immigration figures rose by nearly 250 per cent.

The explanation for this unique period of population movement lies in a number of factors: the political and social instability suffered by much of Europe; the allure of an unpopulated 'virgin land', whose attractions in the early years also included the discovery of gold; the sympathy felt towards subsequent waves of immigrants by US governments composed themselves of the descendants of former migrants.

United Kingdom

The fastest rate of emigration from the UK in the present century took place in 1913 with a registered total of 389 394 persons. Of these, 190 000 were destined for British North America.

Large numbers of foreign workers were brought into Britain in the late 1940s to assist the development of the national economy: perhaps 100 000 by 1948.

Migration from Poland to East Germany by impoverished farm workers in the period before World War I took place at the rate of 300 000 persons a year.

Current statistics are obscured by the fact that a great deal of present day immigration is illegal. Official statistics reveal the fastest current immigration rate to be that existing between the USA and Mexico. In 1975, 62 205 Mexicans obtained US citizenship, nearly twice as many as the next group of foreign nationals (Philippine Islanders) with 31 751 applications.

Legislatures

Fastest dismissal of a parliament

A parliament of Edward I (1272–1307), summoned to Westminster on 30 May 1306, lasted only a single day.

Accession to high office

The Rt. Hon. William Pitt (b 28 May 1759)

acceded to the office of First Lord of the Treasury (ie Prime Minister) on 19 December 1783. He was then aged 24 years 205 days—and had already declined an earlier offer of the post.

Accumulation of high offices

Between the period October 1964 and March 1976 (11 years 5 months) the Rt. Hon. (Leonard) James Callaghan held all four major state offices—officiating, successively, as Home Secretary, Chancellor of the Exchequer, Foreign Secretary and Prime Minister: this in spite of a 3½-year interruption (June 1970–February 1974) when the Labour Party was not in government. He continued in power until May 1979.

Political declarations

Traditionally, each General Election in Great Britain sees a rush on the part of certain constituencies to be the first to declare their result. Yet records are not easy to determine, if only because of the difficulty in comparing constituencies of differing size (a discrepancy somewhat reduced by boundary changes made prior to the 1983 General Election). However, the following are generally accepted as 'record' counts.

General Election

In the days when polling stations closed at 9 pm, the fastest ever result was from the constituency of Billericay, Essex in the General Election of 1959. A declaration came at 9.57 pm—just 57 min after the count (which involved the reckoning up of 52 973 ballot papers) began. The elected candidate, Edward Gardner (Conservative) had a majority of 4822. In contrast, a number of Scottish constituencies took in excess of 36 h.

More recently—the closure of polling stations having been put back to 10 pm—the record would seem to be held by the constituency of Torbay, Devon, which at the General Election of June 1983 declared at 11.10 pm.

Referendum

The referendum held to decide the vexed question of the United Kingdom's continued membership of the European Economic Community took place on 5 June 1975. However, owing to administrative difficulties, the count did not begin until 9 am on the

Pitt the Younger. The most meteoric political career in English history. (BBC Hulton Picture Library)

James Callaghan leaves No 10 Downing Street for the House of Commons. (Keystone)

following morning. Within 2 h the Scilly Islands declared a 74.5 per cent yes vote.

Fastest opening of ballot box

Beyond question, this took place at Cheltenham, Gloucestershire, at the General Election of June 1983, where a ballot box was opened exactly 10 s after the closure of the poll: a celerity explained by the siting of the count in a building used previously as a polling station.

Delays in receipt of ballot boxes in the Scottish constituency of the Western Isles are often occasioned by difficulties in transporting them to the mainland by air or boat.

Reading, writing, quickness of intellect

Human computer

The fastest extraction of a 13th root from a 100-digit number is 1 min 28.8 s by William Klein (b 1914, Netherlands) on 7 April 1981 at the National Laboratory for High Energy Physics (KEK) Tsukuba, Japan.

In the days before electronic calculators, numerous cases have been recorded of accountants who could add up columns of 30 or 40 figures 'in a matter of seconds'.

Rubik's cube

Dr Rubik's famous cube—composed of interlocking coloured squares—attained an enormous vogue in Western Europe in the late 1970s. The extremely fast solution times recorded during contests in England in the early 1980s—some of them below 10 s—should be viewed with scepticism. Frequently, cubes had been insufficiently dislocated or competitors allowed a preliminary period in which to examine the cube.

More reliable indications of speed are provided by the World Championships (established 1981) where there exist standardised dislocation and inspection times. At the 1981 championships in Munich, West Germany, a tie of 38.0 s was recorded between Ronald Brinkman and Jury Frösch. However, in the 1982 World Championships (staged in Budapest, Hungary, on 5 June 1982) Minh Thai, a 16-year-old Vietnamese refugee, recorded a time of 22.95 s.

Crossword solution

The fastest recorded time in which the *Times* crossword (generally admitted to be the most difficult of solution) has been completed under test conditions is 3 min 45 s by Roy Dean, 43, of Bromley, Kent in the BBC 'Today' studio on 19

Minh Thai reduces the world record for the solution of Rubik's Cube to 22.95 s (Popper foto)

Typewriting

The highest recorded speeds on a manual typewriter (including a 10-word penalty per error) are:

1 min	170 words	Margaret Owen, US[1]	New York	21 Oct 1918
1 h	147 wpm	Albert Tangem, US	New York	22 Oct 1923

[1] Presupposing an average of six letters per word, Mrs Owen appears to have been typing at the astonishing rate of over 15 characters/s.

December 1970. For purposes of comparison, this is slightly faster than the world record for the mile.

Typewriting

The record for an electric machine is 9316 words/h on an IBM machine, giving a rate per minute of 149 words, by Margaret Hamma (Mrs Dilmore) in Brooklyn, New York City on 20 June 1941. 149 words/min is the accepted figure even though the arithmetic appears faulty.

In an official test in 1946 Stella Pajunas (now Mrs Garnara) attained a rate of 216 wpm on an IBM machine.

Shorthand

The highest recorded speeds under championship conditions are: 300 wpm (maintaining an accuracy of 99.64 per cent) for 5 min and 350 wpm (99.72 per cent—two errors) for 2 min by Nathan Behrin (USA) in tests in New York in December 1922. Behrin used the Pitman system invented in 1837. Morris I. Kligman, official court recorder of the US Court House, New York, has taken 50 000 words in 5 h—this making a sustained rate of 166.6 wpm.

Records for other shorthand systems tend to be somewhat higher. For instance Arnold Brearley achieved a speed of 309 wpm without error using the Sloan-Duployan system with 1545 words in 5 min at Walsall, West Midlands (9 November 1970).

Morse

The highest recorded speed at which anyone has received Morse code is 75.2 wpm, that is over 17 symbols/s, by Ted R. McElroy of the United States in a tournament at Ashville, North Carolina on 2 July 1959. The highest speed for hand-key transmitting is 175 words/min by Harry A. Turner of the US Army Signals Corps at Camp Crosder, Missouri, on 9 November 1942.

Fastest talker

Although records have been claimed in excess of 300 wpm these should be viewed with suspicion. Whilst it may be possible to speak at this rate, it is virtually impossible to remain articulate. By common consent the world's fastest talker is regarded as Gerry Wilmot, the ice-hockey commentator in the period subsequent to World War II.

Raymond Glendenning, the BBC horse-racing

Raymond Glendenning in full flow at Ascot Race Course in August 1949. (BBC Hulton Picture Library)

commentator, once spoke 176 words in 30 s while describing the course of a greyhound race. Among politicians—a race renowned for high speed exposition—the fastest speed recorded is a 327 wpm burst in a speech made in December 1961 by John F. Kennedy (1917–63), at that time US President.

Patricia Keeling-Andrich recited 403 words from W. S. Gilbert's 'The Nightmare'—maintaining reasonable coherence—in 60 s under test conditions at Chabot College, California, on 16 March 1978.

Reading

Attempts to measure the speed at which people read are notoriously impracticable, owing to the difficulty of estimating comprehension. Thus, people with very high reading speeds (in excess of 1500 wpm) will often claim to have read a 200-page book in half an hour and yet demonstrate an inability to recall its contents. Reading speed-tests exist in which candidates are timed over a set number of pages and a total word count and then questioned on content. However, the questions are frequently of a self-evident nature, and such tests should be regarded with caution.

Extreme, though apparently verifiable, cases exist of persons with a reading speed of 2200 wpm, although this tends to be confined to short bursts. The diarist A.C. Benson (1862–1925) records the case of an acquaintance who was reputed to read five books a day (an average of 1000 pages, approximately 300 000 words). Most people have difficulty in maintaining a rate of 300 wpm.

The romantic novelist Charlotte Lamb (q.v.) claimed on a BBC 'Desert Island Discs' programme (10 September 1983) that she had read *War and Peace* in 3 h.

Writing

Again, similar problems of estimation arise. It is not enough merely to write quickly: one should also remain intelligible. Although the writing speed of authors is discussed elsewhere, the fastest rate of imaginative composition (as opposed to reproduction of an existing text) would appear to be that attained by the novelist Anthony Trollope (1815–82).

Trollope's extraordinary regimen is worth recording in some detail, although as he observed 'rapid writing will no doubt give rise to inaccuracy—chiefly because the ear, quick and true as may generally be its operation, will occasionally break down under pressure'. Woken by a servant at 5.30 am he wrote continuously at the rate of 250 words every quarter of an hour until breakfast, after which he commenced his labours as an employee of the Post Office. The author ought, according to Trollope's *Autobiography*, 'so to have tutored his mind that it shall not be necessary for him to sit nibbling his pen and gazing at the wall before him, till he shall have found the words with which he wants to express his ideas'.

Born in 1812, the son of a failing London barrister, Trollope was brought up amid an atmosphere of debt and privation. It was left to his mother to maintain the family by writing. Eventually he went into the Civil Service, obtaining a position in the Post Office (he is supposed to have been the inventor of the red pillar box) until his retirement in 1867.

Constancy was Trollope's maxim, along with unremitting attention. 'It will be said' he wrote 'that a man who has risen to no higher pitch than mine has attained, has no right to speak of the strains and impulses to which real genius is exposed. I am ready to admit the great variations in brain power which are exhibited by the products of different men and am not disposed to rank my own very high; but my experience tells me that a man can always do the work for which his brain is fitted if he will give himself the habit of regarding his work as a normal condition of his life. I therefore venture to advise young men who look forward to authorship as the business of their lives, even when they purpose that that authorship be of the highest class known, to avoid enthusiastic rushes with their pens and to seat themselves at their desks day by day as though they were lawyers' clerks and so let them sit still until the allotted task shall be accomplished'.

Trollope's fluency became proverbial: he records that he finished *Doctor Thorne* on one day, only to begin *The Bertrams* the next morning.

We can gain some idea of the speed at which he produced by examining his list of publications at the beginning of the 1860s. In 1862 *Orley Farm* was being brought out in serial numbers. At the same time *Brown, Jones and Robinson* was appearing in the *Cornhill Magazine*. In September *The Small House at Allington* followed. 1863 saw the first number of *Can You Forgive Her?* which was published as a separate serial and continued throughout 1864. Also in 1863 came a short novel in ordinary volume form: *Rachel Ray*. In addition Trollope published during this period two volumes of short stories—*The Tales of All Countries*. Not long after, *Miss Mackenzie* arrived in the same form as *Rachel Ray*. The following May *The Belton Estate* began to appear in *The Fortnightly*.

'I quite admit' Trollope wrote disarmingly, 'that I crowded my wares into the market too quickly, because the reading world could not want such a quantity of matter from the hands of one author in such a short space of time.'

Trollope was undoubtedly exceptional. Joyce, in contrast, is alleged to have written large portions of *Ulysses* at the rate of two sentences in an 8 h working day.

Candidates in GCE and University Examinations have been known to fill 24 A4-size pages in 3 h (about 7200 words)—an hourly rate of 2400 words, or 40 wpm.

An unparalleled feat of signature signing was performed by L.E. Chittenden (d 1902), Registrar of the US Treasury. In 48 h (20–22 March 1863) he signed 12 500 bonds worth $10 000 000 which had to catch a steam packet to England. There was, apparently, no possibility of using any facsimile device.

Mention should also be made of the writing speeds achieved by Arthur Christopher Benson (1862–1925), a versatile performer in a number of literary media. The son of a former Archbishop of Canterbury and successively a Master at Eton and a Fellow (later Master) of Magdalene College, Cambridge, Benson is perhaps best remembered for his collaboration with Elgar on 'Land of Hope and Glory'.

Benson could produce an ode, a lyric or a sonnet practically to order. Asked to produce an ode for the thousandth number of the Eton *Chronicle*, he set to at once. 'It is odd what an extraordinary facility and rapidity I have for this kind of thing' he commented afterwards. I

Arthur Benson (1862–1925). Diarist, belletrist ... and also high-speed versifier. (Cambridge Studios)

wrote it in about ten minutes—and though it is not *good* it is not bad at all.'

On another occasion, word came from Windsor Castle that special hymns for the confirmation of Prince Leopold of Battenburg would be appreciated. Benson composed two immediately. 'I wrote them in the train from London to Horsted Keynes.'

Strangely, Benson—who possessed a lofty conception of the role of the *litterateur*—was suspicious of his fluency. He was, he regretted, 'not a wise, tender craftsman ... but a rollicking teller of tales. An artist ought to be more of a *priest*, I think'.

Education

Fastest gaining of professorship
Colin Maclaurin (1698–1796) was appointed Professor of Mathematics at Marischal College, Aberdeen, on 30 September 1717, when aged 19.

Given the prevalence of age-regulations in Further Education, the achievement of Dr Harvey Martin Friedman (b 23 September 1948) is possibly even more noteworthy. Dr Friedman was appointed Assistant Professor of Logic at Stanford University, California, on 1 September 1967—22 days before his 19th birthday.

The subjects of this pair of prodigies should not be surprising. It is calculated that the fastest maturing human intellects are possibly those of mathematicians and logicians. Mathematicians, in particular, seldom achieve their best work after the age of 30.

Quickest examination success
In 1973 it was reported that an anonymous candidate in the Oxford University Final Honour School of Politics, Philosophy and Economics required only a minute to complete his answer to a paper in Logic. The paper apparently consisted of a single question: 'Is this a question?' The candidate is alleged to have written: 'If this is an answer'.

Fastest departure from a university
University life has not always proved congenial to tyro undergraduates. A number of records are preserved at Oxford University of freshmen who made their arrival and took their departure on the same day.

Growth in educational provision
So far as precise figures can be estimated, a record growth rate took place in France in the period subsequent to World War II, when there occurred an explosion in the number of secondary school teachers: from approximately 26 000 in 1950 to in excess of 67 000 in 1967. This represents an increase of 160 per cent in 17 years.

Royalty—fastest deposition
King Virabahu of the Kalinga Kshatriya dynasty of Ceylon (Sri Lanka) was assassinated a few hours after his coronation at Polonnaruwa in 1196.

In a lengthy war of succession the Roman Empire was ruled by four Emperors in a single year: Galba, Otho, Vitellius, and Vespasian in AD 69.

United Kingdom
A record arguably held by the usurper Jane (6–19 July 1553) who accepted the allegiance of the Lords of the Council on 9 July and was proclaimed the next day, as the result of a plot on the part of the Duke of Northumberland. By mid-1553 it had become obvious that the health of the reigning King Edward VI was failing. Northumberland, in May 1553, married his son Guildford Dudley to Lady Jane, eldest grand-daughter of Henry VIII's sister Mary. He then persuaded Edward to leave his throne to Jane and her heirs male. Despite the illegality, and the tenuous nature of Jane's connection, the councillors and judges were compelled to agree. However, when Edward died on 6 July 1553 and Jane was proclaimed Queen, the nation swiftly rallied to the legitimate monarch, Mary Tudor. The usurpers went to The Tower, Jane being beheaded. A single signature of 'Jayne the Queen' survives.

Fastest completion of warfare
The fastest end to hostilities took place in the war fought between the United Kingdom and Zanzibar (now Tanzania) from 9.02 to 9.40 am on 27 August 1896. The 38-min war came about in this wise: Zanzibar had been proclaimed a British protectorate in 1890 and a constitutional government installed under British auspices. By 1896, on the death of the Sultan Hamad bin Thuwaini, the royal palace at Zanzibar was seized by Khalid, a son of the previously deposed Sultan Barghash. The UK battle fleet under Rear Admiral Rawson delivered an ultimatum to Khalid to evacuate and surrender.

This was not forthcoming until 38 min of bombardment had elapsed. Admiral Rawson received the Brilliant Star of Zanzibar (1st Class) from the new Sultan Hamud Ibn Muhammed.

Legal—fastest trials in Britain

The law's briefest delay occurred in the case of Duport Steel and Others *v* Sirs and Others, heard in High Court on 25 January 1980. The appeal was heard on 26 January and went to the Lords on 1 February (am) with the decision given in the afternoon.

Murder trials

A record shared by R. *v* Murray (28 February 1957) and R. *v* Cawley (14 December 1959), both at the Winchester Assizes. On each occasion the proceedings occupied only 30 s of court time.

A prosecution under the Air Navigation Order of 1974 against a pilot at Edinburgh airport was timed at No 1 Sheriff Court, Edinburgh, on 1 March 1977 at 7 s—the time it took Sheriff Skae to utter the two words 'Not Guilty'.

The Emperor Otho (d. AD 69) was remarkable for speedy deposition in the year of four emperors. (BBC Hulton Picture Library)

Miscellaneous human speed records

Knot-Tying

The fastest-recorded time for the tying of the six principal Boy Scout knots (square knot, sheet bend, sheep shank, round turn and two half-hitches, bowline and clove hitch) on individual ropes is 8.1 s by Clinton R. Bailey Sr at Pacific City, Oregon, 13 April 1977.

Knitting

Mrs Gwen Matthewman of Featherstone, North Yorkshire, attained a speed of 111 stitches/min in a test at Phildar's wool shop, Central Street, Leeds, on 29 September 1980.

Leap Frogging

14 members of the Phi Gamma Delta Club of Seattle, Washington, USA, covered 969 km (602 miles) in 126 h 46 min on 20–25 March 1981.

Tailoring

The fastest speed in which the making of a two-piece suit has been completed from sheep to finished article is 1 h 34 min 33.42 s by 65 members of the Melbourne College of Textiles, Pascoe Vale, Victoria, Australia on 24 June 1982. Of the various stages involved in this piece of lightning outfitting, the catching and fleecing took 2 min 21 s. The carding, spinning, weaving and tailoring occupied the remaining time.

Tree-Climbing

As no two trees are exactly alike, record attempts are usually made on a 100 ft spar pole (and back). A record ascent and subsequent descent of 27.93 s (a rate of 10 ft every 1.39 s) was achieved by Clarence Bartow of Grants Pass, Oregon, USA, on 27 July 1980.

Stilt-Running

The record for completing the standard 100 m distance on 30.48 cm (1 ft) stilts is 14.15 s by Masahara Tatsukio in Tokyo, on 30 March 1980.

Potato Picking

The fastest rate at which this vegetable has been picked involved the garnering of 235 US barrels in a $9\frac{1}{2}$ h day by Walter Girois (b 1917) of Caribou, Maine, USA, on 30 September 1950.

Chicken Plucking

Ernest Hausen (1877–1955) of Fort Atkinson, Wisconsin, USA, remains the undisputed world champion. In 1939 he was timed at 4.4 s in the plucking of a medium sized chicken. He reputedly clocked 3.5 s a few years later.

Continued

The record for 12 chickens of adequate size, plucked clean by a team of four women at the annual Plucking Championships held at Marsary Town, Florida, USA, is 32.9 s set on 9 October 1976 by Doreena Cary, Diane Grieb, Kathy Roads and Dorothy McCarthy.

Turkeys, predictably, present more problems to the plucker. A sustained feat of carnage was achieved by Vincent Pilkington of Cootehill, Co Cavan, Ireland, who killed and plucked 100 birds in 7 h 32 min on 15 December 1978. The record for a single bird, neither undernourished nor moulting, is 1 min 30 s on RTE television in Dublin on 17 November 1980.

Ploughing

The fastest recorded time it has taken a ploughman to cover an acre (0.464 ha), taking a specified number of turns and preserving adequate contact with the furrow, is 12 min 9.5 s by Martin Allum. He used a Ransomes 5 Furrow 35.5 cm (14 in) plough, towed by a Ford Model TAZO tractor at the Royal East Berkshire Association's 120th annual ploughing match, held on 29 September 1979 at the Lower Mount Farm, Cookham, Berkshire.

SPORT

Projectile speeds

Unsurprisingly, the fastest speeds in sport are attained not by competitors but by the relevant projectiles.

The highest projectile speed in any moving ball game is 302 km/h (188 mph) in pelota, probably the fastest of all individual ball games. This speed was electronically recorded by José Ramón Areitio at Newport, Rhode Island, USA, on 3 August 1979.

This compares with 273 km/h (170 mph) for a golf ball driven off a tee, and the fastest ever lawn tennis service: 263 km/h (163.6 mph) by William Tilden (USA) in 1931. A number of tennis coaches believe that the service of the US player Robert Falkenburg may have achieved a similar velocity.

The speed of a table tennis ball has never been electronically tested, but speeds of 169 km/h (105 mph) have been estimated before the ball smashed under impact.

Speeds of over 160 km/h (100 mph) have also been recorded in ice-hockey. Robert Marvin Hull (b 1939) struck a puck at 190.3 km/h (118.3 mph) while playing for the Chicago Black Hawks.

The fastest baseball pitcher on record is Lynn Ryan of the California Angels (b 1947) who, on 20 August 1974, achieved a speed of 162.4 km/h (100.9 mph).

This is slightly faster than the highest electronically tested speed for a ball bowled by a

Bill Tilden, the swiftest server in the history of tennis, in action at Wimbledon in the 1929 men's semi-final. (Syndication International)

cricketer. Jeff Thomson, bowling for Australia in the Second Test against the West Indies in December 1975, attained a speed of 160.4 km/h (99.7 mph).

Running

Man's fastest running speed is something over 40 km/h (25 mph). As a statement this may seem curiously imprecise, but despite the advancement of timing and measuring techniques no really accurate data are available on just how fast a man or woman can run. Engaging speed legends exist—such as athletes outrunning race horses—but their plausibility must be regarded as suspect. The problem is to measure speed when an athlete has reached his or her maximum.

What makes a fast runner?

The speed at which one can exchange the position of one's legs is dependent on the speed of the nerve impulses supplying the muscles involved. This means that man has an ultimate capacity to perform this action, beyond which he is incapable of improving. However, as record speeds are continually improving it seems reasonable to assume that man has some way to go before attaining this capacity.

Man increases his speed by increasing his stride length. However, if the stride length is increased to the detriment of leg frequency then the probability is that a slower performance will result. An improvement in speed can only proceed from an improvement in frequency or stride length, without a falling off in either, or if both are improved simultaneously.

The fastest speed recorded in an individual athletics world record is 36.51 km/h (22.69 mph) for Pietro Mennea's 19.72 s 200 m at Mexico City on 12 September 1979 in the World University Games. The speed record for the world 100 m is 36.25 km/h (22.53 mph) by

World running records and speeds

EVENT	TIME		SPEED		NAME	PLACE	DATE
metres	m	s	km/h	mph			
100		9.93	36.25	22.53	Calvin Smith	Colorado Springs	1983
200		19.72	36.51	22.69	Pietro Mennea	Mexico City	1979
400		43.86	32.83	20.40	Lee Evans	Mexico City	1968
800	1:	41.73	28.31	17.59	Sebastian Coe	Florence	1981
1000	2:	12.18	27.23	16.92	Sebastian Coe	Oslo	1981
1500	3:	30.77	25.62	15.92	Steve Ovett	Rieti	1983
5000	13:	00.41	23.06	14.23	David Moorcroft	Oslo	1982
10000	27:	22.24	21.90	13.63	Henry Rono	Vienna	1978

Obviously the speed declines the longer the athlete is running. Note that Mennea and Evans set their records at an altitude of 2240 m (7349 ft). It is noticeable how techniques in middle-distance speed running have improved in recent years. Coe's 1000m record (though run over a distance ten times that of the world 100m record) was achieved at 75 per cent of its speed.

The longer the distance, the greater man's ability to maintain a regular pace. Rono's speed in gaining the world 10000m record was only marginally below that of Moorcroft's in covering half the distance.

Right:
Coe before the race: a study in concentration. (BBC Hulton Picture Library)

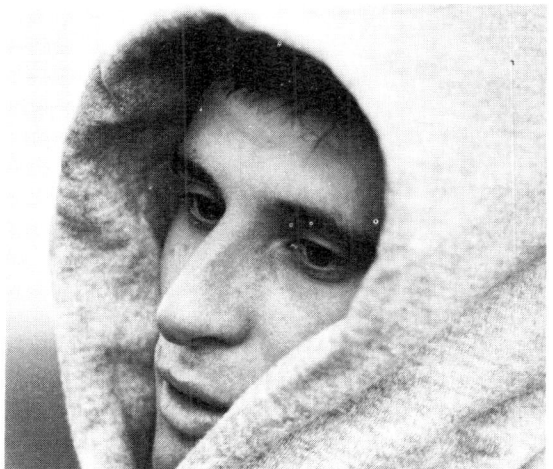

Calvin Smith at Colorado Springs, 3 July 1983. A faster speed of 36.47 km/h (22.66 mph) is reached by the fastest automatically timed 100 m—9.87 s by William Snoddy at Dallas, 1 April 1978, a performance not recognised as a world record as it was aided by a following wind of 11.2 m/s.

Consequently, it appears that human beings run 200 m faster than 100. This is not really correct—the anomaly is the result of the delay taken in reaching peak speed from a standing start. Maximum speed is probably reached at about 40 m (44 yd) and may be sustained until perhaps 130 m (142 yd). Coaches have estimated that top sprinters are able to run at fractionally under maximum speed for approximately 300 m (328 yd).

These figures demonstrate the existence of speed variations within any race. Once an athlete has got over what one coach terms the 'embarrassment' of having to move at speed from a static position, there is not much he can do except to rely on innate muscular memory. If a runner consciously strives for speed, he tends to become tense and his locomotive powers become correspondingly less efficient.

The period of a race after the start is known as the 'pick up'. Some runners can accelerate to peak speed within 15 m (16.4 yd). Others require as much as 40 m (44 yd). Each accelerating stride is longer than the previous one and the strides will increase in length until maximum speed is attained. Then the speed is constant for a relatively brief period of time before decline. No race, even the shortest of sprints, is therefore performed at continuous maximum speed. Even in the 200 m, which produced the world's fastest speed record, athletes achieve their maximum between 30 and 130 m.

However, despite the precision of decimal places of a second of automatic timing there have not been accurate timings at, for instance, 10-m intervals during the race, so that individual sections of the runner's speed can be analysed.

A race in which runners move at a consistently fast overall rate is the 400 metres. Significantly, this shows a falling off in endurance. Very few athletes have been known to run their second 200 m at a faster rate than the first. This becomes obvious when examining the records of some recent Olympic winners. The 1972 winner ran the first 200 m in 21.3 s and the second in 23.3 s—a differential of 2 s. The 1968 winner completed the first 200 m in 21.2 s and the second in 22.6; a differential of 1.4 s. The average differential for all those who competed in the 400 m at Mexico was 1.5 s.

The fastest speed recorded in any individual athletic performance is 37.14 km/h (23.08 mph) for Tommie C. Smith's 19.5 s over 220 yd on a straight track at San Jose, California, USA on 7 May 1966. It is estimated that bend running in the half-lap race adds perhaps 0.4 s to the finishing time.

The fastest speed for any athletics world record is 38.26 km/h (23.77 mph). This was not achieved by a single athlete but by the US team that won the 4×100 m relay at the 1983 World Championships in Helsinki in 37.86 s. This gives a clue to determining man's greatest speed: in a relay only one of the four participants has a standing start: the rest are already running when they receive the baton. Despite the imperfections of baton changing methods, the overall speed is markedly higher than that attained by a single athlete in a sprint race. Experts have estimated that the effect of a standing start at 100 m is to add approximately a second to overall time. Consequently, Calvin Smith's 9.93 might be equivalent to a flying 100 m in 8.93 s. This equates to 40.31 km/h (25.05 mph). While there exists a lack of precise, measured data, experts have continued to argue about the fastest man and the fastest individual performance. Such black American sprinters as Jim Hines, Calvin Smith and James Sandford have all run very fast anchor legs in relay races. Carl Lewis (USA) was timed unofficially at 9.2 s for the last 100 metres of the relay in the match between the United States and East Germany, Los Angeles, California, 24 June 1983.

The fastest women's speed for an individual record is 33.36 km/h (20.73 mph) for Evelyn Ashford's 100 m in 10.79 s at Colorado Springs, USA on 3 July 1983. The fastest record for any team event is 34.62 km/h (21.51 mph) for the 4×100 m relay by the GDR team to win the 1980 Olympic Games in Moscow. The pattern, when compared to men's events, is remarkably similar. By applying the same start factor of 1 s to the women's 100 m record (Ashford's 10.79 s) a speed of 36.44 km/h (22.4 mph) can be adduced.

Getting slower

As men or women run longer distances, the speed at which they run naturally declines. The process of running not only faster but further— ie endurance running—demands complex body changes. The body adapts in two ways:

Firstly, by an immediate increase in the rate and depth of breathing. This has the effect of making more oxygen available in the alveoli. Secondly, by increasing the output of the heart. This is achieved by a greater stroke output and a faster pumping rate which has the effect of pushing more blood to active tissues. This speeds up the transportation of gases from lungs to tissue.

The over-riding problem with high levels of speed is the accumulation of acid products. If the rate of blood flow is excessive the blood will not be fully operational during circulation through the active tissues. This means that the muscle is ultimately starved of oxygen and saturated with deposits of carbon dioxide and waste products. The best middle-distance runners—such as Sebastian Coe and Steve Ovett—are those who have achieved the best way of synthesising these waste products back into the system.

Coe, in particular, has perfected a system of training involving massive muscular activity— weight-lifting, frequent ten-mile runs— interspersed with short rest periods, as a result of which his body has gradually adapted itself to this continual, maximum effort.

Men and women are continuing to better sporting records with amazing frequency. It might be expected that the pace of record-breaking would slow as sportsmen approach some ultimate level of performance. But for the moment, the pace is increasing except in the fastest sprint events. For instance, the world 400 m mark, 43.86 s, has not been bettered since 1968 and the world 200 m record has only been improved once—by Mennea (q.v.) in 1979. By contrast the 800 m record has been improved upon several times, and by more than 2 s. However, it should be noted that the 400 m was recorded at altitude. The *Guinness Book of Records* has now taken to signifying these

Ovett and Coe move through the field in the 1980 Olympic 1500 m final. (All Sport)

favourable conditions in its record tables.

The principal reasons for this increase are probably the increased numbers participating in sports, increased opportunities to compete under favourable conditions, improvements in shoes, surfaces, implements and training.

Coaches have debated how best to produce the 'perfect athlete'. It was suggested, for instance, that to improve speed capacity athletes should be encouraged to run in car slipstreams. The sight of the accelerating car would presumably act as an incentive, not to mention the lessening wind-resistance, although it appears that the runner would be in some danger of carbon monoxide poisoning.

In the late 1960s Russian athletics experts used computer methods in an attempt to determine (via estimation of physique, stamina and so forth) the young Russian athlete with the greatest sprint potential. The chosen runner— Valery Borzov—was then exhaustively trained, using quasi-scientific methods, for sprint stardom. Borzov recorded an Olympic sprint double in 1972, registering 10.14 s for the 100 metres and 20.00 s for the 200.

The number of active athletes throughout the world has increased very rapidly as more and more nations develop sufficiently to include sports and recreation as part of their leisure time, and as people begin to enjoy more leisure. The rise to prominence of African athletes in the period subsequent to World War II was a part of this process. In the first modern Olympic

Games, held in Athens in 1896, only 59 athletes from ten countries contested the track and field events, whereas in Munich in 1972 over 1500 athletes from 104 nations took part. This number would have been higher in 1976 and 1980 had it not been for the boycotts. The World Athletics Championships in Helsinki, 1983, attracted entries from over 150 nations.

Women's athletics, which only began for any practical purposes in the 1920s, is showing an even greater acceleration of standards as the old prejudices against female sports participation decline.

Just as the number of athletes has increased, so the scope for competition has also grown. Top athletes now meet their main rivals more frequently than in the past. Thus the opportunity for bettering record marks has greatly increased.

Moreover, the current athletics vogue has not been neglected by government. Many nations have found it useful for their national prestige to promote sportsmen and provide sports facilities. Indeed, in the Eastern bloc sporting victories over Western nations are frequently held to denote moral (and by implication political) superiority. Improvements to equipment have also materially contributed to higher standards. Tracks have changed to take advantage of modern knowledge. Synthetic tracks consistently provide the best possible conditions, which could only rarely be achieved on the old cinder surfaces.

Training methods have also been subjected to scientific scrutiny. Mileage rates of over 160 km (100 miles) a week are commonplace for distance runners and types of training have become highly specialised as more emphasis is given to the skills appropriate to a particular event. The days of the athletic 'all rounder' who could double up in the 100 yards and the mile continue to recede.

A good diet has been recognised as vitally important, as athletes have learned to eat the right quantities and types of food. The incidence of drug-taking (sprinters consuming amphetamines prior to a race) has also blurred the dividing line between what is an acceptable food and what is an unnatural stimulant. In general, however, men and women are bigger, stronger,

better prepared and ultimately faster than ever before.

The great sprinters

Traditionally, the most famous sprinting events have been the 100 yards and—as metric distances became more commonplace—the 100 metres.

In the 19th century, sprinters set their sights on 10 s, 'even time', as the barrier to beat for the 100 yards. Yet timing procedures were still lamentably unstandardised. *Bell's Life*, the great Victorian sporting paper, records an account in its issue of 28 November 1861 of the final of the Oxford University Sports 100 yards. This event, run on Magdalen College Cricket Ground, was won by a Mr Poole of Trinity College in 'somewhat under 10 seconds'. One wishes that Mr Poole's time-keepers had been rather more precise.

It was not until 1890 at Analostan Island, Washington, that 10 s for the 100 yards was authentically beaten under championship conditions when John Owen Jr won by a foot from Luther Cary in 9.8 s. This mark remained unbeaten during the early years of the present century, the Englishman Arthur Duffy recording 9.8 s in 1901 and W.A. Schick (USA) the same time in 1904.

The years immediately after World War I saw new developments in sprinting techniques: rigorous training schedules, more attention devoted to the business of starting and finishing, and the emergence of a new breed of super sprinters. The Scotsman, Eric Liddell (one of the heroes of the film *Chariots of Fire*) reduced the British record to 9.7 s but he was rather overshadowed by the charismatic American Charlie Paddock, who on six occasions in the 1920s tied the World Record at 9.6 s. This performance was equalled by his fellow countryman Chester Bowman and by the Australian sprinter 'Slip' Carr.

Throughout the 1930s and 1940s the American domination of world sprinting became even more pronounced, with the rise of Mel Patton, Barney Ewell and the compact Edward Conwell, embodiment of the new sprint-starting techniques. At the 1947 British Games Conwell, of whom great things were expected, led the field in 9.6 s. Another of the US team, by way of congratulation, remarked that 'Ed, you sure got a flier'. Conwell was a perfectionist. His reply: 'You goddam s.o.b. I sure got left'. Ultimately Patton reduced the record to 9.3 s in 1948.

Though the 100 yards record continued, periodically, to be lowered (it now stands at 9 s dead) world attention began to transfer itself to the metric 100 metres. Some astonishing times had been recorded for this distance earlier in the century. However, rudimentary timing techniques caused them to be regarded with disfavour, as when the Japanese sprinter Minora Fuji ran an electrically-timed 10.24 s in 1902.

A new sprinting era was ushered in at the 1924 Olympics, when the Englishman Harold Abrahams recorded an inches victory over Paddock in 10.6 s. However, over a period of years, Paddock proved to be the faster man in the 1920s he established a world record of 10.4 s and also ratified a then astonishing 'American noteworthy performance' of 10.2 s for the 110 yards.

The new generation of post-war American sprinters brought new precision to the event. As long ago as 1930 Tolan, running at an event in Canada, had recorded 10.2 but for some reason no application was made to the IAAF for ratification of a record performance. The record did not officially descend to 10.2 until 1948, when Barney Ewell won a race at Evanston, Illinois, in that time.

The 1940s were also remarkable for some legendary sprinting feats which, if they could ever be corroborated, would probably revise our estimate of mankind's top speed.

In May 1949 Mel Patton, running the anchor leg of a 4×110 yards, was timed to cover a flying 100 yards in 8.3 s. Averaged out, this would represent a speed of 39 km/h (24.64 mph).

This feat is matched by an account of the American Athletic Union 100 m final which took place in 1943. Matched against each other were H. 'Barney' Ewell (q.v.) and Hal Davis, co-holder of the world record at 10.2 s. Davis a criminally slow starter, was 3 m down on Ewell at the 50-metre mark but over the second half of the race closed, in an extraordinary burst, to

within a foot. Observers suggested that Davis must have surpassed 40 km/h (25 mph). This, in the light of modern evidence, seems unlikely but it remains an impressive display of human speed.

As sprinting techniques improved it began to take decades rather than years to lower the world record. The Panamanian sprinter Lloyd La Beach was the first person to record 10.1 s for the 100 metres and in the early 1950s actually got to 10 s dead, although this time was never upheld by the IAAF. It was left to the American sprinter Bob Hayes to record the first official 10.0 s at the 1964 Olympic final in Tokyo.

Altitude running assisted the lowering of the record yet further. Jim Hines' 9.95 s at the 1968 Mexico Olympic final was an astonishing achievement, but it would have been even more astounding had the race been run at sea level.

Calvin Smith's 9.93 s, the current world record, which was recorded under normal conditions, suggests that the new wave of American sprinters will succeed in reducing it still further within the next few years.

The middle-distance crown

Although the One-Mile race has long been regarded as a classic distance, speed standards remained mediocre for much of the 19th century. Probably the first man ever to go beneath 4:30 s was the Englishman W.C. Gibbs who won the Inter-Varsity mile of 1868, in what was then the sensational time of 4:28.8. After this, there was no substantial improvement for a dozen years—until a 22-year-old Wiltshireman, named W.G. George, arrived on the scene. He reduced the record to 4:24.2 and, in a series of stages, to 4:18.4. Interestingly, this is approximately the equivalent of a 4-min 1500 m, an extremely mediocre performance by an athlete today.

On 23 August 1886, in a duel with the North-countryman W. Cummings, George pushed the record down to 4:12.75 where it stayed for some time. Until the outbreak of World War I a sub-4:20 mile was still a rarity. Public interest was perenially excited by this classic middle distance event. It was simply that running techniques had yet to adapt themselves to the problems of maintaining a sustained speed over four laps.

The mile had always been an Englishman's event. The new generation of Scandinavian athletes changed all that. In the 1920s Paavo Nurmi, the 'Flying Finn' produced a devastating 4:10.4. The great French middle-distance runner Jules Ladoumègue subsequently reduced this to 4:9.2.

But the new star of middle-distance running was a New Zealander, John Edward Lovelock, a student of Otago University who was studying at Oxford in the 1930s. In 1933 he was competing in the United States against the combined Princeton, Cornell, Harvard and Yale University teams, his principal opponent being the American champion W.R. Bouthron. Lovelock broke new ground with 4:07.6. This was seen as an apogee for mile times but within a year Glenn Cunningham, the 'Iron Horse of Kansas' had cut this by 0.8 to 4:06.8.

But the new challenger to the record was another Englishman, the balding, bespectacled Sydney Wooderson who, at Motspur Park on 28 August 1937, clocked a time of 4:06.4. Wooderson dominated middle-distance running up until the outbreak of World War II and it was not until 1941, with most of Europe war-bound, that news began to leak through from neutral Sweden of two incredible new 'finds'—Hagg and Andersson. In a mile race at Gothenburg that year, the two fought an exciting duel all the way to the tape. The race ended with Hagg lowering the world record to 4:06.2 while Andersson equalled Wooderson's old time.

As the rest of Europe watched from afar, Hagg continued to take seconds off his best time. A final effort, at Malmo, Sweden in 1945, brought it down to 4:01.4. This was felt to be about as sophisticated as middle-distance running could get and the four-min mile was still regarded as a more or less impossible dream: it had taken nearly 80 years to reduce the world best time from 4:30 s to 4:01. But in 1954, at the Iffley Road sports ground in Oxford, in a race distinguished by ingenious pacing techniques, Roger Bannister, a medical student, ran the first sub four-minute mile: 3:59.4. The impossible had been done.

Yet the athletes of the 1960s and 70s left Hagg and Bannister far behind. By 1966 Jim Ryun (who, sadly, never won an Olympic final) had reduced the record to 3:51.1. The New Zealander John Walker's 3:49.4 broke yet another barrier and Sebastian Coe's current world record of 3:47.4 looks as if it may not last very long. The great increase in techniques and endurance—and ultimately of course in speeds—is obvious. In the 70 years betwen 1868 and 1938 the world record was reduced by only 22.4 s. Yet it took only another 45 years to bring it down by a further 19 s. And in the last 30 years the World Record has been reduced by exactly 12 s—about the length of the finishing straight. This improvement in speeds has not merely been the prerogative of champions. Four-minute miles are now a commonplace, with even club athletes dipping below the former 'dream mark'.

Swimming

Swimming is not the most natural of human speed activities. Man was not born to exist in an aquatic environment. Thus his performance in the water is largely a matter of adaptability. Maximum pace remains at under one-fifth of locomotive pace on land. However, competitive swimming is a comparatively recent phenomenon. It appears that man's aquatic speed capacity is not yet fully developed.

At present the fastest speed achieved by a male swimmer is 7.98 km/h (4.96 mph) by Robin Leary (USA) when he completed 50 m in 22.54 s at Milwaukee on 15 August 1981. The female record is 7.03 km/h (4.37 mph) by Dara Torres (USA), this in the completion of a 25.62 s 50 m at Clovis, New Mexico on 6 August 1983.

Significantly, both these records were achieved in straight 50-m pools. The 'turn' in shorter pools can clip as much as a second from final timings.

However, swimming speeds are improving and the rate is remarkably constant. In 50 years the United States records for the 50 yards and the 100 yards have been lowered by 24.5 per cent and 26.4 per cent respectively. The average improvement is close to 1.8 s a decade, or 0.2 s each year. In contrast, running sprint records have improved by less than 10 per cent since the turn of the century.

These figures have led swimming statisticians to speculate that we are still some way from the ultimate in world records since the inception of speed swimming at the beginning of the century. Certainly, the rate of improvement has been phenomenal. In 1956, for instance, 5 min for the 400 metres was bettered by a woman for the first time. Since then this mark has been bettered well over a thousand times. Mankind is getting faster in the water.

Obviously, swimmers do not maintain the same rate throughout races. Even over short distances, competitors find it difficult to maintain 100 per cent effort all the way. This was effectively demonstrated at the Mexico Olympics 100 metres final. Zorn, who held the world record, expended too much energy at the start, leading at the turn, having recorded a 24.4 s 50 metres. He could not maintain the rate.

The best swimmers conserve their energy. The first 58 s 100 m at the butterfly stroke is a good indication of this. Lewis Berry swam the first 50 metres in 28 s and only reduced his rate slightly to complete the second 50 metres in 30 s.

This energy conservation has led to the development of 'even pace' swimming. In some cases the second half of a middle-distance race is swum at a faster rate than the first. Watchers of the sport will have noticed how many American competitors 'kick hard' in the second half of the race. This contrasts interestingly with athletics where it is exceedingly rare for the second half of a race to be run at a faster rate than the first, in events below 1000 m.

What makes fast swimmers?

As we remarked, swimming is an adaptive rather than a natural skill. According to scientific estimates the best swimmers tend to have body weights of 76–84 kg (168–186 lb), heights of up to 185 cm (6 ft 2½ in). One coach has likened the physique of a champion to a racing dog. A low-resting heart beat is also important: the lower the rate the greater the efficiency of the heart muscle. Most Olympic athletes average 50 beats/min. Champion swimmers can dip beneath this rate. The Australian prodigy Dawn Fraser had a pulse rate of only 42 beats/min. A normal rate is *c* 72 beats/min.

Anatomically, human beings are usually divided into three body groups: endomorphs (short of stature and overweight), ectomorphs (tall and thin with light bones) and mesomorphs (who possess square and hard bodies with long

Dawn Fraser, the Australian swimming prodigy. Her pulse rate (42 beat/min) was a major contribution to her speed in the water. (Keystone Press)

trunks). The best swimmers are usually a combination of the latter two categories: ecto-mesomorphs, able to achieve fast bursts of speed in the water, while maintaining an underlying stamina.

A great deal depends on the rate of the stroke. Sprinters have faster arm turnovers than middle-distance swimmers. In a 50-metre race top performers will average a stroke a metre, doing the conventional crawl stroke. Other strokes have slower rates. Berry's butterfly record (q.v.) was obtained at the expense of only 37 strokes.

How can the swimmer be made faster?

According to one coach, swimming speed is improved only by experience in the ability to sprint. The variable nature of performances is demonstrated by D. Dickson's performance in the Tokyo Olympics of 1964.

The swimmer assured his coach that each 100 m he recorded was at 'absolute maximum' speed. However, his times for successive swims were 55.1 s, 54.9 s, 54.6 s and 54.1 s.

Other coaches have stressed the need for the elimination of 'frills' and concentration on faster turns. A properly executed tumble turn can save as much as 0.8 s.

The celebrated trainer Harry Gallagher achieved great success in coaching the Australian team at the 1968 Olympics with a doctored stopwatch. By setting the watch 0.3 s 'on' he convinced his team of the excellence of their performances in training; performances they equalled and excelled in competitions timed with normal watches.

Channel swimming
The Channel Swimming Association's official record for the crossing of the English Channel is 7 h 40 min by Penny Dean (b 1955) of California, swimming from Shakespeare Beach, Dover, to Cap Gris Nez, France, on 29 July 1978.

The difficulties involved in crossing the Channel do not so much relate to distance but to tides and currents and uncertain weather conditions. The

A meeting of the rival coaches: these breakneck races were commonplace in early Victorian England. (BBC Hulton Picture Library)

fastest crossing by a commercial ship, for instance, is merely 53 min 49 s.

Given this reliance on the environment, the crucial factor involved in swimming the Channel is timing. There are four ebb and flow tides of 6 h in a single day. Consequently, the aim must be to start on an outgoing tide and land on the opposite shore on an ingoing one. Too slow (or for that matter too fast) a rate can catch a swimmer on the wrong tide and throw him or her miles off course.

The fastest two-way crossing was completed in 19 h 12 min by Cindy Nicholas (b 1957) of Canada, 4–5 August 1979.

Jon Erikson, 27, a physical training instructor from the USA, completed the first three-way crossing without a break in 38 h 27 min on 11–12 August 1981.

Coaching

The sport of racing a coach and horses reached a peak in the early 19th century before the advent of the railways. In earlier times the condition of roads rendered maximum speeds insignificant, but 18th-century improvements in road surfaces

combined with advances in coach-building techniques effected a drastic improvement in performance. Even then it was as much as coaches could do to cover 32 km (20 miles) in 2 h. This feat was achieved in 1808 when *Patriot* and *Defiance* (the sport encouraged fanciful nomenclature) raced each other from Leicester to Nottingham, the former completing the distance in 2 h 10 min, with a full complement of a dozen passengers.

The zenith of the sport came with the introduction of tarmacadam. However, speed estimation was still complicated by the practice of changing teams of horses at irregular intervals. For instance, in 1888 Mr Selby drove the *Old Times* coach 173 km (108 miles) from London to Brighton and back in 7 h 50 min (average speed 22.19 km/h, 13.79 mph), but he did so with no fewer than eight teams and 14 changes.

Four-horse carriages could maintain a speed of 34 km/h (21 mph) but this depended to a large degree on the alacrity of grooms and the speed with which they could substitute tired teams with fresh ones. A trained team were known to perform this changeover in 48 s flat.

Cricket

Aside from the speed at which the cricket ball is propelled, the factor of principal interest is obviously the run rate. As a day's play in the first class game is of 6 h duration it is possible to arrive at reasonably precise estimations, although variations frequently arise as the result of tardy over-rates.

The fastest rate of scoring in a day's play is 721 runs in 5 h 48 min by the Australian touring side against Essex at Southend on 15 May 1948. The test record is predictably slower—588 runs at Old Trafford, Manchester on 27 July 1936, composed of 398 English runs and 190 by their opponents, India.

Over short periods of time the fastest ever run rate is that recorded by Lancashire in a match against Leicestershire on 13 September 1983. Batsmen O'Shaughnessy and Fowler scored 201 runs in 45 min. The match, however, was dead and the bowling, to say the least, irregular

Individual speed scoring feats centre on the 50 and 100 marks. Clive Inman (b 1936) needed

Denis Compton, scorer of the fastest triple century in cricket history.

only 8 min to score 50 runs, playing for Northamptonshire against Nottinghamshire at Trent Bridge on 20 August 1965, this off 13 balls in 11 scoring strokes. Percy Fender (b 1892) achieved the fastest ever century in 35 min for Surrey against Northamptonshire on 26 August 1920. However, no accurate count was kept of the number of deliveries he received: between 40 and 46. David Hookes, playing for South Australia against Victoria on 25 October 1982 scored a century off 34 balls. The feat, however, took him 43 min.

These very fast run rates are not maintained, the higher a player's score becomes. The fastest double century in first class cricket clocks in at 2 h exactly; by Gilbert Jessup for Gloucestershire *v* Sussex at Hove on 1 June 1903. This figure was equalled by the West Indian captain Clive Lloyd, playing against Glamorgan at Swansea on 9 August 1976.

Denis Compton's fastest ever treble century, for the MCC against North Eastern Transvaal in 1948, took 181 min and involved an overnight break although this must seriously have disturbed his concentration.

The fastest Test Match 'double' (1000 runs, 100 wickets) was achieved by the Indian Kapil Dev (b 1959) between 1978–80, during Test series against Pakistan, the West Indies and England.

Minor cricketing records are even more astonishing: one should not assume that speed is the prerogative of Test cricketers. For instance, Vivian Crawford (1879–1922) took only 19 min to score a century in a minor game in 1899.

As regards team run rate, in the match between the Royal Naval College, Dartmouth and Seale Hayne Agricultural College in 1923, K.A. Sellar and L.K.A. Block were set to score 174 runs in 105 min but achieved the requisite number of runs in 33 min, thus averaging 5.27 runs/min.

Cycling

There are two entirely different sets of speed records for cycles (pedal cycles propelled only by the rider). The highest speeds ever measured for unassisted machines are all just under the US road speed limit of 88.5 km/h (55 mph), as detailed in the relevant section of 'The Technical World' on a later page. Much higher speeds can be reached by riders cycling behind a car or

other vehicle provided with a windbreak to cut down the cyclist's wind resistance (in fact, with care, the airflow behind the lead vehicle can be made to curl round and help thrust the cyclist along). The highest speed recorded under these very artificial conditions is 226.1 km/h (140.5 mph) set by Dr Allan V. Abbott, of San Bernardino, California, on 25 August 1973. He rode behind a windbreak mounted on a 1955 Chevrolet, and the speed was measured over 1.21 km (0.75 mile).

The one-hour record for a rider behind a windbreak lead vehicle is 122.862 km (76.343 miles) set by Leon Vanderstuyft of Belgium on the Montlhéry (Paris) motor circuit on 30 September 1928.

The introduction of pacing was a significant, though perhaps artificial, development in the history of the sport. Initially promoters put out single riders. Subsequently tandems were brought in to keep pace with exceptionally speedy riders. Finally, multiple pacing machines were constructed, the ultimate being a 15-man 'quidecuplet' manufactured in the USA at the end of the last century.

By this time, as cycle racing became a successful sporting attraction, each rider possessed his own series of pacers, often provided by the tyre company to any rider whose cycle was fitted with the company's products. In the 1890s the Dunlop company had 60 such employees who were used in races and record attempts.

Today, the most popular form of cycling is probably road racing, which reaches its most sustained demonstration in the annual Tour de France. The fastest average speed was the 37 km/h (23.2 mph) recorded by Jacques Anquetil in 1962.

In the Tour of Britain, now known as the Milk Race, Fedor den Hertog recorded an average speed of 40.55 km/h (25.20 mph) in 1971. The record for the Lands End to John O' Groats race is 1 day 22 h 39 min 50 s—average speed 29.57 km/h (18.39 mph) by Mick Coupe on 28–30 June 1982. This is a true average, the 'tours' not including sleeping time.

Association Football

Goalscoring

Controversy surrounds the fastest goal in

Association Football, some authorities claiming that allowance should be made for the time taken for the pressure of the stop watch and the speed of the referee's reflexes.

Given this caution, the quickest goal ever scored in first class football occurred after 4 s in the game between Bradford City and Tranmere Rovers on 25 April 1964. The scorer was Jim Fryatt of Bradford.

Three players have scored goals after only 6 s:

Barrie Jones for Notts County against Torquay United in a Third Division game, 31 March 1962.

Keith Smith for Crystal Palace against Derby County in a Second Division match at Derby, 12 December 1964.

Albert Mundy, for Aldershot in a match against Hartlepool, 25 October 1958.

Torquay's Pat Kruse headed into his *own* goal after only 6 s in a match against Cambridge United, 3 January 1977.

In amateur football, wind-assisted goals in which the ball was blown over the head of startled keepers have been recorded in 3 s. A recent instance was by Andrew Meadows playing for Riley High School, Hull, against Kelvin Hall High School, on 4 March 1977.

The fastest goal in an FA Cup Final came after only 40 s in the 1895 tie between Aston Villa and West Bromwich Albion. Jackie Milburn netted after 45 s in the 1955 final for Newcastle against Manchester City.

Among more sustained rates of scoring, John McIntyre, playing for Blackburn Rovers against Everton in a First Division game on 16 September 1922, scored four goals in 5 min. Ginger Richardson, the West Bromwich Albion centre forward, performed the same feat in a match against West Ham in November 1931.

Fastest rise through the football league
Northampton Town took only four seasons to climb from the Fourth Division to the First Division between 1961 and 1965.

Rugby Football

H.L. Price, playing for England against Wales at Twickenham in 1923, scored a try direct from kick-off without any other player managing to touch the ball.

In the Rugby League game, David Watkins, playing for Salford against Barrow in 1972, scored 13 points in 5 min—comprising three tries and two conversions.

Golf

Because of substantial variations in the length of courses, speed records in golf are of little intrinsic value, even those involving rounds completed under par.

Robert Williams, playing on a course at Eugene, Oregon, in 1971 completed an 18-hole course (5495 m, 6010 yd) in 27 min 48.2 s, but indulgent judges allowed him to strike the ball while it was still moving. The record for a stationary ball is 31 min 22 s by Len Richardson, a South African athlete of Olympic fame, at a 5685 m (6248 yd) course at Cape Town, November 1931.

Speed records achieved by groups of players are virtually meaningless, but it is worth noting that 43 players representing Borger High School, Texas, completed the 18-hole, 5586 m (6109 yd) Huber Golf Course in 10 min 11.4 s on 11 June 1976.

A speed endurance record was probably that established by Ian Colston, 35, at the Bendigo Golf Club, Victoria, Australia on 27–28 November 1971. Colston played 22 rounds and five holes in 24 h, ie 401 holes at an average rate of 16.7 holes/h.

Greyhound Racing

More properly, dog speeds should be classifiable elsewhere but it should be pointed out that many of the speeds are obtained as the result of human agency. That is, if we did not train greyhounds so exhaustively, it is unlikely that they would run as fast.

Confusion existed over maximum greyhound speeds until the advent of precise methods of measurement. Greyhounds racing at Southland, West Memphis, Tennessee, were timed by radar at speeds approaching 74 km/h (46 mph). The best handtimed speed, previous to this, was the 67.14 km/h (41.72 mph) by 'The Shoe' on the straight track at Richmond, New South Wales.

The Saluki: probably the world's fastest untrained dog. Used in Arabia to hunt gazelles it has recorded a speed of 69 km/h (43 mph). (Syndication International)

It was estimated that the dog covered the last 100 yd in only 4.5 s, achieving 73.15 km/h (45.45 mph). This is almost exactly twice as fast as the best human 100 yd.

The highest greyhound speed recorded in Great Britain is 63 km/h (39.13 mph) by 'Beef Cutlet' along a straight 457 m (500 yd) course at Blackpool, Lancashire on 13 May 1933. The fastest photo-timing over 500 yd is 28.96 s at the Brighton Stadium by 'Monday's Bran', on 4 August 1979, 56.83 km/h (35.31 mph).

Over hurdles, the fastest photo-timing was the 61 km/h (37.64 mph) by 'Wotchit Buster' also at Brighton on 22 August 1978.

As remarked earlier, the greyhound is artificially trained. The saluki, or Arabian gazelle hound, probably the world's fastest untrained dog, has achieved speeds of 68 km/h (43 mph), which suggests that in competition it would probably be appreciably faster.

Foxhounds are capable of remarkable sustained speeds. In an interesting experiment, at the end of the 18th century, a number of race horses and foxhounds were matched against each other on a 4-mile course at Newmarket. The winning hound recorded an average speed of 50 km/h (31 mph).

Horseracing

The fastest speed ever recorded by a race horse is 69.52 km/h (43.26 mph) by 'Big Racket' over 0.25 mile of the Mexico City course on 5 February 1945. On a British course the 4-year-old 'Indigenous' ran 1.01 km (0.62 mile) in 53.6 s (67.16 km/h, 41.73 mph) over the Epsom course, Surrey, in June 1960.

This record was hand-timed, thus leaving a substantial margin for error. Ten years later, 'Raffingora' was electronically timed over the same distance at 53.89 s.

The record for the English Derby, the cynosure of the five classic races, is 2 min 33.8 s for the 2.4 km (1.5 mile) Epsom course. This was achieved by the Aga Khan's horse 'Mahmoud', running at an average speed of 56 km/h (35.06 mph) in 1936. 'Apelle' recorded a hand-timed 2 min 33 s in the 1928 Coronation Cup race, run over the same course. 'Bustino' recorded an electronically timed Coronation Cup win of 2 min 33.31 s in June 1975.

These speeds are remarkably constant, probably because horseracing, an ancient sport, has been concentrating on speed techniques for over two centuries. The sport reached a high point of development at a comparatively early stage. Seventeenth-century enthusiasts had realised that certain systems of mating produced much faster horses and the concept of the thoroughbred soon came into favour. Ancestries are far from disparate. All thoroughbred race horses are descended in direct male line from one of only three of the 200 Arabian, Turkish and Barbary steeds imported to England during the 17th and 18th centuries.

The greatest feat of steeplechasing was achieved by 'Red Rum' who completed the Aintree Grand National Course (7242 m, 4.5 miles, 30 jumps) in 9 min 1.9 s in 1973. This represents an average speed of 47.96 km/h (29.80 mph) and would undoubtedly have been faster, had the animal not been carrying 66 kg (10 st 5 lb).

The standard of speed in trotting, or harness racing, the type of horseracing in which the rider is towed along in a small cart, has been rising steadily as improved breeding methods have produced faster horses.

Above:
The Aga Khan leads 'Mahmoud' into the winner's enclosure after the completion of the 1936 Epsom Derby. (BBC Hulton Picture Library)

'Red Rum's' exploits were even the inspiration for poetry. This tribute comes from the wall of the winner's enclosure at Aintree. (BBC Hulton Picture Library)

THE GRAND NATIONAL 1977

RED RUM

SOME HORSES COME. SOME HORSES GO, WHOSE NAMES WILL LAST FOR YEARS.

AND ONE OF THESE IS WITH US NOW WHOSE FEAT BROUGHT FLOODS OF TEARS.

THREE TIMES HE WON ROUND AINTREE AND HIS SPIRIT DID NOT FADE.

HE WAS SUBLIME AND GENTLE AND A TOUCH OF CLASS DISPLAYED.

SO LET US NOT FORGET THIS HORSE. STAND UP AND BEAT THE DRUM.

WHEN TALES OF AINTREE SHALL BE TOLD THE ANSWER IS RED RUM.

A major step forward came with the introduction of bicycle wheels for the cart, or 'sulky'. These had the effect of reducing vibration and the chance of overturning on fast bends. Smaller than earlier wheels, they allowed the driver to sit lower behind the horse and reduce wind resistance.

Equipped with these innovatory techniques, 'Lou Dillon' became the first horse to break the 2 min mile with a time of 1 min 58.5 s in 1903.

Thereafter improvements came slowly. In 1938 the record figures set by 'Greyhound' had only descended to 1 min 55.25 s. This was considered unbeatable until in 1969 a 2-year-old named 'Nevele Pride' recorded 1 min 54.8 s at Indianapolis.

Ice Hockey

This fast team sport preserves some appropriately speedy records. Kim D. Miles scored after only 3 s for the University of West Ontario against Guelph, Canada, on 11 February 1975.

As for the rate of scoring, Toronto recorded eight goals in 4 min 52 s against the New York Americans on 19 March 1938. The individual record is a hat-trick in 21 s by Bill Mosienko of the Chicago Black Hawks against New York Rangers on 23 March 1952.

In Great Britain, Kenny Westman of the Nottingham Panthers scored three goals in 30 s against the Brighton Tigers on 3 March 1955.

Skiing

The highest speed claimed for any skier is 208.09 km/h (129.30 mph) by Franz Weber (Austria) at Silverton, Colorado, on 23 April 1983. Kristan Culver (USA) achieved the fastest female speed—194.38 km/h (120.78 mph) on the same date and at the same location.

The highest average speed in an Olympic Downhill race was in 1976 on the Patscherkofel Course at Innsbruck, Austria, set by the Austrian Franz Klammer who recorded 165.482 km/h (102.826 mph) on 5 February 1976.

Skiing speeds have improved markedly since World War II, a process that began with the introduction of metal skis in the 1950s.

This was followed by fibre-reinforced plastic skis and finally by a metal/plastic combination which quickly dominated the Alpine market.

Skiing is a sport possessing considerable attractions to the speed statistician. As the sole

Austrian skier Franz Klammer. His 165.482 km/h (102.826 mph) is the highest average speed in an Olympic downhill race. (All Sport)

object is to career down a steep, predetermined course faster than anybody else, great attention is paid to accurate methods of timing. In top class races the timing device is set off at the start by the skier's leg and a magic eye beam is broken at the finish to record the time electronically to 0.01 s. This accuracy is absolutely necessary as modern ski races are often decided by such delicate margins.

Bobsleigh and Tobogganing

The two principal forms of sleigh riding on ice are bobsleigh riding and tobogganing, both of which have inspired serious competition for over a century.

The fastest bobsleigh speed ever recorded was by the four-man American team on Lake Placid, USA, in 1969. They covered the mile-long track in 1 min 4 s, representing an average speed of 90.53 km/h (56.25 mph).

Speeds of 128 km/h (80 mph) have been recorded on the luge—a variety of toboggan, in which the sled is ridden in a sitting position instead of the rider lying prone.

The record for the Cresta Run at St Moritz, Switzerland—the oldest toboggan club in the world (founded 1887)—is 53.24 s (average 82.02 km/h, 50.96 mph) by Poldi Berchtold of Switzerland on 9 February 1975. Speeds of 145 km/h (90 mph) are occasionally achieved on the faster parts of this twisting 1212-metre (1325 yd) course.

Skating

The foremost criterion for speed roller skating is a smooth skating surface. Curiously, the fastest speed attained during an official world record is 41.48 km/h (25.78 mph) when Giuseppe Cantarella recorded 34.9 s for 402 m (440 yd) on a Sicilian road on 29 September 1963.

The world mile record on an ice skating rink is 2 min 25.1 s by the Italian Ferretti at Inzell, West Germany, on 28 September 1968.

Rowing

The Boat Race
Rowing speeds in the annual competition between Oxford and Cambridge Universities vary considerably, being dependent on such factors as wind speed and general weather conditions. The race record time for the present 4 mile 374 yd course is 16 min 45 s by Oxford in 1984. This represents an average speed of 24.28 km/h (15.09 mph).

The fastest pace is probably obtained at the very start of the race. The Oxford eight reached the mile post in 1978 after 3 min 31 s (fractionally better than Steve Ovett's world 1500 metre record)—an average speed of 27.45 km/h (17.06 mph).

Henley
At the Henley Royal Regatta the record time for the 2212 m (1 mile 550 yd) course is 7 min 40 s by the Irishman Sean Drea in 1975.

Other events
The highest recorded speed on non-tidal water for 2000 m is by an East German eight in 5 min 32.17 s (21.66 km/h, 13.46 mph) in the FISA Championships on the River Meuse, Belgium, in 1980.

The Rev Sidney Swann (1862–1942) sculled the English Channel in 3 h 50 min on 12 September 1911.

Loch Ness (36.5 km, 22.7 miles in length) has been traversed by an individual—George Parsonage of Edinburgh—in 2 h 43 min 34.1 s in 1975. A junior coxed eight could only manage the distance in 2 h 35 min 38.2 s.

The fastest ever recorded punting speed is an appreciably slower 12.2 km/h (7.6 mph).

Water Skiing

A record speed of 230.26 km/h (143.08 mph) was established on 6 March 1983 in NSW, Australia by Christopher Massey. Donna Patterson Brice (USA) set a female record of 178 km/h (111.11 mph) at Long Beach Marine Stadium, California, on 21 August 1977.

The fastest pace attained by a British skier over a measured kilometre is the 131.2 km/h (81.5 mph) of Billy Rixon on Lake Windermere in 1973.

Elizabeth Hobbs recorded 122.18 km/h (75.92 mph) in the same circumstances in 1982.

The fastest barefoot water ski run (estimated by defining an average from two runs) was Lee Kirk's 177.06 km/h (110.02 mph) at Firebird Lake, Phoenix, Arizona, on 11 June 1977. His fastest run was at 182.93 km/h (113.67 mph).

Boxing

In any estimation of the fastest speed in which a bout has been completed, it is important to draw a distinction between the fastest *knock-out* and the fastest *fight*. For instance, a knock-out in 10.5 s (including a 10 s count) occurred on 29 September 1946 in Maine, when Al Couture struck Ralph Walton while the latter was adjusting his gum-shield in the corner of the ring. Obviously, Couture was more than half way across the ring from his own corner at the opening bell—a move of doubtful legality.

The shortest fight on record took place in a Golden Gloves tournament at Minneapolis, Minnesota, on 4 November 1947. Mike Collins floored Pat Brownson after a single punch had been thrown and the contest was stopped without a count, 4 s after the opening bell.

The fastest officially timed knock-out in British boxing is the 11 s (including a 10 s count) when Jack Cain beat Harry Deamer at the National Sporting Club on 20 February 1922.

The fastest completion of a title fight, in which competitors are more evenly matched, was when the referee stopped the fight after 63 s when Michael Dokes (USA) beat Mike Weaver (USA) for the WBA title on 10 December 1982.

The length of the fight between Muhammad Ali (then known as Cassius Clay) and Sonny Liston at Lewiston, Maine, on 25 May 1965 was given as 1 min by ringside announcers. However, video tape recordings denote a time of 1 min 52 s, including the count.

The fastest ever World Title Fight took place on 7 April 1914 in New York, when Al McCoy knocked out George Chip in 45 s to win the Middleweight crown.

In the British Lightweight Championship fight of 20 November 1961, Dave Charnley took only 40 s to knock out the challenger David Hughes.

The fastest removal of a Heavyweight crown was at the expense of Leon Spinks, USA, who held his title for only 212 days in 1978.

Indoor Games

Darts

Darts is not by nature a speed sport, the objective being victory rather than celerity. Nevertheless, several spectacular attempts have been made to improve the rate at which darts are thrown.

The fastest time taken for a match of three games of 301 is 1 min 58 s by Ricky Fusco (GB) at the Perivale Residents' Association Club, Middlesex, on 30 December 1976.

The record time for going round the dart board clockwise in double at arm's length is 9.2 s by Dennis Gower at Hastings, Sussex in 1975, an average rate of more than two darts/s.

Significantly, the record for this feat at the standard throwing distance (2.7 m, 9 ft) in which the aspirant is required to retrieve his own darts, is 2 min 13 s—by Bill Duddy at The Plough, Harringay, London, on 29 October 1972.

Billiards

A great deal of effort has been expended in the pursuit of the fastest century break; a record attributed to the Australian Walter Lindrum who recorded an unofficial century in 27.5 s in Australia in 1952. His official record is 46 s in Sydney in 1941.

In the bar billiards game, the fastest rate of scoring was 11 700 in 10 min on a timed table by Thomas Clayton at The Greyhound, Battersea, London, on 18 June 1974. The record scoring rate in a league game was 24 340 in 17 min by John Stevens at the Ampthill Hotel, Southampton, on 25 January 1979. The highest score in 24 h (admittedly by a five-man team) is 1 359 370 by players representing the G.D. Searle 'A' team at High Wycombe, Buckinghamshire, on 16–17 March 1979.

Marbles

The record for clearing the ring of 49 marbles (between 1.75 and 1.90 m (5.75 and 6.25 ft) in diameter) is 2 min 57 s by the Toucan Terribles—Britain's foremost marbling ensemble—at Worthing, Sussex in 1971.

Pool

The record time for potting all 15 balls in a speed competition is 47 s by Ross McInnes at the Kirkhall Hotel, Gorebridge, Midlothian, on 4 March 1983.

Franz Weber. The world's fastest skier launches himself into space. (All Sport)

The late John F. Kennedy. World's fastest talker on the campaign trail in Georgia, 1960. (Syndication International)

John, Paul, George and Ringo: their second single, *Please Please Me* emerged out of the fastest recording session of all time. (Syndication International)

Pietro Mennea—arguably the world's fastest human. (Syndication International)

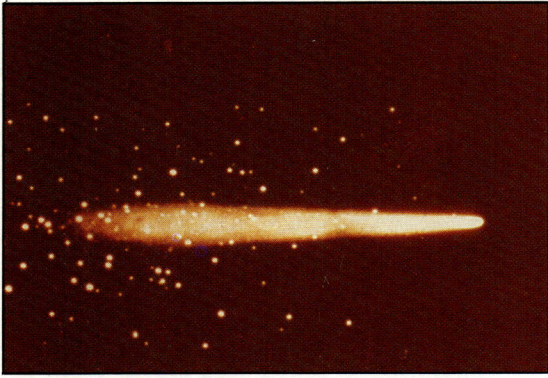

Halley's comet, brightest of the regularly returning comets, passes near to Earth in 1986 but does not return again until 2062. On each visit it is readily visible from Earth (because of the growth of the bright tail, caused by the Sun) for about two years, during which it travels some 1800 million km (1118 million miles), travelling fastest at the point of perihelion (closest to the Sun).

Boeing's HiBEX high-acceleration rocket vehicles were flown from White Sands Missile Range, New Mexico, USA, from 25 February 1965. There was no need for a parachute to cushion the complex electronic systems: the acceleration during motor burn was higher than the deceleration on crashing back to Earth! (Boeing)

Right:
Eruption at night at Hekla, Iceland; expulsion velocities are about 90 m/s (200 ft/s), and in the distance can be seen a river of lava probably moving faster than humans could run. (Picturepoint)

Lower right:
One of the most beautiful galaxies is NGC 224, Messier 31, better known as the Andromeda galaxy. Some 2.2 million light-years distant, it is the most remote object visible to the naked eye. But we see it in a way that may be difficult to comprehend. It is so large that light takes about 150 000 years to cross it, so we see the near side (the galaxy is almost edge-on) about 150 000 years older, ie more recently, than we see the far side. (Caltech and Carnegie Institute, Space Frontiers)

Far right:
The 615-km/h (382-mph) Bell XV-15, the fastest convertiplane, is seen here with its pivoted engine/propeller units in the act of rotating forwards for high-speed flight, supported by its small wing. This arrangement might be used for anything from a battlefield attack aircraft to a large passenger liner. (Bell Aerospace)

Current holder of the official LSR, Richard Noble has a splendid car in *Thrust 2*. (National Motor Museum)

Left:
Convertibles tend to have high drag, but the odd Panther Six has always been marketed as a 200-mph (322-km/h) car—almost three times the permitted maximum on the highways of its native Britain. (National Motor Museum)

Below:
Small dark rectangles show the positions occupied by the heads of Jan Russell (nearest the front, right) and Butch Stanton in pedalling *White Lightning*, the fastest of all bicycles.

PART 2

THE TECHNICAL WORLD

by Bill Gunston

This chapter is divided into three main sections: land, water, and air and space. It covers everything that might be called a vehicle, the 'land' section also including lifts (elevators), ski lifts and transport by pipeline. It also has a sub-section entitled 'skimmers' in which are grouped power-driven vehicles that glide over ice and snow or are supported over land by an air cushion but not guided by tracks (tracked ACVs—air-cushion vehicles—come under the general heading of Guided Land Transport). Clearly, there is no place in this section for skaters, skiers, horse-drawn vehicles or sedan chairs, but we have admitted sailing ships, sand yachts and various other vehicles without an inbuilt source of power. Even so, there were some fine lines to be drawn; for example, while the 'land' section includes a wealth of off-the-road vehicles, armoured fighting vehicles such as tanks are dealt with in a special chapter, Weapons. Here also will be found data on bullets, shells, missiles and other implements of war.

This photograph shows the launch of a TOW anti-tank missile which pierces armour by projecting a fantastically fast jet. (General Dynamics, Hughes Aircraft)

Speed acceleration comparison

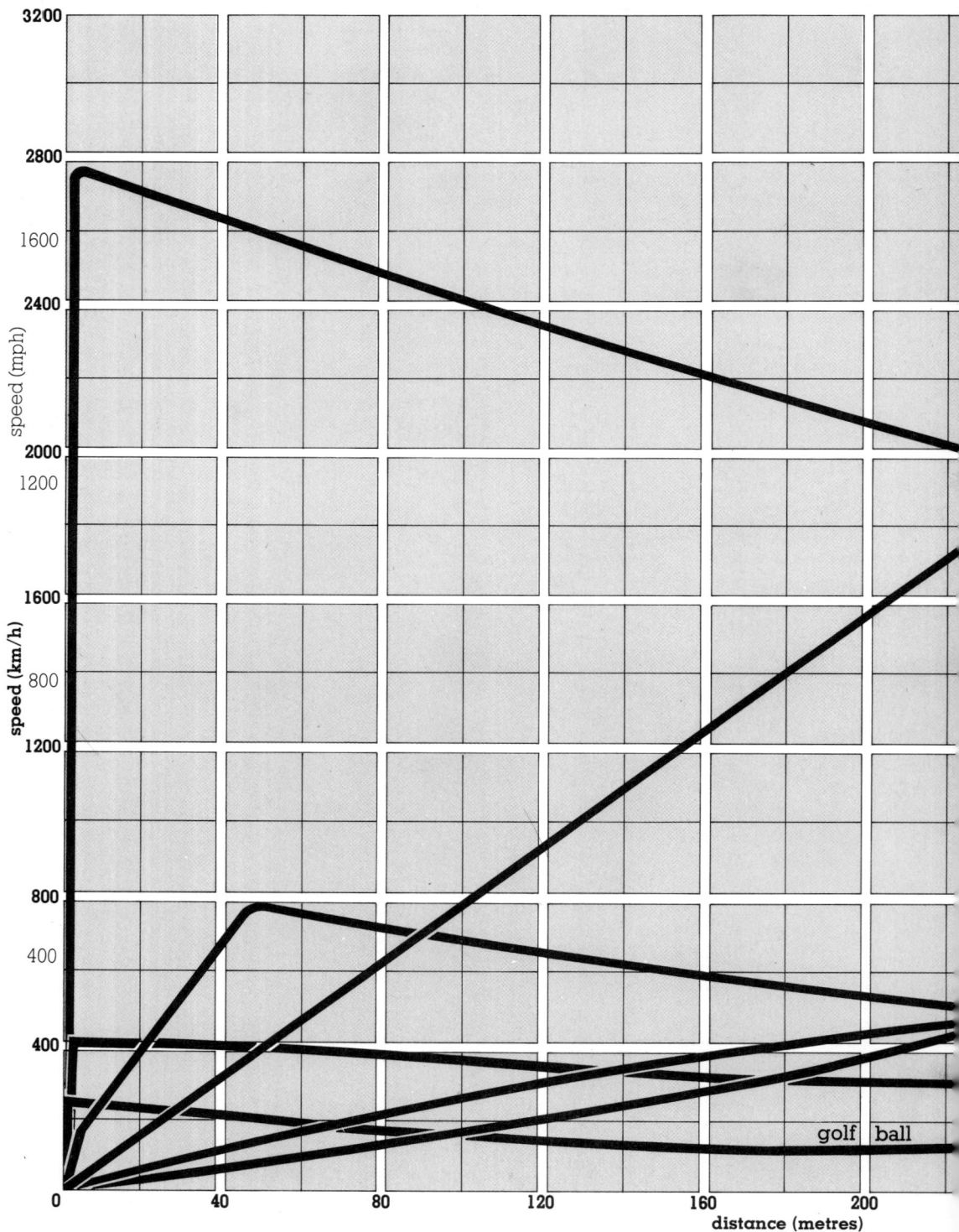

golf ball

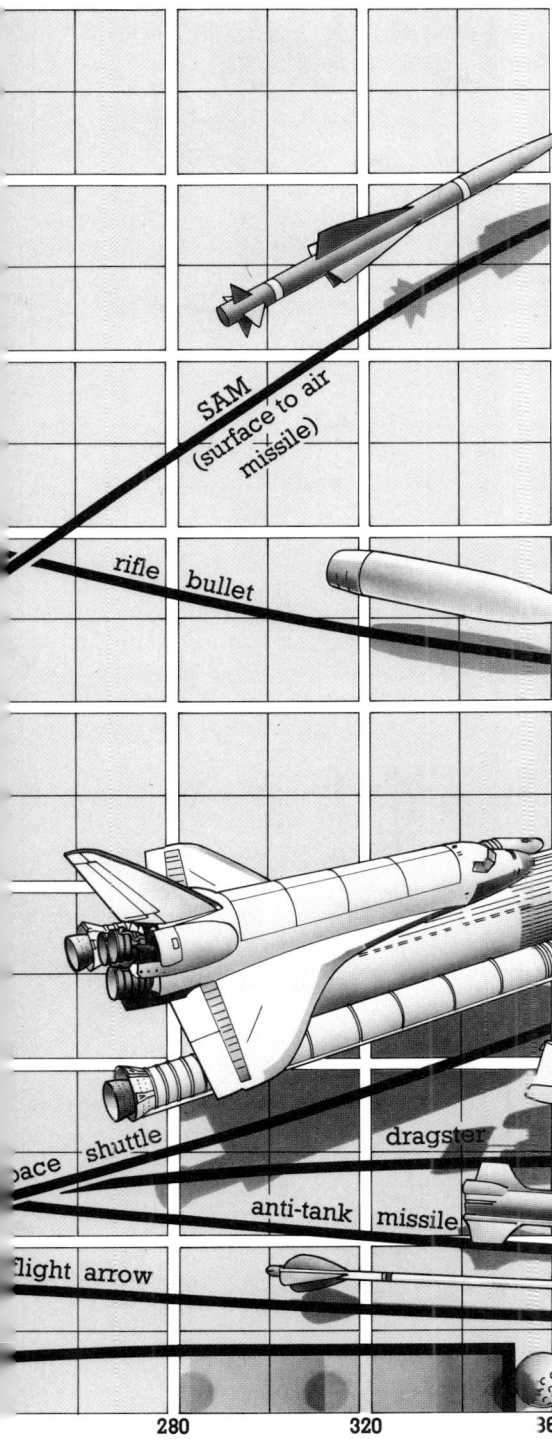

This diagram shows how different things accelerate from rest at the start of their travel. The rifle bullet accelerates very quickly indeed, and reaches its maximum velocity in less than 1 m; but from the moment it leaves the muzzle it slows down. As it gets slower, the deceleration (rate of slowing down) gets less, thus its plot of speed against distance travelled is a gentle curve. The flight arrow and golf ball are similar, in that they accelerate to full speed very quickly and subsequently slow down. The golf ball, struck for maximum distance, goes very high and in falling back its speed may remain roughly constant or even increase, until (depending on how far it goes) its speed is suddenly slowed by striking the ground. The anti-tank missile is initially given a sharp kick, and then accelerates quickly under the thrust of a short-duration rocket. The SAM, however, has a powerful, long-burning rocket and reaches its peak speed just 'out of the picture'. The dragster, likewise, is still accelerating when it goes through the vital quarter-mile mark, also just out of the picture. At about this point it would manage to overtake the arrow, fired at the same instant the dragster began its run. And the item which takes longest of all to cover the first 100 m is the Space Shuttle, which just keeps on accelerating until it is going fast enough to go into orbit.

SAM
(surface to air
missile)

rifle bullet

space shuttle

dragster

anti-tank missile

flight arrow

280   320   360

LAND

Road vehicles

Under this heading are grouped mechanically propelled land vehicles that are not guided by a fixed track. Cars, trucks and buses, and motorcycles are obviously important categories; but it so happens that the fastest and most exciting cars are not intended to run on roads and could do so only illegally and with the greatest difficulty. The section also includes special cars and trucks specifically intended to run where there are no roads—over marshes and deserts, for example—as well as amphibious vehicles of which one of the more unexpected examples is a regular large-size tractor which purposefully made its way from France to England driven by its large rear tyres spinning in the sea. Is an enthusiastic roller-skater clutching a small rocket in each hand a road vehicle? Not in this book!

Car speed records

As far as this book is concerned, the most important class of cars—a loose word which in most English-speaking countries is also applied to such quite different vehicles as rail passenger coaches and freight vehicles running on railed tracks in mines—are those designed to break speed records. This major category is therefore dealt with first; but what a chequered history greets the researcher into the story of the LSR (land speed record)! Half the time the Americans set their own records and refused to recognise those set in Europe, while the French—traditionally the home of the sport's governing body—refused to consider any speed submitted by the United States. Records were set, only to be rejected because the car had no reverse gear, or had only three wheels, or was propelled by a jet blasting out of a nozzle instead of by driving its wheels. The best way to handle the story is strictly chronologically without regard to type of vehicle.

1770 Though many mechanically propelled land vehicles are mentioned in writings dating back to about 800 BC, the earliest of which details are known was a military tractor built at the Arsenal in Paris in 1769 by French artilleryman N-J Cugnot and tested in early

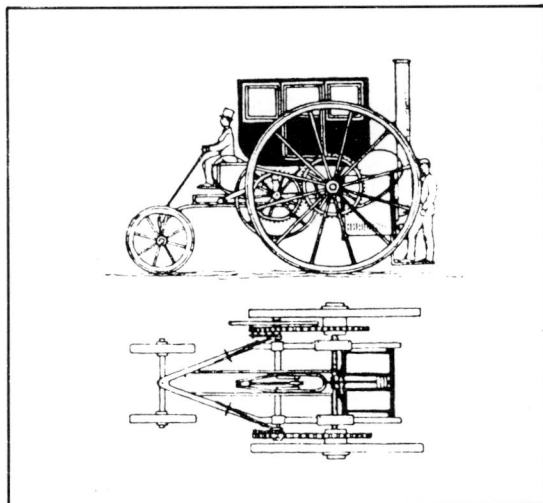

Contemporary drawing of Trevithick's 1803 steam vehicle, popularly called the London Carriage.

1770. Driven by a simple steam engine working on the steerable front wheel, this three-wheeler was a remarkably good effort which survives to this day in the Paris Conservatoire des Arts et Métiers. (According to some authorities it is Cugnot's second, larger tractor which survives.) Speed is given as 3.5–4.0 km/h or about 2½ mph.

1803   Among at least 25 pioneers of steam road vehicles Richard Trevithick stands out as the first to run a reliable passenger vehicle, four years after his first steam train and seven years after his original high-pressure mobile steam engine which on Christmas Eve 1801 ascended Camborne Beacon, Cornwall, with at times as many as eight people hanging on. The 1803 steam car had a traditional coach body high off the ground above giant driven wheels and was reputed to reach 'eight or nine miles in the hour'.

1830s   In this decade several commercial steam coaches and omnibuses were operating in England at speeds claimed to exceed 24 km/h (15 mph). The chief operators, Gurney and Hancock, both claimed speeds in excess of 32 km/h (20 mph), and Nathaniel Ogle's 1830 coach was reputed to reach 51 to 56 km/h (32 to 35 mph), almost certainly a considerable over-estimate.

1898   No mechanical road vehicle is known to have exceeded the speeds claimed for the 1830-vintage British coaches until 68 years later.

Benz's pioneer petrol-engined tricycle of 1885 did not exceed 'two German miles' (about 9 statute miles) per hour (14.5 km/h). But in November 1898 a hill-climb trial near Paris triggered off not only the first-ever accurately timed speed records (for road vehicles, and probably for any kind of vehicle) but also a ding-dong battle between two rivals who set six world car speed records in five months. The first meeting was on 18 December 1898, at the Parc at Achères, north-west of Paris, where there already existed a measured stretch of good straight road where rival *automobilistes* often raced. For a record attempt, cars were flagged off individually. When they saw the starter's flag drop, two timekeepers at the kilometre mark started their stopwatches, and so did a second pair a kilometre further on. This gave speeds for the standing-start kilometre (0.62 mile) and for the 'flying kilometre' entered at near maximum speed. The winner of this first event was the comte Gaston de Chasseloup-Laubat, the only contestant with an electric car, whose lumbering 1.4-tonne (3205 lb) battery-DC car was clear winner at 57 s for the flying kilometre, an average of 63.16 km/h (39.25 mph). The comte's great rival, the Belgian Camille 'Diable Rouge' Jenatzy, was unable to be present, but he threw down an instant challenge leading to a further meeting on 17 January 1899; Jenatzy recorded 54.0 s or 66.66 km/h (41.42 mph), promptly beaten by the comte at 51.2 s, 70.3 km/h (43.69 mph), despite the motor burning out some seconds from the finish. On 27 January Jenatzy hit 44.8 s, 80.34 km/h (49.92 mph), to which the comte replied with an improved Jeantaud car with streamlined body which did the flying kilometre in 38.8 s, or 92.7 km/h (57.6 mph). The newspapers thought the Belgian Red Devil had no chance of bettering this. Little did they know he had built a fantastic blue torpedo-shaped electric car, *La Jamais Contente* (the never satisfied), and on 1 April 1899 he drove it like a bullet on a new speed course—but the timekeepers were not ready. With fresh batteries Jenatzy was back on 29 April and set the first mark at over 100 km/h: the time of 34.0 s was equivalent to 105.9 km/h or 65.79 mph. His standing-start kilometre was faster than the record flying kilometre of 18 December!

1902 The Hon. Charles S. Rolls failed to beat the *Jamais Contente* time, and William K. Vanderbilt Jr exactly equalled it, but during the annual *Semaine de Vitesse* (speed week) at Nice a

Jenatzy's *La Jamais Contente*, the first road vehicle to exceed 100 km/h (62 mph). (*La Nature*, Mary Evans Picture Library)

Driver Fred Marriott removed his cap before setting a record on 23 January 1906 in this Stanley Steamer. (National Motor Museum)

startling figure was set by the steam car of Léon Serpollet. In 1889 he had patented the flash boiler in which high-pressure steam was produced almost instantly by feeding water through coils of red-hot tubes. On 13 April 1902 he brought a streamlined four-cylinder car to the famed Promenade des Anglais and quietly covered the flying kilometre in 29.8 s, equal to 120.8 km/h (75.06 mph). But petrol (gasoline) hit back, in the form of the thunderous 60 hp Mors. In July one was driven by Belgian baron de Caters at exactly Serpollet's speed. On 5 August Vanderbilt took a Mors down the Ablis/St Arnoult road at 122.44 km/h (76.08 mph). On 5 November Henri Fournier's Mors knocked off 0.2 s, at a speed of 123.28 km/h (76.6 mph), and a mere 12 days later M. Augières—to the disgust of the famous professional Fournier—borrowed a car from the Mors works and set 29 s dead, or 124.13 km/h (77.13 mph). The last two records were on a course at Dourdan where a new electrical timing apparatus had been set up and approved by the ACF (Automobile Club de France). The passage of the front wheels across electric cables triggered the start and stop of the watches, and timing was certified within 0.01 s, which was certainly not the case with human observers.

1903 Predictably, refusal of the ACF to approve foreign claims was to lead to trouble. In 1903 the Hon. Charles S. Rolls reached 133.32 km/h (82.84 mph) on the Clipstone, Nottinghamshire, estate of the Duke of Portland; the baron de Forest logged 135.33 km/h (84.09 mph) at Dublin's Phoenix Park, and Rolls returned to Clipstone to notch up 136.36 km/h (84.73 mph), but none was recog-

nised. Near Ostend, however, Belgian Arthur Duray's 26.8 s (134.33 km/h, 83.47 mph) was admitted, as was his later attempt on 5 November at Dourdan which just equalled the 26.4 s set by Rolls. Duray's car was a Gobron-Brillié with 13.5-litre engine.

1904 Virtually all records so far had been made in France by sportsmen. The scene was suddenly changed when Henry Ford decided winning the LSR was 'the best kind of advertising'. He took a vehicle called the Ford *Arrow*, which had already killed one driver. A mere open chassis, with a giant 16.7-litre engine but no gearbox, differential or rear springs, it thundered almost totally out of control ('when I wasn't in the air I was skidding') across the ice of frozen Lake St Clair, near Detroit, on 12 January 1904. His time for the mile was 39.4 s, equal to 147.03 km/h (91.37 mph). But nobody had marked out a kilometre, and the ACF refused to recognise the US timing authority, though nobody ever doubted the accuracy of the claim and Ford's courageous run is today almost universally admitted. Most lists also include the 148.52 km/h (92.3 mph) set 15 days later by Vanderbilt in a beautiful white Mercedes. He drove it on the fine beach at Daytona, Florida, a venue popular for the next 30 years. The ACF disallowed this, but ratified the 152.542 km/h (94.78 mph) of the Gobron-Brillié works driver, Louis Rigolly, on the Nice promenade on 31 March. On 25 May baron de Caters at last got an official record in his 90 hp Mercedes on the Ostend/Nieuport road at 156.25 km/h (97.25 mph). On the same course the 100 mph barrier was passed, on 21 July, by Rigolly in a streamlined Gobron-Brillié, clocking 21.6 s or 166.65 km/h (103.55 mph). On 13 November the same road echoed to the roar of the 100 hp Darracq of Paul Baras, at 168.21 km/h (104.52 mph).

1905 Britain entered the lists on 25 January

when A.E. Macdonald covered the mile at Daytona in a six-cylinder Napier in 34.4 s, or 168.42 km/h (104.65 mph). This was during the Florida Speed Week, an annual meeting at which many LSR records were set during the 1920s. On the same day Macdonald was humbled by a rich Bostonian, Herbert Bowden, who had built a car with two Mercedes engines in tandem and made a single run timed by six watches, all agreeing within 0.1 s to give a figure of 176.62 km/h (109.75 mph)—but the Speed Week authorities disqualified it on the grounds that the car exceeded their weight limit of 1000 kg (2205 lb), and of course the ACF ignored it anyway. So the next official record was 174.46 km/h (109.65 mph) set on 30 December on the Arles/Salon road by Victor Hémery in a new V-8 Darracq.

1906 The Stanley brothers, of Massachusetts, came to Florida's Speed Week with the *Rocket*, which used some parts from the regular production Stanley Steamer touring cars (which were so respected that the first Royal car journey was made in one by Edward VII). Beating Louis Chevrolet, they set 28.2 s for the mile, a remarkable 205.35 km/h (127.6 mph); this was rejected by the ACF, but the august French body did accept the kilometre time of 18.4 s, or 195.65 km/h (121.57 mph). The date was 23 January.

1907 Daytona's beach was in poor shape, and the modified Stanley *Rocket* crashed at a speed estimated by onlookers at between 212 and 319 km/h (132 and 198 mph). Amazingly driver Marriott survived, but this was the end of steam's challenge—and of LSR attempts for two years.

1909 By this time the banked circuit of Brooklands was in use, with Holden's electrical timing able to give results to within 0.001-0.002 s. The first record here was Hémery's 202.7 km/h (125.95 mph) set on 8 November by *Blitzen* (lightning), a superb Benz of the marque that dominated speed attempts until World War I.

1910 Flamboyant barnstormer Barney Oldfield bought *Blitzen*, took it to Florida and on 16 March did the mile in 27.33 s, 211.27 km/h (131.275 mph), though ignored by the AIACR, the international authority that succeeded the ACF. By 1911 this new body had a sensible new

rule: LSR claims in future had to be the mean of two runs in opposite directions. It was now the turn of the Americans to be insular; until 1920 they went on setting their own one-way records, at speeds higher than the two-way ones.

1911 Oldfield sold *Blitzen* to another barnstormer, 'Wild Bob' Burman. After two intense seasons of grass and dirt racing all over the USA it came back to Florida and on 23 April set 25.40 s for the mile or 228.09 km/h (141.73 mph).

1913 In 1910 the Italian Fiat company built a massive car with a 300 hp airship engine. They claimed it reached 290 km/h (180.19 mph) on Long Island in April 1912. This is doubtful, but in foul weather on 8 December 1913 Arthur Duray certainly averaged 213.02 km/h (132.37 mph) over the kilometre at Ostend in this car—only to break down on the return run.

1914 L.G. Hornsted of Britain set a new two-way record in a Benz at Brooklands, his runs at 128.16 and 120.23 mph giving a mean of 199.72 km/h (124.10 mph). This was less than Hémery's existing one-way record of five years previously, while the Benz advertising gave the new record as 128.16!

1919 On 12 February Ralph de Palma covered the mile at Daytona in 24.02 s, 241.200 km/h (149.875 mph), but did not make a return run. His V-12 Packard was almost a regular road car, with even an electric starter.

1920 Tommy Milton, works driver for the Duesenbergs, schemed a car with two engines side-by-side. On 27 April he set a mile record at 251.11 km/h (156.03 mph). Not until 1926 was this beaten by an AIACR-accepted two-way record.

1922 Kenelm Lee Guinness—whose initials became famous through sparking plugs—set a two-way record at 130.35/137.15 mph, the mean being 133.75 mph (215.25 km/h). The car was a V-12 Sunbeam, at Brooklands on 17 May. This contrasts with various speeds up to 180 mph claimed for Sig. Haugdahl's *Wisconsin Special* which, though a fine car, never even achieved official recognition in its native USA.

1923 Malcolm Campbell, probably the greatest name in the LSR story, bought the

350 hp record-holding Sunbeam and entered it at a meeting at Fanöe, Denmark; he set two-way figures of 219.37 km/h (136.31 mph) for the kilometre and 221.64 km/h (137.72 mph) for the mile, but the AIACR refused to recognise the figures even after they themselves had checked the timing system.

1924 The Moto Club de France held a speed meet at Arpajon on the Paris/Orleans highway. On 6 July René Thomas with a V-12 Delage duelled with a monster Fiat driven by Ernest Eldridge of Britain. The Frenchman set an average of 230.55 km/h (143.26 mph) for the kilometre and 230.64 km/h (143.31 mph) for the mile. Eldridge thundered down the road to set 234.98 km/h (146.01 mph) for the kilometre and 233.68 km/h (145.2 mph) for the mile—but Thomas complained the Fiat had no reverse gear and the Briton was disqualified. But Britain's star was now firmly in the ascendant. On 25 September Campbell took his completely rebuilt Sunbeam both ways along the wet beach at Pendine, South Wales, to average 235.22 km/h

(146.16 mph), over the kilometre, the first of his nine accepted LSRs.

1925 From the start of this year extremely detailed AIACR rules were in force governing not only LSR timing systems but such details as the gradient of the course, certificates from surveyors, and the requirement that the two runs must be within 30 min of each other. The only record this year was Campbell's successful assault on his own figure on 21 July in the old Sunbeam, raising the record to 242.800 km/h (150.869 mph) for the kilometre.

1926 Sunbeam joined two six-cylinder Grand Prix units to form a single engine which, though of only 4 litres capacity, was supercharged to give over 300 hp. On 16 March Henry Segrave set 245.15 km/h (152.33 mph) at partial throttle and with leaps through the air up to 14.9 m (49 ft) long across the Southport beach. But J.G. Parry Thomas had built a more streamlined car, *Babs*, with a World War I aero engine, a 400 hp Liberty. On 27 April he set a record at Pendine

at 272.46 km/h (169.3 mph); on the following day he got the engine running better and reached 275.23 km/h (171.02 mph).

1927 From 1925 Campbell had been toiling to build a 'clean sheet of paper' LSR car, regardless of expense. The result was the first *Bluebird*, with a Napier Lion aero engine tuned to a little more than the usual 450 hp. Dozens of companies were involved in the car's design and construction, and on 4 February Campbell roared across soggy Pendine to set an average of 281.45 km/h (174.883 mph). This was slower than he hoped, mainly because of a desperate one-handed fight caused by a bad bump which lifted him into the slipstream, tearing his goggles from his eyes. All the time he knew Segrave was working with Sunbeam on a fantastic new car with twin engines, but before this reached the starting line poor Parry Thomas was killed on 3 March when *Babs* went out of control at Pendine at the end of a double run, incidentally breaking the final timing wire and thus robbing the gallant Welshman of a new record. Segrave

heard the news aboard the liner *Berengaria*, bound for Daytona. His beautiful crimson car, better streamlined than previous contenders, was billed as '1000 hp', but in fact the Matabele ex-World War aero engines put out about 435 hp each. On 29 March Segrave set a splendid new record at 327.97 km/h (203.792 mph) having first—with consummate diplomacy—at last brought the AAA and AIACR together so that the record should be internationally accepted.

1928 Campbell had rebuilt *Bluebird* with a Lion boosted to 875 hp and a more streamlined body, and on 19 February took it down the Daytona beach at 214.7 mph in foul weather to end in an airborne trajectory and skid. Not stopping to change tyres he went straight back, into wind, at 199.9 mph; the average of 330.06 km/h (206.956 mph) just gave him the record. Segrave's success in getting AIACR recognition triggered off American contestants, and on 22 April Ray Keech overcame immense problems with the awesome White *Triplex* (it had three old Liberty aero engines totalling 81

Above:
Segrave's 1927 Sunbeam was the first of the carefully thought out LSR cars, designed and built regardless of expense. (National Motor Museum)

Left:
Nobody can approach the prolonged LSR effort of Sir Malcolm Campbell, whose *Bluebird* cars were world famous. Here, his 1928 car is being pushed out for a demonstration run at Brooklands. (National Motor Museum)

Campbell was the first LSR driver to use the dried salt lake at Bonneville, just east of the Utah Great Salt Lake, where he is seen at the start of a run in his shapely 1935 *Bluebird*. (National Motor Museum)

litres) to set a record that just beat Campbell at 334.02 km/h (207.552 mph) at Daytona. Three days later Frank Lockhart was less fortunate: his beautiful Stutz *Black Hawk* (actually painted white) had only 3 litres but was doing some 220 mph when it crashed. Lockhart was killed.

1929 Segrave and designer J.S. Irving had left Sunbeam and created a wonderful golden car powered by a Lion boosted to about 925 hp, driving through twin propeller shafts with Segrave seated low down between them. At Daytona on 11 March *Golden Arrow* almost effortlessly pushed the LSR up to 372.48 km/h (231.446 mph). On the following day the White *Triplex* had a go but crashed, killing driver Lee Bible and a photographer.

1931 Sunbeam's great *Silver Bullet* driven in 1930 by Kaye Don had been a flop, and Sir Henry Segrave (knighted for the 1929 record) had been killed attacking the water speed record.

This left the redoubtable Campbell, who had *Bluebird* completely rebuilt yet again, lower and more streamlined and with the Lion tuned to 1450 hp. On 5 February at Daytona he raised the record to 396.04 km/h (246.09 mph), like Segrave being knighted on his return.

1932 With minor improvements, Sir Malcolm Campbell went back to Daytona and set a figure of 408.73 km/h (253.97 mph), on 24 February.

1933 Campbell replaced the Lion by a Rolls-Royce R V-12 rated at some 2300 hp (just as the Supermarine company had done five years earlier with its Schneider Trophy seaplanes) and had no difficulty, apart from wheelspin, in reaching a mean of 438.48 km/h (272.46 mph) on 22 February.

1935 Having spent 1934 rebuilding the old *Bluebird* with the help of Reid Railton, Campbell was ready for another try at Daytona on 7 March and, despite poor conditions, reached a mean of 445.49 km/h (276.816 mph).

Fed up, he went to the dried salt lake of Bonneville, Utah, and at this new venue on 3 September he made two runs at 304.311 and

Pushing out the modified *Thunderbolt* from the Bean factory at Tipton, Staffordshire, in the summer of 1938. Later the radiator was removed, the nose sealed and the fin removed. (Associated Press, National Motor Museum)

297.947 mph. The average was the coveted over-300 figure at which Sir Malcolm had said he would hang up his helmet: 301.129 mph (484.62 km/h). He did not quite retire, but went for and gained the water speed record.

1937 Capt George E.T. Eyston had built a formidable car, *Thunderbolt*, with two of the mighty R engines putting 4700 hp into the two pairs of rear wheels. At the front were four wheels in tandem pairs, all steering as in a modern 'juggernaut' truck. On 19 November Eyston took the untested car over the Bonneville salt at an average of 502.12 km/h (312.00 mph), knowing this was just the start.

1938 By this time another Briton, John Cobb, was in the running with a beautiful car designed by Reid Railton and powered by two diagonally mounted Lions. But Eyston was first off the mark; in a slightly modified *Thunderbolt* he set off on 24 August, but the timing failed. The brilliant sunlight, polished aluminium car and white salt resulted in the photocell on the surveyed course failing to trigger on the return run. So in a black-painted *Thunderbolt* a fresh attempt was made on 27 August and the result was a mean of 556.01 km/h (345.49 mph). On 15 September Cobb took out his sleek silver Railton and replied with 563.59 km/h (350.20 mph). But Eyston had taken the fin off his monster, and sealed the nose by converting to ice-tank cooling with no radiator, and on the very day after Cobb's record he covered the mile in 10.1 s one way and 10.04 the other, an average of 575.34 km/h (357.50 mph).

1939 Unlike Eyston, Cobb was able to return to Bonneville, and on 23 August he made two splendid mile runs at 9.76 and 9.81 s, an average of 590.58 km/h (366.97 mph). The speed for the kilometre was, unusually, even better: 595.04 km/h (369.74 mph). Meanwhile, the Daimler-Benz works at Stuttgart housed the T 80, a six-wheel car with a DB 603 aero engine destined never to get to Bonneville, nor demonstrate its optimistic planned 725 km/h (450 mph).

Dawn of a new era as Craig Breedlove poses with his three-wheeled, jet-propelled *Spirit of America* in 1963. (P.J.R. Holthusen collection, National Motor Museum)

1947 Now called Railton-Mobil Special, Cobb's car returned to the salt flats with higher gearing and better tyres and notched up the magic '400' with one run which hit 415 mph at the end of the mile. But the average was pulled down by wheelspin and bumps, and came out as 634.396 km/h (394.196 mph). This was the end of an era. Cobb's mark stood for 17 years.

1960 By this time a shoal of Americans were going for the LSR. None succeeded, some crashed and one lost his life. Then came Micky Thompson's neat blue *Challenger*, powered by four scrap Pontiac V-8 car engines with blowers to wring 700 hp from each. On 9 September he made a run at 406.6 mph; then a drive shaft fractured, and the vital return run never came.

1963 The last disallowed record, and the first of the new jet era, came on 5 August when Craig Breedlove, a dragster king from California, steered *Spirit of America* at 388.47 mph one way and 428.37 on the return, at Bonneville. The mean was 655.72 km/h (407.45 mph), and today this is included in most LSR listings; but to the 1963 officials the vehicle was not a car at all. It was more like a jet fighter without wings, having three wheels and a General Electric J47 turbojet of some 5000 lb thrust taken from a scrapped Sabre fighter. Such vehicles were relatively cheap to build, and sidestepped most of the problems encountered by legal cars with four wheels, and shaft drive. The successors to the AIACR, the FIA, therefore rewrote the rules

and provided for three LSR categories: four wheels, at least two of them driven; four wheels propelled by jet; fewer than four wheels, propelled by jet.

1964 On 17 July Sir Malcolm Campbell's son, Donald, made two runs across Lake Eyre, Australia, clocking exactly 648.73 km/h (403.1 mph) on each run. His car was a completely different *Bluebird*, with four wheels all driven by a 4400 hp Bristol Siddeley Proteus 705 gas turbine identical apart from the drive system to the turboprop used in the Britannia 102 airliners of BOAC. It cost something like £2 million to get the car to the start line, probably an all-time record. Tests began at Bonneville in August 1960 but Campbell crashed at about 360 mph. A second car had to be built, and this was mistakenly taken to the lake in Australia where the LSR was just grasped after heartbreaking difficulties. Nevertheless, this was to be a great year for the record. On 2 October the projectile-like *Wingfoot Express* built by Walt Arfons and powered by an afterburning Westinghouse J46 turbojet was piloted by Tom Green to a mean of 664.98 km/h (413.20 mph). Three days later *Green Monster* built by young brother Art Arfons was propelled by its much more powerful afterburning General Electric J79 at 396.3 mph on the outward trip and at 479 on the return, to give a mean of 698.49 km/h (434.02 mph). On 13 October Breedlove started up a more powerful J47 in *Spirit of America* and set a mark at 754.33 km/h (468.72 mph). Two days later he tried again and pushed the record to 846.97 km/h (526.28 mph), the biggest jump ever. The

Art Arfons' *Green Monster*, which was actually red, white and blue-green, was one of the most 'backyard' of all LSR cars, costing only $15 000. This included the powerful ex-fighter turbojet, which filled the centre of the car, so that Arfons had to sit beside it! (Holthusen collection, National Motor Museum)

The J46 did little for jet fighters, but its 3175 kg (7000 lb) of thrust pushed *Wingfoot Express* to a new record on 2 October 1964. The harpoon-like projection on the side of the nose is an aircraft-type airspeed sensor. (Holthusen collection, National Motor Museum)

braking parachute failed on the return run, the wheelbrakes naturally burned out and Breedlove zoomed five miles off course and into a lake, slicing a thick telephone pole en route. Breedlove calmly swam ashore and announced 'For my next act I'll set myself on fire'. But 1964 was not yet over: on 27 October young Arfons thundered off in *Green Monster* and by brute force made his runs at 515.98 and 559.18, a mean of 863.75 km/h (536.71 mph).

1965 Under the new FIA rules contenders flocked to the salt flats for the October 'season'. First away was Bobby Tatroe in a completely different *Wingfoot Express*. This had a battery of 15 JATO (jet-assisted take-off) rockets at the rear, plus five more on each side, and demonstrated great acceleration—with an impressive amount of flame—but short endurance. Its best performance was on 22 October when, by firing the rockets in sequence, Tatroe did a kilometre at 767.01 km/h (476.6 mph). Trying for the mile he fired the rockets in quicker sequence and reached about 580 mph at the half-way mark, when all rockets burned out! More successful was Breedlove's completely new *Spirit of America—Sonic I*, which had four wheels and a J79 jet. On 2 November this easily did the kilometre at an average of 893.96 km/h (555.483 mph). Five days later Art Arfons replied with a mile at 927.87 km/h (576.553 mph), with a hair-raising tyre-burst and collision at the end of the return run. Only five days later a quite different record was set by one of the most beautiful LSR cars ever built. *Goldenrod* was a welcome return to wheel drive, and it was the sleekest thing on wheels despite containing a row of four Chrysler V-8 hemi-head engines of about 600 hp each. On 12 November Bob Summers climbed into the tiny cockpit in the tailfin and, without ever getting into top gear, set an average of 658.67 km/h (409.277 mph). This still stands as the non-jet record. The year 1965 rivalled 1964 as a vintage LSR year. Three days later Breedlove got into *Sonic I* and covered the mile at 593.178 one way and 608.201 on the return, to gain the satisfying average of 966.574 km/h (600.601 mph).

1967 Art Arfons tried to reply in *Green Monster* but on 17 November crashed at about 610 mph—suffering merely a face cut by flying salt!

1970 After years of effort, backed up by a rocket dragster that swept all before it, Gary Gabelich climbed into the first of a new breed of LSR car with a long needle-like body, liquid-propellant rocket engine and rear wheels on tubular outriggers. The engine of *The Blue Flame* was fed with concentrated hydrogen peroxide, which decomposes instantly into superheated steam and oxygen, and with LNG (liquefied natural gas) burned in the liberated

oxygen. Thrust was variable up to 22 000 lb, but was normally throttled to about 13 000, equivalent at full speed to about 25 000 hp. On 23 October Gabelich almost effortlessly averaged 1014.51 km/h (the first over 1000 km/h) for the kilometre (630.388 mph). The average over the mile was 1001.667 km/h (622.407 mph).

1976 The highest speed reached by a lady driver is 843.323 km/h (524.016 mph) set on 6 December by Mrs Kitty Hambleton (née O'Neil) of the USA. She was driving the rocket-powered S.M.1 *Motivator* across the Alvard desert, Oregon. She is judged to have touched 966 km/h (600 mph).

1979 On 18 December a three-wheeler very similar to *The Blue Flame* (which has four wheels) set a figure more than 100 mph faster than the official LSR! Named *The Budweiser Special* for its chief sponsor, it was driven by Stan Barrett, a film stuntman, over a course at Rogers Dry Lake, California, part of the vast complex occupied by the US Air Force Flight Test Center, Edwards Air Force Base and NASA's Dryden Flight Research Center. The

electronic timing gear operated over a base of a mere 15.85 m (52 ft) but there is no doubt of the accuracy of the result, which was 1190.377 km/h (739.666 mph). The run did not qualify as an LSR because it was made in one direction only and over a shorter than the stipulated distance.

1983 On 5 October Richard Noble of Great Britain set a new LSR over the measured mile at 1019.468 km/h (633.468 mph). His car, *Thrust 2*, was powered by a Rolls-Royce Avon afterburning turbojet taken from a scrapped RAF Lightning fighter. It had reached 615 mph almost a year previously, showing excellent

Left:
Breedlove's second *Spirit of America* was a completely new car, subtitled *Sonic I*. Though it failed to reach the speed of sound by a wide margin, it was the most projectile-like LSR car ever. (Holthusen collection, National Motor Museum)

Below and right:
With *The Blue Flame*, Gabelich not only turned to rocket propulsion but firmly picked on the three-wheel layout with external rear suspension. (Holthusen collection, National Motor Museum)

stability despite returning to the traditional car configuration of a proper body with four inboard wheels. The venue was the Black Rock Desert of Nevada, USA.

Below:
Richard Noble is the first British holder of the LSR (land speed record) for almost 20 years. His car, pictured in colour on page 72, made its run across Nevada's Black Rock desert as if on rails. (National Motor Museum)

Foot of page:
A good claimant for the title 'The Fastest Man on Earth', stuntman Stan Barrett has yet to do a two-way run, meeting the requirements of an official LSR, but his single run in December 1979 just exceeded the speed of sound in the cold conditions prevailing, and certainly did no harm to sales of Budweiser beer. (Holthusen collection, National Motor Museum)

The future The struggle to go ever faster on land is now firmly split into two categories: the wheel-driven cars and the jets, which are hardly cars at all. Wheel drive poses much greater and more costly problems. Engines are likely to give up burning mere petrol (gasoline) and will be made to run on more energetic witches' brews such as the nitromethane mixtures used by dragsters. Tyres have always been a crucial factor in LSR attempts, and the need to transmit the drive power and resist the centrifugal force at perhaps 2500 to 4000 rpm is far beyond the capability of any ordinary tyre. LSR tyres are usually thin, to reduce weight and centrifugal stress, but must stand up to severe abrasion and wheelspin. Though obviously very slim, the body must press the wheels firmly on the ground to minimise wheelspin; wings can be used, 'lifting' in the downwards direction, but this increases drag. To beat the 409 mph set by *Goldenrod*—which in fact set a speed of 673.517 km/h (418.504 mph) over a shorter than LSR distance—will not be simple. On the other hand the rocket ships are relatively cheap, rely on plenty of existing technology and sidestep most of the mechanical problems. One difficulty could be the need for aerodynamic controls to ensure that the car runs true and upright. At over 1207 km/h (750 mph) even small undulations could cause the whole car to take off, while differences in level between the left and right wheels could impart a rate of roll enough to make the car roll right over. Fortunately, body lift can raise the whole car, except the nose wheel, well clear of the ground. This happens with *Budweiser*, whose rear wheels had at least 0.25 m (10 in) of free space between them and the ground at full speed. Thus, no rolling moment could be imparted, easing the control problem. It would seem straightforward to build a car to reach 1609 km/h (1000 mph).

Private cars
Before 1900 a typical maximum speed for a car sold to the public was 19 km/h (12 mph), on a good level road. There was little to choose between petrol (gasoline), steam or electric-battery propulsion. This speed happened to be the legal limit in Britain, and similar speeds (such as 20 km/h) were common limits elsewhere until well into the present century.

But attainable speeds rose very swiftly, and by 1905 it was not uncommon to find 100 km/h or 60 mph claimed, without exaggeration, in motor advertising. From then onwards it became difficult to distinguish between private cars and racing cars. By 1930, when the LSR was getting near 400 km/h (say, 250 mph), cars capable of 161 km/h (100 mph) were on sale to the public with mudguards, lights and all other legal equipment. Since then, private car speeds have not risen greatly, though a very few expensive cars are in the 290 km/h (180 mph) class. Of course, such speeds can very rarely be attained—legally or otherwise—on public highways, and the performance is of value chiefly in acceleration, which remains fierce at the 160 km/h (100 mph) level at which most cars are near their limit. In the early 1980s the car generally regarded as the fastest in production for use on highways was the Lamborghini Countach series which then had a brochure speed of 315 km/h (195.7 mph); at least eight motoring magazines have independently recorded speeds of 305.7 km/h (190 mph) or more for the Countach S or P400. Almost the same speed has been reached by the same independent drivers with the Aston Martin Bulldog. A speed exceeding 322 km/h (200 mph) is claimed for the British Panther Six, a six-wheel car with a large Cadillac engine, but this is a bit of an oddball built only to special order. The claimed record speed whilst towing a production caravan (trailer) is 201.02 km/h

Broadly similar to many squat 'mid-engined' ultra-fast cars, the Lamborghini Countach 500S has more 'poke' (power) than most, and has for several years been a claimant for the title 'The fastest car you can buy'. (National Motor Museum)

The C 111–III, or C 111 Mk III, is a research vehicle for Daimler-Benz at Untertürkheim, and among its many records is that of the world's fastest diesel vehicle of any kind, including trains. (DB, National Motor Museum)

(124.91 mph) by an Aston Martin Le Mans driven by Robin Hamilton on the derelict runway at RAF station Elvington on 14 October 1980.

Racing cars

There is no simple listing of 'fastest' racing cars; as fully explained in *The Guinness Book of Car Facts and Feats* the sport of motor racing is organised into road, track, hill-climb, sprint, dragster, rally and other divisions, and many of these are further subdivided into car categories. Normally the fastest racing cars—as distinct from dragsters, which can rapidly attain even greater velocities—are those built to Grand Prix formulae defining the allowable size of engine and certain other parameters. Since 1966 Grand Prix rules have prohibited engines of larger capacity than 3 litres (183 in³), or only half this capacity if supercharged, yet output is often in the neighbourhood of 500 hp. The German Auto-Union and Mercedes cars of 1937–38 could attain nearly 200 mph, and Auto-Union driver Bernd Rosemeyer was killed in 1938 in a specially prepared car at an estimated 435 km/h (270 mph). Cars not subject to Formula restrictions frequently have more than 1000 hp, an example being the Porsche 917 series which have not only won the 24-hour Le Mans race (1970) but have been timed at speeds exceeding 370 km/h (230 mph) on straights, the highest accepted figure being 413.6 km/h (257 mph) on

the French Paul Ricard course in 1973. The fastest known lap speed is 403.878 km/h (250.958 mph) set in 1979 by Dr Hans Liebold driving a special Mercedes-Benz (the C 111–IV) on the Nardo, Italy, circuit. The related C 111–III with a turbocharged 3-litre diesel engine holds the world diesel record with a speed of 327.3 km/h (203.3 mph) on the same circuit on 29 April 1978. The current record for cars with electric propulsion is 281.73 km/h (175.061 mph) by a Class 2 (500–1000 kg laden) three-wheeler, *Battery Box*, at Bonneville in 1974. As this used lead/acid batteries it was heavy for its power; a faster electric car is clearly possible using higher-energy storage batteries. The steam car made a mild comeback in the 1960s but no builder attempted to challenge the Stanley Steamer figures set by Marriott in 1906–7.

Dragsters

This special class of competition car is built to accelerate as rapidly as possible from rest on a straight course. The usual objective is to cover the standing-start quarter-mile (402.34 m) in the shortest possible time. The car thus has the greatest possible installed power for the lowest possible laden weight. There are two classes: wheel drive and jet/rocket. The former is limited by wheelslip, despite the use of giant rear tyres called 'slicks' which are spun prior to the start by harsh use of the accelerator to coat them with molten rubber. All the fastest wheel-drive cars have engines of at least 5 litres capacity (8 is not uncommon) running on special mixtures which often contain no petrol (gasoline) at all but are based on methanol and nitromethane, giving power for the vital few seconds of 1500–

2000 hp. The lowest time for the standing quarter by a wheel-drive car is 5.637 s, giving an average speed of 256.95 km/h (159.66 mph), by D.G. 'Big Daddy' Garlits at the Ontario, California, meet in October 1975. Terminal velocity, measured electronically at all important events, was in this case 403.45 km/h (250.69 mph). Because of variation in the acceleration the highest terminal velocity may not correspond with the shortest time. In fact the highest recorded terminal velocity is 411.33 km/h (255.59 mph) by Jerry Ruth and 411.31 km/h (255.58 mph) by a lady, Shirley Muldowney. All these performances are dramatically eclipsed by the jet dragsters. Timing depends critically on attainment of peak thrust almost instantaneously on being given the start signal, and the record in 1981 was the outstanding 3.94 s by Sammy Miller in his *Vanishing Point*, with HTP (high-test hydrogen peroxide) rocket propulsion. The average speed was thus 371.39 km/h (230.77 mph) and the terminal velocity 579.36 km/h (360.0 mph). Even this is not the highest terminal velocity ever. That honour went to the LSR holder Craig Breedlove in *English Leather Special* at 607.936 km/h (377.754 mph). In fact, as the rocket continues to thrust briefly after passing the quarter-mile point this run may well have topped 400 mph. Elapsed time, however, was 4.65 s, well outside Miller's record.

Other cars

Stock-car racing encompasses a spectrum of events from meetings in which the objective is to knock out one's rivals in collisions to the prestigious NASCAR (US National Association for Stock Car Racing) at which stock sedans (saloons) reach speeds which nudge 200 mph. In the former style of 'race' it is not uncommon for the winner to limp over the finish line at walking pace, and speeds seldom exceed 72 km/h (45 mph). As a contrast, in the 1979 Busch Clash Race at the banked Daytona Speedway (one of the modern high-speed circuits where cars can be driven flat out) the winner's average speed throughout was 312.83 km/h (194.384 mph). Speeds of fairground dodgems vary from 11 to 21 km/h (7 to 13 mph).

Motorcycles

Compared with cars, motor cycles tend to have engines with fewer cylinders (except for the most expensive modern superbikes) and a considerable proportion are two-strokes, with one firing stroke per cylinder on each revolution of the crankshaft. The speed of the earliest accepted machine (Daimler, 1885) was a maximum of 10 km/h (6.2 mph). The first to be marketed in quantity, the 1894 Hildebrand und Wolfmüller, could go at twice this speed provided there were no hills.

MOTORCYCLE MILESTONES

In 1920, after many years of wrangling about rules, the Fédération Internationale Motocycliste at last controlled all competitive aspects of two-wheelers on a world basis, since when the FIM has ratified the following world speed records:

1920 Ernest Walker (994 cc Indian) at Daytona Beach, USA, 167.67 km/h (104.19 mph).
1923 Claude F. Temple (996 cc British Anzani) at Brooklands, England, 174.58 km/h (108.48 mph).
1924 Herbert Le Vack (867 cc Brough Superior) at Arpajon, France, 191.59 km/h (119.05 mph).
1926 Claude F. Temple (996 cc OEC Temple) at Arpajon, 195.33 km/h (121.38 mph).

1928 Oliver M. Baldwin (996 cc Zenith JAP) at Arpajon, 200.56 km/h (124.64 mph).
1929 Herbert Le Vack (995 cc Brough Superior) at Arpajon, 207.33 km/h (128.83 mph).
1930 Joseph S. Wright (994 cc OEC Temple) at Arpajon, 220.99 km/h (137.32 mph); Ernst Henne (735 cc BMW) at Ingolstadt, Germany, 221.54 km/h (137.66 mph); Joseph S. Wright (995 cc OEC Temple JAP) at Cork, Ireland, 242.50 km/h (150.65 mph).
1932 Ernst Henne (735 cc BMW) at Tat, Hungary, 244.4 km/h (151.87 mph).
1934 Ernst Henne (735 cc BMW) at Györ, Hungary, 246.069 km/h (152.904 mph).

1935 Ernst Henne (735 cc BMW) on Frankfurt/Munich autobahn, 256.046 km/h (159.104 mph).
1936 Ernst Henne (495 cc BMW) on Frankfurt/Munich autobahn, 272.006 km/h (169.021 mph).
1937 Eric Fernihough (995 cc Brough Superior JAP) at Györ, 273.244 km/h (169.791 mph); Piero Taruffi on the Brescia autostrada, Italy, 274.181 km/h (170.373 mph); Ernst Henne (495 cc BMW) on Frankfurt/Munich autobahn, 279.503 km/h (173.680 mph).
1951 Wilhelm Herz (499 cc NSU) at Ingolstadt, 290.322 km/h (180.403 mph).
1955 Russell Wright (998 cc Vincent HRD) at Christchurch, NZ, 297.640 km/h (184.950 mph).

1956 Wilhelm Herz (499 cc NSU) at Bonneville, USA, 338.083 km/h (210.081 mph).
1962 William A. Johnson (667 cc Triumph) at Bonneville, 361.400 km/h (224.570 mph).
1966 Robert Leppan (1298 cc Triumph) at Bonneville, 395.270 km/h (245.616 mph).
1970 Don Vesco (700 cc Yamaha) at Bonneville, 405.250 km/h (251.818 mph); Calvin Rayborn (1480 cc Harley Davidson) at Bonneville, 410.370 km/h (254.992 mph); Calvin Rayborn (same machine and place) 426.400 km/h (264.960 mph).
1975 Don Vesco (1496 cc Yamaha *Silver Bird*) at Bonneville, 487.502 km/h (302.928 mph).
1978 Don Vesco (2032 cc Kawasaki *Lightning Bolt*) at Bonneville, 512.734 km/h (318.598 mph).

As this book went to press no dragster bike had broken the seven-second barrier, the best figure being 7.08 set in 1980 by Bo O'Brochta on a Terminal Van Lines Kawasaki. (Roger M. Gorringe)

There are no clear answers to the questions of which are the fastest catalogued road machine and the fastest track racer. In the former category the author of *The Guinness Book of Motor-Cycling Facts and Feats*, L.J.K. Setright, offers the 1979 Dunstall Suzuki GS 1000CS, which he personally tested at 248.15 km/h (154.20 mph)—though he confusingly also calls the 6-cylinder Honda, CBX 'the fastest ... of all the world's production motorcycles'. The fastest road bike with engine modifications is the Bimota SB3, catalogued and tested at 256.8 km/h (159.6 mph). Candidates in the second category include all the main current Japanese racing bikes (Kawasaki, Suzuki and Yamaha) which are geared to achieve rather more than 300 km/h (186.41 mph) under favourable conditions.

Drag-racing bikes
Motor cycles accelerate faster than any other common road vehicles. The fastest road machines by Honda (CBX and CB1100R), Kawasaki (Z1100GP) and Suzuki (GS 1000CS) can cover the standing quarter-mile (402.336 m) in about 11.5 s and cross the finish at about 185 km/h (115 mph). But purpose-built drag bikes can do much better. They are long machines because most have several engines in a row, often highly supercharged and burning specially formulated nitromethane fuel. The power is put into a rear wheel carrying a slick (special smooth drag tyre, which is 'burned in' by spinning it against the ground before the start to coat it with molten rubber) with a width of about 200 mm (8 in). There are two sets of (unofficial) world records for motor-cycle drag racing: elapsed time and terminal speed. The former is the time taken to cover a quarter-mile from a standing start; the speed is instantaneously measured as the bike crosses the finish line. Curiously, the highest terminal speed has very seldom also been that for the fastest run. In 1984 the record time was 7.08 s, giving an average speed from the start of 204.571 km/h (127.118 mph), set by Bo O'Brochta of the USA on a 1200 cc supercharged Kawasaki at Ontario, California, in 1980. The record terminal speed was 321.06 km/h (199.5 mph), reached on two separate occasions in 1978 and 1980 by Russ Collins of the USA on his bike *Sorcerer*, with two 1000 cc four-cylinder Honda engines; his best elapsed time, however, is 7.62 s.

Pedal cycles
The record for any human-powered vehicle is

87.60 km/h (54.43 mph), just under the US legal highway limit, by *White Lightning*, a streamlined tandem tricycle pedalled by Jan Russell and Butch Stanton at Ontario Speedway, east of Los Angeles, on 7 May 1978. Ralph Therrio set the single-rider record in 1977 at 79.47 km/h (49.38 mph).

Wind-propelled land vehicles

This is probably the best place to include speeds of wind-propelled land vehicles. One of the volumes of the English historian Samuel Purchas, written in about 1615, described use in Korea of wagons fitted with sails. About 1630 at least two large (28 passenger) land yachts were made in the Netherlands by Simon Stevin, one reaching 35 km/h (21.7 mph) on a journey from Scheveningen to Petten (this was presumably an estimated maximum). In 1827 one of the 'Charvolants' (carriages towed by multiple kites) built by Viney and Pocock was said to have covered a mile in three minutes (20 mph). The 1981 record for a sand yacht is 92.84 km/h (57.69 mph) over the measured mile, set in 1956, though in 1976 an American wheeled yacht reached 142.26 km/h (88.4 mph). The record for an ice yacht, with skate runners, is still the 230 km/h (143 mph) set in 1938. In contrast, a rocket-propelled ice sled, *Oxygen*, was driven over Lake George, NY, on 15 February 1981 at 399.0 km/h (247.93 mph). A braking parachute was rather important.

Commercial vehicles

There are few authentic or meaningful speed feats in this category. There was fierce speed competition in the horse era, but motor buses and trucks are invariably designed for economy and reliability, and urban traffic speeds are in any case usually low. Until the fuel crisis of 1973 it was common for long-distance buses and heavy goods vehicles to be designed to a governed speed of 70 mph (exceptionally for buses, 80 mph), or either 100 or 120 km/h. Since 1973 a limit of 55 mph or either 80 or 85 km/h has been more common.

Guided land transport

This category includes all transport systems in which the vehicle is steered automatically along a predetermined path by some form of guideway or track. By far the most common is the conventional railway (US, railroad), technically known as the duo-rail system. Much less common are monorails, tracked hovercraft, tube and pipe conveyance, aerial ropeways and various other schemes.

Railways

One cannot be dogmatic about where and when the first railway was built. The Greek Periander built a paved track across the Corinth isthmus for the haulage of ships, and some archaeologists believe the wheeled cradles were guided by grooves. By the 14th century wood and iron tracks were common in mines in central Europe. The advantages of a prepared track are chiefly that it can support a much higher intensity of loading than a wheel resting on the ground, and it gives roughly the same performance in all weathers, instead of being muddy and rutted in wet conditions. The greater intensity of loading means that the wheel hardly sinks into the track, and this greatly reduces deformation of the surfaces in contact which dramatically lowers the rolling friction. For this reason, a given tractive effort (pull) can move a train much heavier than the limit that the same pull could move with wooden wheels on soil or rubber pneumatic tyres on a road. Thus, other factors being equal, trains ought in theory to be faster than road vehicles.

Until the first years of the 19th century all railroads were worked by the muscle power of labourers or draught animals. It was Cornishman Richard Trevithick, who appears at the beginning of the 'Car Speed Records', who in 1803 built what is believed to have been the first steam railway locomotive. It was to run on 0.914 m (3 ft) gauge angle-iron track at Coalbrookedale ironworks, Shropshire. There is no certainty that it ever ran, but Trevithick's second engine, built in 1804 for the Pen-y-Darran ironworks in Glamorgan, certainly did. On 22 February 1804 it hauled 10 tons of iron over a 15.3 km (9.5 mile) route to win a 500-guinea bet for the local ironmaster. More than that, 70 cheering passengers also rode on the wagons, which were estimated to have worked up to 8 km/h (5 mph) on good stretches, though the trip took four hours because of overhanging branches and rocks on the line.

Many locomotives were built, mainly in England, before the Stockton & Darlington

This engraving shows the *Rocket*, one of the most famous railway locomotives of all time, as it was originally built. Later it was several times modified, and after being sold in 1836 to Lord Carlisle's Railway, Cumberland, it was altered again. (*Rail in Britain*, Mary Evans Picture Library)

Railway was opened on 27 September 1825. This was the first public steam railway, all previous undertakings having been on private industrial sites such as mines and ironworks. Steam was used for freight trains only, passenger vans being hauled by horses until 1833. The S & DR's *Locomotion No 1* was the first locomotive to have coupled wheels: all four wheels were joined by coupling rods, so that the entire weight of the engine was available for adhesion.

The most famous of all the early steam locomotives was Robert and George Stephenson's *Rocket*, built to compete in the Rainhill Trials of October 1829 to select a locomotive type for the Liverpool & Manchester Railway (the first all-steam public railway, and the first to make front-page news around the world and launch the age of 'railway

mania' that saw fantastic expansion of the new mode of transport). The *Rocket* was a light engine, with just two quite large driving wheels, but it met all the conditions and without a train set the impressive and accurately measured speed record of 46.8 km/h (29.1 mph). A year later, at the opening ceremonies of the same line, *Rocket* ran over William Huskisson MP, who, fatally injured, was rushed to hospital by the engine *Northumbrian* at a speed forever afterwards optimistically recorded as 57.9 km/h (36 mph).

By this time locomotive designers appreciated that steam engines can be built either for speed or for tractive effort. In general the former type, for passenger use, has driving wheels that are few in number but of large diameter; the freight loco has many driving wheels of small diameter, all coupled together. Thus, when designing for pure speed at the expense of poor pulling power, engineers tended to make their driving wheels as large as possible. Usually the driving axle was placed roughly half-way along the locomotive, which meant it had to be under the boiler. The larger the wheels, the higher the axle (and boiler) had to be off the ground. To keep within the

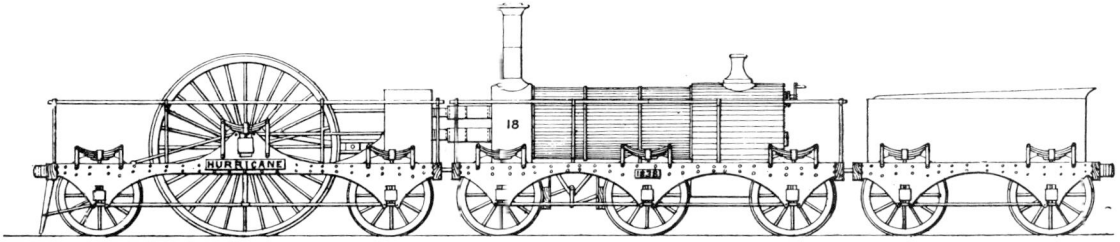

Over a century ago the way to make trains go faster was to increase the diameter of the driving wheels, but the boiler got in the way of the axle. With *Hurricane* and the slightly different *Thunderer* the ultimate was reached: the driving wheels were put on a separate frame ahead of the boiler. (*Rail in Britain*, Mary Evans Picture Library)

allowable height of the loading gauge the boiler thus had to be slim, reducing its ability to raise steam. One engine had equal-size boilers above and below the driving axle! Thomas Crampton, an engineer on Britain's Great Western Railway, designed an engine with the driving axle right at the back, behind the firebox; his engines were popular all over Europe and set many speed records (one of which appears in the complete listing of progressive railway speed records, pp. 96–8). Going to the other extreme, the R & W Hawthorn company built for the same railway an engine called *Hurricane* with gigantic driving wheels on a small truck pivoted ahead of the rest of the engine. Its problems included excessive slipping, because there was so little weight on the driving wheels. The expected speeds were not attained, and Mr Brunel regretted buying it.

Throughout the second half of the 19th century railway speeds were progressively pushed up, invariably with very light trains and usually by locomotives with a single pair of very large driving wheels. Increasingly, rail speed records were set by special trains; and they came to be of two kinds, the peak instantaneous speed and the fastest time over a particular route. The latter obviously can run into thousands of different 'records' and cannot be discussed here; many of them are included in *The Guinness Book of Rail Facts and Feats*, uniform with this volume. It must be admitted that few accomplishments of man's technical creations are as shot through with unreliable data, hearsay, exaggeration and sheer mythology as record speeds by rail. Not

until the early years of the present century were any kind of speedometers used—and even then often not in the locomotives but in the special dynamometer coaches used only on test runs—and there are numerous cases on record of the speeds indicated by these instruments failing by considerable margins to agree with those logged by experienced timers of trains who were riding in the passenger coach(es). Today, however, virtually every speed is recorded by accurate instrumentation.[1]

Thus, the rest of this sub-section is concerned not with the fastest times over any particular route but with the highest briefly recorded speeds. As in this century several distinct forms of locomotive have come into use, a separate section is devoted to each. This allows discussion of important achievements which would not appear in a list of absolute progressive world rail speed records.

Steam

One of the more fundamental limitations to the speed attainable by a steam locomotive is the operating speed of the motion. Questions of mechanical balance, the inertial forces of heavy pistons, rods, connecting rods, coupling rods and valve gear, and the ability of the steam to pass into and out of the cylinder, all tend to make reciprocating steam engines inherently much slower than internal combustion engines (the all-rotary steam turbine is an exception). Thus, to go fast early designers built large driving wheels, accepting thereby a severe limitation in pulling power. All rail records from 1830 to 1900 (with hardly any exceptions, and none for absolute speed) were gained with locomotives having a single driving axle with wheels of some 2.44 m (8 ft) diameter.

[1] The art of train timing is not lost, however. In almost every country armies of new train-timers are busy with ever more sophisticated equipment. For those who merely enjoy knowing roughly how fast their train is going, a rudimentary speed figure in Britain and many other countries can be obtained by counting the telephone posts passed in 66 s (for km/h) or in 41 s (for mph).

Tank engines are remembered as suitable for slow suburban services, but the Bristol & Exeter's No 41 (sister to No 46, illustrated) set a world speed record at 81.8 mph in 1854 which was not broken until 1889. The 2.74m (9ft) driving wheels were the largest in regular use in Britain. (British Rail)

The first authentically logged record was gained on 13 November 1839 by the 2–2–2 *Lucifer* of the Staffordshire & Grand Junction Railway, which in regular service reached 91.33 km/h (56.75 mph). It was descending Madeley Bank just south of Crewe which was to be the location of most of the highest speeds reached on the subsequent LNWR and LMS.

Then followed three records on the lately completed main line of the Great Western Railway, with a gauge of 2.1336 m (7 ft). On 20 June 1845 the 2–2–2 *Ixion* reached 98.2 km/h (61.0 mph) between Didcot and Reading, where the track is almost dead level (though the whole of this GWR route has always been beautifully laid and suitable for the countless high-speed trains that have used it). On 1 June 1846 another 2–2–2, *Great Western*, reached 119.9 km/h (74.5 mph) going down the quite gentle bank west of Wootton Bassett, Wiltshire, and over the same stretch of line the larger 4–2–2 *Great Britain* was timed at 125.5 km/h (78 mph) on 11 May 1848.

The next authenticated record was 131.64 km/h (81.8 mph) achieved by a 4–2–4 (a most unusual wheel arrangement) tank engine, the *No 41* of the Bristol & Exeter (later merged into the GWR), in June 1854, whilst going down the steep bank from Whiteball Summit to Wellington, Somerset.

In spite of many attempts, no authentic record beat this figure for 35 years! In 1889 one of the

Still in running order at Swindon, the GWR's *City of Truro* is almost certainly the first locomotive to have hauled a normal passenger train at 100 mph (160.9 km/h). (John Marshall)

many French Crampton 2–4–0s, on the main line from Paris to Dijon and the Mediterranean, touched 144 km/h (89.48 mph) just outside Paris between Montereau and Sens. The line here follows the River Yonne and is virtually level.

Two claims exceeding 100 mph for runs in May 1893 on the New York Central & Hudson River Railroad are not now regarded as justified. The peak of 144.84 km/h (90 mph) for a 4–2–2 (No 117) of the Midland Railway near Plumtree south of Nottingham in March 1897 was timed by the eminent Charles Rous-Marten—first of the great train-timers—and is indisputable, but the oft-quoted 164.63 km/h (102.3 mph) for the 4–4–0 *City of Truro* of the Great Western is now regarded as possibly inaccurate. The claimed speed was reached on 9 May 1904 whilst descending Wellington bank, just as had the 4–2–4 tank 50 years earlier, during a series of intensely competitive 'races' with the London & South Western to see who could get transatlantic passengers from Plymouth to London first. On this occasion *City of Truro* averaged better than 'even time' (a mile a minute) from Plymouth to Bristol, and the general consensus based on accurate passing times is that this train did set the first record at over 160.9 km/h (100 mph).

Despite numerous contenders no clear improvement was forthcoming until in the first half of the 1930s The Milwaukee Road—the Chicago, Milwaukee, St Paul & Pacific Railroad—began deliberate acceleration of passenger expresses on its very easily graded and well-laid track across northern Illinois, Wisconsin and into Minnesota. On 29 July 1934 a regular 4–6–4, No 6402 of the F6 class, with a five-car train, averaged 149.05 km/h (92.62 mph) for 98.8 km (61.4 miles) and reached a peak of 166.56 km/h (103.5 mph). This led to a series of special locomotives, as noted below.

Controversy surrounds the highest speed reached by a special lightweight 4–4–4 built by the Baltimore & Ohio, oldest and most consistently pioneering of the US railroads, which is claimed to have attained 183.5 km/h (114 mph) soon after completion in 1934. The next unchallenged steam record was 173.8 km/h (108.0 mph) set by a Gresley A3 4–6–2, *Papyrus*, on the fastest stretch on the LNER (London & North Eastern), the southwards descent from

WILLS'S CIGARETTES

"CORONATION SCOT" EXPRESS, L.M.S.R.

Desperate to beat the rival LNER, the LMS flogged *Coronation* down the bank to Crewe at an alleged 114 mph (183 km/h) on 29 June 1937. Then it made the 158-mile return trip to London in 119 min.

Stoke Summit towards Peterborough. This was achieved on 5 March 1935, and together with rivalry with the LMS (London, Midland & Scottish) spurred new high-speed locomotives and trains from 1935.

These soon set numerous British national steam records, but the world figure was in May 1935 pushed up to a remarkable 200.4 km/h (124.5 mph) on the Deutsche Reichsbahn (German State Railway), which had built two exceptionally large locomotives purely for running at the highest possible sustained speeds on the special FD (extra fare) expresses between Berlin and Hamburg. Nos 05.001 and 05.002 were giant 4–6–4s with driving wheels 2.3 m (over 7 ft 6½ in) diameter, which by this time was most unusual. General development of steam engines had enabled the running speed to be considerably increased, so that express locomotives could have numerous relatively small wheels and thus great pulling power. With the 05 class the Germans intended to keep all the power and add even more speed. Fully streamlined, the first of these great machines knocked all previous ideas of steam performance for six, and in regular service (with relatively light trains) could hold speeds close to 100 mph. The great British train-timer Cecil J. Allen was aboard on one run which reached 96.5 km/h (60 mph) in just 2.4 km (1.5 miles), 113 km/h (70 mph) in 4.43 km (2.75 miles) and 129 km/h (80 mph) in under 6 km/h (4 miles) of level track.

In Britain the LNER built a class of streamlined Gresley-designed 4–6–2s, the A4 class, which set a new level of speed on the East Coast route.

On 27 September 1935 the first, *Silver Link*, made a Press run during which it twice reached 181 km/h (112.5 mph). Trying to beat this, the LMS flogged their first streamliner, No 6220 *Coronation*, down the bank from Whitmore, past Madeley (site of the 1839 record) to Crewe. The company claimed 114 mph (183.46 km/h); three experienced timers did not record over 112.5 mph (181 km/h), but accepted that the peak may have momentarily been the claimed figure. But the descent leads immediately over the sharp points to Crewe station, and despite furious braking the train hit the points at 91.7 km/h (57 mph), causing fractured rail chairs and piles of smashed crockery!

Going back to June 1935 the Milwaukee Road in that month may have set a speed of 206 km/h (128 mph) with the first of a superb new class of fully streamlined 4–4–2s for working *The Hiawatha* express between Chicago and Minneapolis/St Paul. These were by far the most powerful 4–4–2 locomotives ever built (for example, the combined heating surface of their boilers and superheaters exceeded by a wide margin that of the monster German 4–6–4s) and they were the first locomotives in the world designed for sustained 100 mph running on every trip. The 128 mph was never fully authenticated, but there are countless records of 193 km/h (120 mph) being reached in regular service. These oil-fired flyers were so successful the trains grew longer and heavier, and a class of more powerful streamlined 4–6–4s had to be built to pull heavier trains at the same speeds.

The famous *Mallard*, claimed by Britain as the fastest steam locomotive of all time, still exists and is usually pictured with wheel valances removed, cylinders exposed and a bell on the front. Here she is as she looked in late 1938. (Museum of British Transport, Clapham)

These likewise were capable engines, holding sustained speeds up to 120 mph.

There remains one isolated speed record which still stands as the accepted maximum ever reached by steam, so far as precisely measured speeds are concerned. Sir Nigel Gresley was determined that the LNER should set a figure that would be hard to beat, and a series of 'brake trials' culminated on 7 July 1938 with an A4, No 4468 *Mallard*, being run down the bank from Stoke Summit, with a train plus dynamometer car for accurate instrumentation, at virtually full throttle and the highest steam consumption (40 to 45 per cent cut-off). The train worked up quickly to 100 mph, and then went on to cover five miles (mileposts 94 to 89) at an average of over 193 km/h (120 mph), with a peak at 202.8 km/h (126 mph). Later *Mallard* was renumbered 60022, but today she is in York Railway Museum restored to 1938 appearance.

At her peak speed this locomotive was running much faster than any previous steam locomotive, the driving wheels turning at over 500 rpm. It so happened that this gruelling run caused severe damage to the middle-cylinder big-end and crankpin, but this could have been avoided. Subsequently more modern steam locomotives operated at even higher rotational speeds, the record probably being achieved by some of the best steam power ever produced, the Class J 4–8–4s of the Norfolk & Western. These were the last steam express locomotives built for a US railway, and they reached speeds up to 177 km/h (110 mph) despite having driving wheels only 1.78 m (5 ft 10 in) diameter. For sheer combined speed and power no steam locomotives could equal the Union Pacific's giant Challenger class of 4–6–6–4s and the smaller Pennsylvania T-1 class of 4–4–4–4s. Not including its 193-ton tender, one of the latter hauled a passenger train weighing 1000 long tons (1120 US tons) at an average speed of 164 km/h (102 mph) for 111 km (69 miles), typical of their regular working performance; but they were soon swept away by diesels.

The Pennsylvania, incidentally, used the most powerful steam-turbine locomotive ever built— and it was not only economical but able to sustain 160.9 km/h (100 mph) with trains as heavy as those worked by the T-1s. There were dozens of other turbine locomotives, including a

Above:
The most weighty and powerful Atlantics (ie, 4–4–2 wheel arrangement) ever built, the splendid Alco *Hiawatha* class were the first locomotives ever built to exceed 100 mph (160.9 km/h) every day. They were so successful that the railway—full name, the Chicago, Milwaukee, St Paul & Pacific Railroad—soon had to add extra coaches and buy bigger locomotives! (Milwaukee Road)

Below:
This splendid turbine locomotive showed great performance and satisfactory reliability on the Pennsylvania RR in 1944–49, but was swept away by diesels. In theory a steam-turbine locomotive can be very fast. (Altoona area public library, Pennsylvania)

STREAMLINED PROPELLER RAILCAR

"DENVER ZEPHYR" DIESEL FLYER

pair built for the Union Pacific theoretically capable of 201 km/h (125 mph); but, though free from most of the inherent speed restrictions of other steam motive power, none set any records.

Diesel

Like the steam-turbine variety the diesel locomotive has no fundamental speed limitation beyond that of the rolling vehicle itself. Numerous solutions have been tried to the problem of linking the crankshaft of the engine to the driven wheels. In smaller sizes a plain mechanical drive via a gearbox has proved satisfactory, as in buses and trucks. Other common schemes include hydraulic transmissions, giving an infinitely variable speed ratio, and the most common method of all, the diesel-electric in which the engine drives a generator supplying current to traction motors. Diesel locomotives and railcars entered service before World War I, but it was not until the 1930s that internal-combustion engines began to surpass steam traction in the matter of speed on rails.

In fact, one outstanding achievement in 1931 was an aberration outside the mainstream of rail travel, and the vehicle never entered revenue passenger service. It was a streamlined railcar designed in Germany by Dipl-Ing F. Krückenberg, who was convinced the standard steel duo-rail system could carry much faster vehicles (he was so right!). It was almost an aircraft fuselage on rails, because though 28.96 m (95 ft) long it weighed a mere 17.25 tons and was carried by just two pairs of small wheels 20 m (65 ft 7 in) apart. Propulsion was by a 600 hp V-12 airship engine driving a four-blade pusher propeller. On 21 June 1931, between Karstadt and Dergenthin on the main Berlin/Hamburg line used for so many other speed

records, it was opened up to full power and reached 100 km/h (62.1 mph) in the first kilometre (0.62 mile)! The speed continued rising to 230 km/h (143 mph) on level track, a figure not reached again on rails for more than 20 years.

In 1932 a more practical diesel railcar-set appeared on the DR (German state railways) after prolonged research. Called *Der Fliegende Hamburger* (The Flying Hamburger) it was a two-car set, with careful streamlining and powered by a Maybach V-12 diesel of 410 hp in each unit, with electric traction. As the total weight was only 77 tons, it achieved a level of performance, both speed and acceleration, much higher than ordinary trains of the period. Fully furnished for 102 passengers with a luxurious buffet section, toilets and luggage space, it reached a speed of almost exactly 200 km/h (124.3 mph) on test. It entered service in spring 1932 and after a shakedown period was booked to average 125 km/h (77.6 mph) over the entire journey Berlin/Hamburg, which meant holding 160.9 km/h (100 mph) over the faster sections. During the subsequent four years other diesel railcar sets, often worked in pairs as a four-car train, linked Berlin with Cologne, Munich and other cities on even faster schedules.

The German railcars helped trigger off a gradual introduction of high-speed diesel trains in the USA. The first, commissioned by the Union Pacific Railroad, was the M-10000 *City of Salina*; only a few weeks later came the first *Zephyr* on the Chicago, Burlington & Quincy road. Both were streamlined three-car sets with articulated bogies joining each pair of cars so that the whole train ran on four bogies. Both trains were powered by large slow-running

WILLS'S CIGARETTES

SANTA FE 'SUPER CHIEF' DIESEL FLYER

engines designed to run for years with no major trouble, driving a generator supplying electric traction motors. Nobody could foresee that these were the first of a new breed of train that would sweep away steam traction throughout North America, though their shiny new image and dramatic speed created headlines from coast to coast.

In early tests the Union Pacific train set a national rail record at 193 km/h (120 mph), and demonstrated its ability to average over 160.9 km/h (100 mph) for long distances. On 26 May 1934 the *Zephyr* made a remarkable demonstration run from Denver to Chicago over the shortest route, 1637 km (1017 miles), in 14 hours at an average speed of 124.9 km/h (77.6 mph), with long stretches at the magic 100 mph.

Such performance attracted more passengers, all eager to ride at similar speeds. The result was that diesel-electric traction had to be applied to long and heavy trains, and the first was the *City of Denver* run jointly by the Union Pacific and the North Western, again between Chicago and Denver. This used a streamlined triple-unit locomotive of 6000 hp to haul a very heavy train at speeds unattainable with any other form of traction at that time, with running close to the 100 mph level over the flat prairies in order to average nearly 113 km/h (70 mph) over the 1688 km (1049 mile) route including a climb in the Rocky Mountains to a mile above sea level. The Burlington route likewise lengthened its *Zephyr* into the *Denver Zephyr* with 12 passenger cars hauled by a 3000 hp twin-unit locomotive. On 23 October 1936 this train, with ten cars only, covered the shorter (1017 mile) route in a remarkable 12 h 12.5 min, at an average of 134.1 km/h (83.35 mph). Long

distances were covered at over 100 mph and the highest speed on the run was 186.7 km/h (116 mph).

Sadly, this was the speed peak of US railroads. Though the colourful diesel went from strength to strength, and hauled such famous trains as *The Super Chief, El Capitan*, Rock Island *Rockets, Hiawatha* and *Twentieth Century Limited*, standards of track maintenance and other problems resulted in a slow decay and a fall-off in performance.

In Germany the quest for speed resulted in 1935 in a developed three-unit train being built on the Krückenberg principles, with single axles instead of bogies but very much heavier than the 1931 car and weighing in all 123.5 tonnes. Each car had a 400 hp Maybach diesel driving through one of the first hydraulic transmissions (such a drive had been pioneered on the original car, whose propeller had been removed and replaced by wheel drive in 1933). Even though the power/weight ratio of the three-car unit was much lower than that of the single-unit car it was only fractionally slower, and following prolonged trials reached 215 km/h (133.6 mph) in June 1939.

This remained the record for diesel traction until 12 June 1973, by which time almost the whole world's railways had gone diesel and in some countries had raised average speeds to not far short of 160.9 km/h (100 mph). Unlike the steam era little attention had been paid to speed records, the overall improvement in times of ordinary trains being far more important; but by the 1970s important advances in vehicle dynamics were opening the way to rapid further acceleration. British Rail developed a radical Advanced Passenger Train, described later. In parallel a more conventional High-Speed Train (HST) was built, with non-tilting cars and diesel-electric propulsion by a short power car at each end containing a 2250 hp Paxman engine and with a streamlined cab. During tests on the excellent former LNER main line between York and Darlington in 1973, the first HST demonstrated its ability to exceed its design speed of 125 mph (201 km/h). On 6 June it reached 210.8 km/h (131 mph); on 11 June it attained 227 km/h (141 mph), and the highest figure reached was 230 km/h (143 mph) on 12 June. Production HST.125s have in general been held to the published maximum, but on special occasions (or, exceptionally, when making up time) have shown their full capabilities. A special round trip Bristol–London–Bristol on 7 May 1977 (to mark the Queen's Silver Jubilee) covered the 189.3 km (117.7 mile) journey in 68 min 20 s up and 67 min 35 s down, the latter giving an overall start/stop average of 168 km/h (104.4 mph); cruising speed was close to 206 km/h (128 mph) throughout.

Gas turbine

As previously noted, few steam-turbine locomotives were built, and the same is true of those with gas-turbine propulsion. As explained in the air speed section, gas turbines are basically turbojet engines with as much energy as possible extracted from the jet and put into a shaft drive. Some experimental rail and tracked air-cushion vehicle (TACV) units have even been propelled by turbojets, as described presently.

All the earliest gas-turbine rail motive power comprised large and powerful locomotives without any special high-speed capability. The Swiss Brown Boveri company built the first examples, one of which was used by British Rail, which then also bought a 3000 hp locomotive from Metropolitan-Vickers. By far the largest gas-turbine locos were the monster 408-US ton (370 tonne) two-unit machines, used very successfully by the Union Pacific for

heavy freight haulage; they were each rated at 8500 hp.

The first modern lightweight gas-turbine passenger trains were the Turbotrains built in Canada with small aircraft-type (Pratt & Whitney of Canada PT6) engines. These were the first trains to have passenger coaches designed to tilt on bends to improve passenger comfort (unlike the British APT they were simply suspended from pivots high above the centre of gravity), and also the first complete trains powered by multiple small gas turbine engines. They gave prolonged trouble but eventually entered revenue service with Canadian National with their fastest timing being 144.8 km/h (90 mph) average over a 500 km (311 mile) stretch between Guildwood (east of Toronto) and Dorval (west of Montreal).

The first prototype of the British Rail APT (Advanced Passenger Train) was powered by ten 300 hp Rover (British Leyland) gas turbines with electric transmission, grouped five at a time in power cars at the ends of the train. After five years of research this ran in 1972, and on 10 August 1975 reached 244.6 km/h (152 mph) on the Western Region, east of Swindon. In October 1975 it ran from London to Leicester, 159 km (99 miles) over a difficult route, in 58 min despite a blanket speed restriction to 201 km/h (125 mph). Production APTs are referred to in the next subsection.

Today the most important gas-turbine trains are the TGV type (Train de Grande Vitesse, high-speed train), of the SNCF, the French national railways. Though made up of conventional non-tilting cars, connected together by sharing common bogies joining the ends of adjacent vehicles, the TGV has been designed for sustained running at 300 km/h (186 mph). The first SNCF gas-turbine train, tested from 1970, reached what is today the humdrum speed of 201 km/h (125 mph), with hydraulic transmission (one was sold to the USA for Amtrak service). The TGV uses multiple engines and electric transmission, like the original APT, and from 1972 quickly set some very impressive speed records. Its drawback, compared with APT, is that the non-tilting cars cannot negotiate curves at very high speeds without severe passenger discomfort, so the TGV needs

British Rail's APT-E experimental advanced passenger train is seen here on test in 1972. The lumps above the first and last cars are the exhaust cowls for the multiple small gas turbine engines. It was confidently planned that passenger service would begin in 1975 at an initial 250 km/h (155 mph), but the whole APT was abandoned in 1983. (British Rail)

France's SNCF cheated by building a completely new route for its outstanding TGV (Train de Grande Vitesse) linking Paris and Lyons, thus avoiding the limitations of previous routes surveyed over a century ago. The regular average speed of 255 km/h (158.5 mph) has been far exceeded by an experimental train. (La Vie du Rail)

very straight track. Such track exists south of Bordeaux, and here on 8 December 1972 the prototype TGV sustained 318 km/h (197.6 mph) on level track.

On 26 February 1981 the SNCF's T6V.PSE experimental high-speed train reached 380 km/h (236 mph) near Tonnerre, the highest-ever speed on ordinary service track. From 1983 the production TGV trains have been running to a 2 h schedule between Paris and Lyons using new high-speed track; this is a start-to-stop average of 255 km/h (158.5 mph). A photograph appears above and on the book jacket.

Electric

Though miniature electric locomotives were tested from 1835 it was not until 1881 that a useful permanent public electric railway was opened. In theory electric traction should be the fastest of all rail motive power forms, since there are no speed limitations other than those of the basic vehicle (assuming current can be collected successfully) and the energy to drive the train does not have to be generated on board. No speed worthy of note, however, was attained until a special high-speed vehicle was built in 1901 by the original pioneer of electric railways, the German company Siemens und Halske.

The test car rode on two bogies and had a ratio of power to weight unprecedented on any rail vehicle. On test in 1901 it easily reached 162.5 km/h (101 mph), but the heavy unsprung weight of the traction motors caused damage to the track of the Prussian State railway. Two further locomotives were therefore constructed with more but lighter traction motors, and these were tested in 1903 on the military line at Marienfeld–Zössen near Berlin. The 12-wheel car with Siemens power reached 201 km/h (124.9 mph) on 6 October 1903. The other, with power equipment by AEG, reached 210 km/h (130.5 mph) on 23 October. The ponderous weight of traction motors was still a problem, and it held back very powerful locomotives for some time, those that were built all having the motors fixed to the frame and driving via cranks and coupled driving wheels as in steam locomotives.

These speeds were not equalled in regular line service, until in 1938–39 extremely light and powerful three-car electric trains were put into use on Italian State Railways. On 27 July 1938 a speed of 201 km/h (124.9 mph) was reached during an 83 min run from Rome to Naples (213.9 km, 132.9 miles), and on 20 July 1939 a peak of 203 km/h (126.1 mph) was attained during a run from Florence to Milan, 315 km (195.7 miles) in a remarkable 115 min.

The SNCF, French railways, were rebuilt almost from scratch from 1945, and turned into one of the finest networks in the world. Large mileages were electrified, initially at 1500 volts DC supplied via overhead catenary, and new classes of compact but very powerful locomotive were built from 1950. It was decided to do high-speed tests to ascertain what problems existed in picking up current from the catenary and to verify the predicted riding of the locomotive on ordinary (but well-laid) track. Calculations showed that, with the new breed of electric

locomotive, changing the gear ratio of the drive between the traction motors and the axles would enable extremely high speeds to be reached. This is equivalent to changing the small wheels of a steam freight locomotive for the large wheels of a passenger express, the speed being gained at the expense of reduced pulling power.

The trials which followed may have been just slightly 'pushing their luck' in that they explored a realm of speed never before approached in any form of rail travel, and still never equalled in regular service. It must be emphasised that the locomotives were standard production types, apart from the altered ratio of the gearing, and they were in each case pulling a short train of three ordinary cars of passenger stock, over metals used by heavy traffic (the test trains were booked into convenient slots in the timetable). These runs did more than anything else not only to probe the limitations of flanged steel wheels on ordinary rails but also to raise the speed sights of rail engineers in many countries.

The first trials took place on the main (former PLM) line from Paris to the Mediterranean, between Dijon and Beaune, in early 1953. Using Co-Co (two bogies each with three powered axles) engine No 7121, weighing 106 tonnes and with a one-hour rating of 4300 hp, the tests culminated on 21 February 1953 with a run during which 240 km/h (149 mph) was held for 5 km (over 3 miles), with a peak at 242.8 km/h (150.9 mph). Following further tests, a change of gear ratio and a change of venue to the straight and level line south from Bordeaux, a second programme was completed in 1955. On 28 March Co-Co No 7107, a sister to No 7121, reached the amazing speed of 330.9 km/h (205.6 mph) between Facture and Morceux. On the following day the smaller 81 tonne, 4000 hp Bo-Bo No 9004 reached exactly the same speed. There was no damage to locomotives, rolling stock or track, and of course to reach such a speed current collection had to be effective.

These trials made all subsequent rail speeds—until very recently—anti-climax. Despite global research, and a ceaseless upgrading in the speeds of ordinary trains in many countries, it was almost 20 years before the SNCF figure was again reached on conventional track, and then it was by a special research car many years away from possible public use. The speed reached was

410 km/h (254.76 mph), on 14 August 1974, during tests on a LIM research vehicle of the US Department of Transportation at a special laboratory track at Pueblo, Colorado. The LIM (linear induction motor) is widely regarded as the preferred system of propulsion for future high-speed guided land transport. In principle an ordinary electric motor 'unrolled', it usually takes the form of current-carrying coils on the vehicle (corresponding to the stator of the motor) which react against metal in the track, typically a shallow wall of aluminium, which corresponds to the rotor. The LIM is noiseless and devoid of friction or mechanical wear, and suffers from no speed limitation. With enough power, speeds of up to 800 km/h (500 mph) could become commonplace, the main limitations being due to the drag and noise of the airflow past the vehicle.

Though not records, the following electric railway speeds are worthy of mention:

By far the greatest programme of increasing rail speeds by building new lines has been that of Japan, which adopted the brute-force method of constructing completely new routes, without sharp curves or other speed restrictions, and equipping them with electric multi-unit trains of unprecedented power. The new Shin–Kansen network opened with the New Tokaido line between Tokyo and Osaka on 1 November 1965. Each train comprises 16 long and heavy cars with every axle powered and a total of more than 12 000 hp, sufficient for speeds of up to 210 km/h (130.5 mph), with newer sections cleared to 255 km/h (158.5 mph). The usual time from Tokyo to Osaka is 3 h 10 min for the 516 km (320.6 miles), an average of 163 km/h (101.3 mph) including a stop at Nagoya. Later Shin-Kansen routes have similar performance. These lines required the solving of major problems not previously encountered, including use of sealed toilets serviced at night (when the wheels are also re-ground to the correct profile) and sealed cars to protect passengers against violent pressure changes on passing other trains, especially in tunnels.

The highest speed reached by a regular passenger train in the USA is 251 km/h (156 mph), by the first prototype of the Metroliner. These trains, built by the Budd Company, famed for its all-metal rail passenger cars, were designed for the North-East Corridor linking New England (Boston) via New York and Philadelphia to Baltimore and Washington, the world's busiest route. Like the Japanese expresses they are big and heavy, and hardly streamlined at all, but have such power they can accelerate very rapidly, reaching their normal running speed of 201 km/h (125 mph) in two minutes from rest. The maximum speed was explored in a run on 24 May 1967.

In 1974 the DB (German state railways) broke its long-standing national train record during trials with the first TE 403 four-car set, yet another multi-unit express with overhead pantograph for current collection. Half the weight of Metroliner cars and much better streamlined, these neat luxury trains cruise at 201 km/h and can reach 230 km/h (143 mph).

In late 1976 South African Railways set a record for 1.067 m (3.5 ft) gauge lines by running a regular electric loco with a special design of bogie and modified drive gears at 200 km/h (124 mph); the speed could have been higher.

Britain's production type APT (Advanced Passenger Train) at last entered service in December 1981, on the West Coast route between London and Glasgow. Electrically propelled, unlike the prototype, with power cars in the centre of the train, these comfortable and technically very advanced trains demonstrated sustained running at around 258 km/h (160 mph) on their first revenue service between Glasgow and Carlisle on 7 December 1981. Much higher speeds would have been possible, but the entire programme was abandoned after 20 years of work in 1983, largely because of endemic unreliability caused by poor quality control.

Other propulsion

Several early railways used the atmospheric or vacuum propulsion method in which the train is drawn along by a piston running in a pipe between the rails, connected by a bracket passing through a slit in the pipe sealed (except at the bracket) by flexible leather, and with air sucked out of the pipe ahead of the train. Part of the folklore of railways is that on 19 August 1843 a runaway train on the short atmospheric line from Dalkey to Dun Laoghaire, Ireland, reached 136.8 km/h (85 mph). But no measure-

Bertin & Cie in France formed a subsidiary company to develop what they called Aérotrains, sliding along a concrete track of inverted-T form on cushions of air. This early vehicle reached about 200 km/h (124 mph) and later, with a rocket added, 345 km/h (214.4 mph). (Bertin)

ment was possible, and the most that can be said is that it probably *seemed* like such a speed.

Purely as an experiment, and to set a startling national record, the New York Central fitted an ex-US Air Force bomber engine pod, containing twin General Electric J47 turbojets, above the forward roof of a Budd railcar. After carefully inspecting the track near Bryan, Ohio, the car was let loose and reached 295.9 km/h (183.85 mph), covering a five-mile stretch in just 1 min 39.75 s (average 291 km/h, 181 mph).

The first series of TACV (tracked air-cushion vehicle) trials took place in France, with vehicles and track produced by the Société Bertin and known as Aérotrains. After five years of testing, a special company, Société de l'Aérotrain, was formed in 1965 and its research vehicles set several speed records. The original Aérotrain 01 reached speeds around 200 km/h with an air propeller and finally 345 km/h (214.4 mph) with jet propulsion in December 1967. In the same month the small 02 vehicle attained 378 km/h (234.9 mph), and in January 1969 this was fitted with a small booster rocket and, despite the short length of the test track, reached 422 km/h

(262.2 mph). The largest Aérotrain, the 80-seat Orleans type, cruised at 250 km/h and could reach 435 km/h (270 mph).

Other TACV test vehicles have reached the 480 km/h (300 mph) level, though the Grumman TACV of the US Department of Transportation has not so far been fitted with the large (6350 kg, 14 000 lb thrust) JT8D jet engine intended to give it a speed of 579 km/h (360 mph). For the 1990s and beyond much is expected of Maglev (magnetic levitation) vehicles, if possible using refrigerated superconducting coils to sustain the magnets that raise them a few centimetres above the guideway. Germany and Japan are leaders in this area, and as far back as February 1976, a German (Krauss Maffei and MBB joint development) Maglev car exceeded 400 km/h (248.5 mph). At the time of writing, the highest

One of two pioneer Maglevs in Japan, this car ran on a test track at Yokohama in January 1976. The High-Speed Surface Transport project by Japan Air Lines is intended to link city centres with airports. (JAL)

speed attained by a Maglev, and the highest known speed attained by any normal guided land vehicle, is 517 km/h (321 mph), reached on 21 December 1979 by the ML-500 test car of Japanese National Railways on its 7 km (4.3 mile) track at Miyazaki. It is the intention to use Maglev support instead of wheels on a new route to back up the already overcrowded New Tokaido line. The Tokyo-Osaka schedule is to be one hour, a start-to-stop average of about 500 km/h (311 mph).

Rocket sleds
Since the late 1940s the US Air Force has conducted research (for example, into problems of escape from high-speed aircraft) using rocket-propelled vehicles sliding on railed tracks at Holloman AFB (Air Force Base) near Albuquerque, New Mexico. Most of the tests have reached supersonic speed, even with a human 'pilot' aboard. The all-time record was reached in a test on 19 February 1959, without a human aboard, when the peak velocity was 4972 km/h (3090 mph). This is by a wide margin the highest speed ever reached by any large vehicle running across the Earth's surface.

Conveyors, pipes and lifts
A typical speed for the thousands of aerial ropeways used for transporting people, raw material and waste products from mines and quarries is 5 km/h (3.1 mph). Ski lifts generally move rather faster, at about 6.5 km/h (4 mph). Some of the largest installations are much faster; the longest and fastest in the world is believed to be the Teleférico Mérida to the summit of Pico Espejo (4764 m, 15 630 ft) in Venezuela, which has two 45-passenger cars pulled at 35.08 km/h (21.80 mph). Indoor conveyors vary greatly. For transport the speed can be as high as 11 km/h (6.8 mph), while for process work and assembly of parts it may be a mere 0.073 km/h (0.045 mph, 20 mm/s, 4 ft/min). Among the faster types are pneumatic tube conveyors, delivering at up to 40 km/h (25 mph). Piped

material can travel at any speed up to over 150 km/h (93 mph) for water. Crude oil usually flows at about one-tenth this speed, though less-dense and less-viscous petroleum products can be pumped in a large pipe at speeds which in the centre of the pipe reach 80 km/h (50 mph). In contrast, suspended solids such as fluid capsules and coal seldom travel at above 11.25 km/h (7 mph, 10 ft/s) because pumping energy losses soon become uneconomic; a study for a 724 km (450 mile) pipe carrying 1100 short tons (998 t) of coal in dense phase per hour by pneumatic transport found that the rate of energy loss by pumping was higher than the rate at which energy was supplied by the delivered coal!

By far the fastest lifts are those for face-workers in deep mines, the top ten all being in diamond mines in South Africa. Winding speed to some extent is at the discretion of the operator but the cage in a 2072 m (6800 ft) shaft at Western Deep, Transvaal, can operate at 1095 m (3595 ft)/min, or 65.8 km/h (40.9 mph). This is almost twice the speed of the fastest public lifts, in the Sunshine 60 Building, Tokyo, which run to the 60th floor (240 m, 787.4 ft level) at 609.6 m (2000 ft)/min, or 36.56 km/h (22.72 mph). Even at this speed, ear-popping can be a painful problem.

MARINE VEHICLES

Some classes of speed on water are covered in greater detail in *The Guinness Book of Yachting Facts and Feats*, *The Guinness Book of Motorboating Facts and Feats*, and *The Guinness Book of Ships and Shipping*.

Though the ship is man's earliest vehicle, no useful numerical speed information exists prior to the mid-19th century. There have been many estimates—or rather guesstimates—of the peak speeds attained by various early sailing craft and, especially, rowed galleys which could invariably overhaul any vessel relying on sail alone. Though some students of early ships, and fiction writers, have suggested speeds for the fastest galleys of up to 15 knots (27.8 km/h, 17.27 mph) there is no reason to believe that two-thirds of this speed was ever exceeded. A

number of authorities doubt that any early ship using sail alone ever exceeded 9 knots (16.68 km/h, 10.36 mph).[1]

By the mid-19th century intense commercial competition had led to faster ships and attempts at measuring their speed. As it is at the mercy of the wind, and in fact proceeds according to a very complex interaction between several forces along a path arbitrarily determined by the man at the helm, there is no slick figure for the 'speed' of any sailing vessel. One more meaningful figure is the length of the day's run measured by taking a sextant shot of a heavenly body at two times 24 h apart (normally separated by six 4 h 'watches') and calculating the great-circle distance between the two fixes thus obtained. The usually quoted 'best day's run' is that reported for the square-rigger *Champion of the Seas* (sometimes incorrectly called *Sovereign of the Seas*) for a 23 h 18 min period in December 1854. Unfortunately, even this claim is of doubtful value. The distance has been reported variously as 410.7, 465 and 467 nautical miles; and the speeds which result by calculation of up to 20.04 knots are today no longer regarded as credible.

Most authorities are inclined to believe the claim of Capt Enright of the clipper *Lightning* for 430 nautical miles in one 24 h period in March 1857, giving an average speed of 17.92 knots (33.2 km/h, 20.63 mph), though this also is extraordinary. The highest speed ever actually measured over a 4 h watch is believed to be the 17.5 knots (32.4 km/h, 20.15 mph) by the enormous *Preussen* (Prussia), a five-masted square-rigged barque of 1903. The same speed was also claimed by several other much earlier and smaller ships of the clipper family, including the *Cutty Sark*, but without confirmation. In-service average sailing speeds of the fastest clippers were in the region of 7 knots (13 km/h, 8 mph).

One of the significant sailing journeys of the clipper ships was the circumnavigation of the globe from northwest Europe to Australia via the Cape of Good Hope and back via Cape Horn, a total distance conventionally taken as 29 600 nautical miles (54 855 km, 34 085 miles).

[1] Still almost universally used by marine and even air travel, the knot is one nautical mile (1853 m, 6080 ft) per hour; other values include 0.5144 m/s and 1.15152 mph.

Though everyone seems willing to accept the claim, the clipper *Lightning*'s longest-ever day's run under sail is variously given as 430 nautical miles (495 miles) and as 436 miles. (Lithograph in Macpherson collection, Mary Evans Picture Library)

Right:
Great yachts racing in 1896: the British royal yacht *Britannia* (left) in contention against the record-breaking *Satanita*. (Beken of Cowes)

The best time ever was 133 days set by *James Baines*, a mean of 9.27 knots. Today a vessel could be built to beat this; the best single-handed time is the 169 days by Alain Colas in trimaran *Manureva*, 7.29 knots (13.51 km/h, 8.40 mph), with the best day's run no less than 326 nautical miles (13.58 knots, 25.17 km/h, 15.64 mph).

Racing with large cutters (yachts) started in the 1890s, and the highest speed ever measured with this class was by one of the first, and largest: *Satanita* of 1893. On smooth water she was timed at a steady 17 knots (31.5 km/h, 19.58 mph). Since then, while conventional sailing vessels have rarely reached such a speed, unconventional types such as catamarans, trimarans, proas, hydrofoils and windsurfers have exceeded it. Despite many claims, the only authenticated speed records now accepted are those measured by instrumentation approved by a competent national authority, and on this basis the following are current sailing speed records:

The fastest waterborne sailing craft, whose speed has been measured according to the specified conditions, is the proa *Crossbow II*, built solely for the purpose and useless for normal sailing (because such an asymmetric craft cannot sail with the wind on the other side, and so has to lower sail and be towed back to the start). Her best-ever speed over the measured 500 m (1640 ft) course was 33.40 knots (61.89 km/h, 38.46 mph) achieved on 4 October 1977. A year later she was unofficially estimated to have reached 45 knots (83.4 km/h, 51.8 mph).

The fastest practical sailing craft is almost certainly the catamaran *Beowulf V*, timed in 1974 at a claimed 31.4 knots (58.19 km/h, 36.16 mph). This speed is not internationally accepted, but is certainly far in excess of the best recorded by other cats (such as *Icarus*, a hydrofoil cat which never exceeded 21.6 knots even in a wind of almost the same velocity). Much contention surrounds the claims of *Monitor*, a hydrofoil sailing boat which in 1956, during trials for the US Navy, was said to have nudged 40 knots and reached speeds roughly twice that of the wind.

For three years the windsurfing (boardsailing) record was 22.95 knots (42.53 km/h, 26.42 mph) set by Clive Colenso on 22 October 1979. There were at least 40 attempts to break this record, many by Colenso, before it succumbed to the outstanding 27.82 knots (51.52 km/h, 32.01 mph) set on 13 October 1982 at Weymouth, England, in a Force 7 gale by Pascal Maka of France.

Power boats

The term power boat is normally reserved for high-speed sporting motorboats, and this class continues to be important in long-distance ocean racing. It came into existence owing to the roughly parallel developments of the planing-bottom hull (then called the hydroplane) and internal-combustion engine, which sharply improved the ratio of power to weight. Prior to the planing bottom the rapid increase in drag of a displacement vessel—which rises approximately in proportion to the cube of the speed—appeared to make 40 mph forever unattainable. Today we know this is not the case, but with the planing-bottom boat skimming across the surface the speed quickly reached almost 60 mph in T.O.M. Sopwith's *Maple Leaf IV* in 1913.

During the 1920s speeds almost doubled, so that the pre-eminent power-boat races, for the Harmsworth Trophy, became dangerous; in 1930 *Miss England II* struck a submerged log and sank, Sir Henry Segrave being drowned, and a year later the same boat was overturned by the wash of her American rival. Water speed records are usually the average of at least two runs in different directions; they are not normally quoted in knots. The following are significant water speed records or attempts since that year:

POWER BOAT MILESTONES

1932 *Miss America IX*, driven by long-standing Harmsworth competitor Gar Wood, reached 179.76 km/h (111.7 mph). Later in 1932 Kaye Don replied in *Miss England III* at 192.64 km/h (119.7 mph). Wood returned with a new boat, *Miss America X*, to set the figure of 201.00 km/h (124.8 mph).

1937 The loss of Sir Henry Segrave in *Miss England II* in 1930 had retarded British attempts on the water speed record, but in 1935 Sir Malcolm Campbell retired from land speed record attempts and, to everyone's surprise, announced he was going for the water record. He had a beautiful new boat built, named *Bluebird* like his cars and powered by a Rolls-Royce R engine similar to that in his last car. On a test at full speed in August 1938 the engine cut dead at 130 mph; the boat had risen so high out of the water the cooling-water scoop had sucked nothing but air and the engine had seized. The aim of getting both records with the same engine was impossible, but after an engine-change Campbell pushed the record to 208.41 km/h (129.5 mph).

1938 Campbell raised the record to 210.66 km/h (130.9 mph).

1939 Campbell set his final record at 228.04 km/h (141.7 mph).

1950 There were no further attempts until in this year Stanley Sayres of the United States set a new record at 257.98 km/h (160.3 mph) in *Slo-mo-Shun IV*.

1952 Sayres raised the record to 282.27 km/h (178.5 mph). Meanwhile, Britisher John Cobb—like Segrave and Campbell a holder of the land speed record—had entered the lists with the first of a new breed of jet boats, the engine being a de Havilland Goblin turbojet. Named *Crusader*, the compact craft appeared likely to set a wholly new level of performance over water. On 29 September 1952, at about 331.5 km/h (206 mph), *Crusader* dived into the water and disintegrated, killing the driver.

1955 Sir Malcolm Campbell's son Donald now took up the challenge with another jet boat, *Bluebird K7*. This had twin front sponsons (planing floats) and was propelled by a Metrovick Beryl turbojet. He raised the record to 325.57 km/h (202.3 mph) and then to 348.10 km/h (216.3 mph).

1956 Campbell raised the figure to 363.07 km/h (225.6 mph), in the course of which one run was made at 460.27 km/h (286.0 mph).

1957 Campbell raised the record to 384.79 km/h (239.1 mph).

1958 Campbell raised the record to 400.08 km/h (248.6 mph).

1959 Campbell raised the record to 418.91 km/h (260.3 mph).

1964 Campbell again raised the record to 444.66 km/h (276.3 mph).

1967 On 4 January Campbell rounded off a month of testing with a fresh record attempt. The slightly modified boat was travelling at 527.9 km/h (328 mph) when it somersaulted and disintegrated. Campbell's body was never found. Later in the year (30 June) Lee Taylor Jr of the United States took the record in *Hustler* (one Westinghouse J46 turbojet) at 459.00 km/h (285.21 mph).

1978 Having set an unequalled but imprecisely measured speed around 556 km/h (345 mph) in 1977, Kenneth Peter Warby set the current water speed record at Blowering Dam Lake, NSW, on 8 October 1978 at 514.39 km/h (319.627 mph) in *Spirit of Australia*. In 1984 at least five contenders were known to be preparing new jet boats to attack the record.

Right:
Donald Campbell is seen here in the cockpit of *Bluebird* together with his famous mechanic, Leo Villa, who had previously worked for his father, Sir Malcolm. Villa had been riding with him on the Oltranza Cup Race on Lake Garda which Campbell won in June 1951. (Leo Villa)

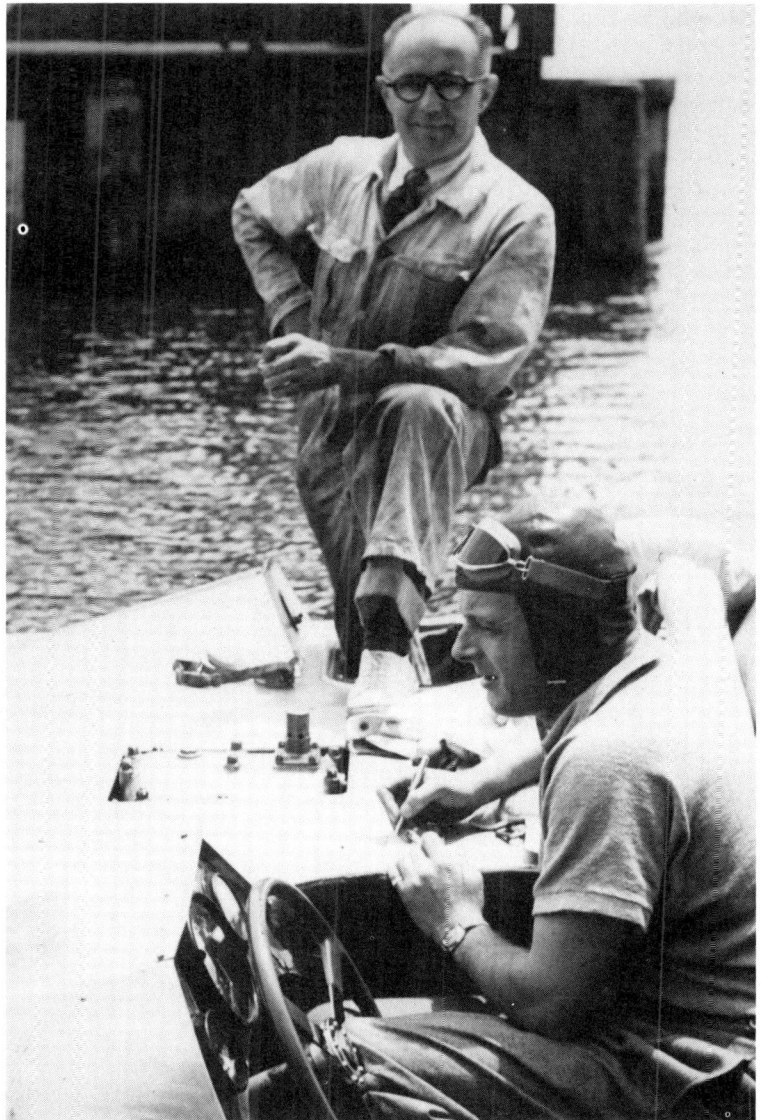

There are numerous internationally controlled classes for other powered sporting boats, as set out in *The Guinness Book of Motorboating Facts and Feats*. The classes include various inshore categories with different engine sizes, inflatable craft, air propeller and immersed propeller classes, and separate categories for offshore boats able to race at sea. In the latter group the diesel-engined figure of 126.1 km/h (78.36 mph) is notable for having been set in 1924, and the record for air-propeller propulsion has stood at 155.88 km/h (96.86 mph) since 1951. Waterjet propulsion, important with hydrofoils and ACVs as noted later, is not yet an established class for records. The record for an immersed water propeller is 325.76 km/h (202.42 mph) set by Larry Hill of the United States in his supercharged hydroplane *Mr Ed* off Long Beach in 1973. Sue Williams, also of the USA, drove the unlimited hydroplane *U–96 KYYX* through a measured mile on Lake Washington, Seattle, at 262.392 km/h (163.043 mph) on 26 July 1978 for the women's world record.

Merchant ships

Speeds were seldom greater than 5 knots (9.3 km/h, 5.8 mph) until well into the second half of the 19th century. Then competition, especially for the passenger trade across the North Atlantic, led to very great increases in installed power, much greater than necessitated by the increasing size of ship. Enormous sections of the hull were occupied by as many as 24 steam boilers, thousands of tons of coal and giant reciprocating engines, often of the triple-expansion type in which the steam is passed through successively larger cylinders to improve efficiency. But the fight for extra speed was hard: the power needed rises approximately with the cube of the speed, and it was a balance between coal consumption and passenger-appeal. No ship could economically reach 20 knots (37 km/h, 23 mph).

Then in 1889 Charles Parsons formed his own company at Newcastle-upon-Tyne and produced a series of improved steam turbines, in which steam expands past fixed and rotating blades to turn a shaft. Unlike the reciprocating engine this could run at very high speeds. In 1894 Parsons set out to build the fastest ship in the world. The result was *Turbinia*, a trim launch 31.5 m (103 ft 4 in) long. At first she had a very poor performance, and the cause was eventually traced to cavitation, a phenomenon which ruins the performance of many propellers rotated at high speed under water and indeed causes rapid erosion of the propeller's surface. (Cavitation is the formation of small transient empty bubbles, filled not by air but by a

At the great Jubilee Review of the assembled fleets at Spithead in 1897 the first turbine ship, *Turbinia*, saucily streaked among the grey monsters at speeds double anything seen previously. (Beken of Cowes)

vacuum, which appear suddenly and just as suddenly disappear, the 'implosion' acting on the propeller like a small hand-grenade.) Cavitation has been a problem in almost all high-speed craft driven by water propellers, and with *Turbinia* the answer was a major rethink. The turbine was taken out and replaced by three turbines, one high-pressure, one intermediate and a large low-pressure machine. Each drove its own prop shaft, and on each shaft were arranged three screws, quite widely spaced; thus there were nine propellers in all. Refloated in 1897 she amply fulfilled all expectations, reaching over 34.5 knots (63.94 km/h, 39.73 mph), almost twice as fast as anything else afloat.

The Royal Navy soon got Parsons to put the steam turbine into warships, the first being a destroyer, *Viper*, which reached 37 knots (68.57 km/h, 42.61 mph). A much bigger gamble was the early decision of the Cunard Steamship Company to adopt the (literally revolutionary) propulsion for two giant new transatlantic passenger liners, *Mauretania* and *Lusitania*. The former, on her trials in 1907, staggered the world by steaming steadily at 27.4 knots (50.78 km/h, 31.55 mph), roughly twice as fast as other large liners of the day. Parsons' new turbines were also put into the Royal Navy's radically advanced new battleship

SS *Persia*, the first Cunarder to have an iron hull, typified the mid-19th century transatlantic passenger liners which had all the steam and sail power they could muster. She took the Blue Riband in July 1856 at 13.82 knots (25.6 km/h), taking just over 9 days Liverpool–NY.

After trying the new Parsons turbines in the 19 524-ton *Carmania* in 1905, the Cunard line commissioned two giant new liners, *Lusitania* and *Mauretania*, the largest and fastest in the world. *Mauretania*, seen here, held the Blue Riband from 1907 until 1929! (Beken of Cowes)

Dreadnought, the first to have multiple heavy guns in pivoting turrets, which on test in 1906 achieved 21 knots (38.9 km/h, 24.2 mph), enough to overhaul any other battleship with the greatest ease.

The notional, but highly coveted, prize for the fastest liner on the North Atlantic is the Blue Riband, and *Mauretania* held this for 22 years, longer than any other ship. The Riband passed in 1929 to the Norddeutscher Lloyd sisters *Bremen* and *Europa* at fractionally above the old Cunarder's speed (though when she was 20 years old *Mauretania* pulled out a bit of extra power and sustained 29 knots going to the rescue of a crippled cargo vessel), and in 1935 the gigantic new French *Normandie* set a figure just

What Parsons did for Cunard it could also do for the Royal Navy, and with the most famous of all battleships, HMS *Dreadnought*, HM ship designers also introduced the revolutionary main armament of five twin-12-inch turrets. (Beken of Cowes)

over 30 knots with turbo-electric propulsion, her four steam turbines driving electric generators which supplied current to electric motors driving the four propellers. In 1936 competition came with the Cunard company's equally enormous *Queen Mary*, with almost the same speed as *Normandie*. Slightly larger, *Queen Elizabeth* was also capable of similar 32-knot speeds, but normally steamed at a more economical 29.

In 1952 the United States Lines completed its biggest and last passenger liner, *United States*. Smaller than the 'Queens' but even more powerful, she was the fastest passenger liner ever built, with a measured speed of 41.75 knots (77.37 km/h, 48.08 mph) claimed during a sustained stretch at 38.32 knots (71.01 km/h, 44.12 mph). Such speeds were fine for publicity purposes, but by the 1950s sea passengers were less interested in speed, and in any case the number of transatlantic sea passengers was rapidly declining (and has now reached effectively zero, even cruise passengers flying out to the ship). With increasing price of oil fuel,

SS *United States* was the fastest passenger liner ever built, discounting much smaller modern hydrofoils and hovercraft. Registered at 53 329 tons, she added almost 4 knots (7.4 km/h) to transatlantic Blue Riband speeds, but soon succumbed to jet travel. (Beken of Cowes)

later passenger vessels were designed to slower speeds, and in recent years have been limited to speeds still further reduced, typically in the region of 25 knots. The fastest commercial displacement craft are without exception those carrying containerised freight, which for reasons of economy have grown to great size in order to reduce unit transport costs. All the largest, in the 40 000 to 70 000 ton sizes, were gas-turbine propelled to cruise at some 33 knots (61 km/h, 38 mph). In 1973, for example, *Sea-Land Commerce* crossed the Pacific from Yokohama to Long Beach at an average 33.27 knots (61.65 km/h, 38.31 mph). The 'fuel crisis' brought a switch to diesels, and reduced speeds.

Hydrofoils and ACVs (hovercraft) are dealt with later.

Warships

The requirements and economics of warships are naturally different from those of merchant ships, though today's inflation hits both equally hard. No warship displayed an interesting speed until at the turn of the century the Royal Navy decided that the Parsons steam turbine was too good to ignore, and ordered two torpedo-boat destroyers with this form of propulsion. Still not quite convinced that the turbine would perform as predicted, Their Lordships at The Admiralty forced Parsons' company to deposit a bond of £100 000—then a colossal sum, much more than the price of the ships—against failure. Parsons deposited the money, built HMS *Viper* and was on board when she was timed at just over 37 knots (68.57 km/h, 42.61 mph). The myopic Admiralty hardly deserved her.

This speed—which may not be impressive on a motorway but looked remarkable enough to Queen Victoria's Navy—was to remain for ever a typical upper limit for all displacement warships. Most destroyers in both world wars could not quite attain it, though there were one or two exceptions, notably some classes of Italian cruisers and French destroyers. Probably the fastest cruiser of all time was Italy's *Alberto di Giussano*, first of a class of 6000-ton vessels with steam turbines of 95 000 hp, which on trials in 1931 reached 42.05 knots (77.9 km/h, 48.42 mph). During World War II it became a British morale-boosting joke that Italian warships had all their guns facing aft, and could run away faster than any other ships, but in fact in service their speeds were well down on the trial figures, so that, for example, HMAS *Sydney* caught and sank *Bartolomeo Colleoni*, sister to *Giussano*, which on paper looked an impossible feat.

Perhaps the fastest large displacement vessels of all time were the French destroyers of the *Fantasque* class built in 1931–36. All far exceeded their published design power and speed, and could sustain high speeds in actual service, though their endurance was short. The fastest of the class was *Le Terrible*, the only one to have traditional Yarrow boilers, which on acceptance trials in 1935 sustained 45.25 knots (83.86 km/h, 52.10 mph). Modern high-speed surface warships, such as carriers and their destroyer escorts, can reach about 34 knots in good weather.

The French destroyer *Le Terrible* was the fastest conventional displacement ship ever built. By sheer brute power she thrust her hull through the water at over 45 knots (83.86 km/h, 52.1 mph) in 1935. Every marine vehicle faster than this skates across the surface. (Musée de la Marine)

Fastest of all displacement warships are the various high-speed motorboats, including MTBs (motor torpedo boats), MGBs (motor gun boats), US Navy PT boats, German S-series Schnellboote (known to the Allies as E-boats) and modern boats with gas turbine propulsion replacing the former reciprocating engines. Even the vastly increased power of gas turbines has not resulted in much increase in speed, because the boats have got bigger, though the fastest precisely published speeds have been those for the Royal Navy's *Brave* class, built in the 1950s and now in reserve. Each powered by three Proteus turbines, the same engine as used in the Britannia airliner, they exceeded 52 knots (96.37 km/h, 60 mph). Fastest of the traditional piston-engined boats was probably MTB.102, of 1937, which like the *Braves* was built by the Vosper company, with a speed of 47.8 knots. Typical maxima in calm water for a German S-boat was 39 knots, and for an American PT boat 41.5 knots.

A special class, where speed is concerned, is the submarines. All the early (pre-1900) designs could hardly go faster than a good swimmer, but the internal-combustion engine transformed the picture and by 1905 typical speeds were 13 knots on the surface and 5 to 8 knots (on electric motors) submerged. Speeds rose only slightly by World War I, except for a series of giant submarines of the Royal Navy which for some reason were designed to keep up with the surface fleet. Powered by large steam turbines (imagine the problems of two giant boilers inside a submarine!) the K-class could steam on the surface at 25 knots. After hectic preparations,

USS *Tigrone*, the last wartime submarine to be stricken from the US Navy (in 1975), typifies traditional lumpy design. Submerged she was noisy, and could not exceed 10 knots (18.5 km/h). (USN)

USS *Hawkbill*, SSN-666 of the Sturgeon class, typifies modern nuclear-powered attack submarines, almost perfectly streamlined (the large rectangular sail is narrow and well-rounded, and the projecting tubular mast is retractable). Submerged, she is quiet even at more than 30 knots (55.6 km/h) (USN)

such as shutting off the funnels, they could dive; the crew then slowly roasted from the heat of the furnaces while the speed dropped to 9 knots on electric motors. No submarine ever again equalled this speed on the surface, though American and Japanese submarines of World War II could exceed 20 knots. But then a series of fundamental developments transformed the entire picture. The first was the realisation in Germany in 1942 that it was not speed on the surface that mattered but speed when submerged. The radical new Type XXI U-boat of 1944 was slightly slower on the surface than the standard mass-produced Type VIIC, but once it had dived, it switched in electric motors of an unprecedented 5000 hp, giving a sustained underwater speed of 16.8 knots (faster than on the surface). The smaller Type XVIIA and XVIIB had radical new Walter turbines driven by concentrated hydrogen peroxide (a technology used in German rocket motors) and could reach 26 knots submerged. After 1945 the Allies copied these designs, but in the United States two further dramatic advances were achieved. The traditional hull shape was replaced by an almost perfectly streamlined shape (which actually gave far more interior room, because the section was a generous circle) called variously a 'teardrop' or 'spindle' hull. Instead of a bluff conning tower on top, a slim 'sail' was provided—so slim, its alternative name is a 'bridge fin'. The first of the new vessels was USS *Albacore*, commissioned on 5 December 1953. Her performance opened up a new era in submarine development, a 15 000 hp electric drive giving her an underwater speed of 33 knots; for the first time the submarine became 'flown' like an aircraft with the ability, for example, to loop. The third great advance was nuclear propulsion, which by a factor of at least ten multiplied the energy in a submarine's fuel, and thus the practical installed engine power. Since 1957 all American submarines have been driven by steam turbines supplied by nuclear boilers, with submerged speeds of about 30 knots. Almost certainly the world's fastest submarines are the US Navy's *Los Angeles* class of attack submarines, which are slightly smaller and better streamlined than the various Poseidon-missile classes, yet have exactly double the installed power. Submerged speed is classified, but has been guesstimated at over 40 knots (74 km/h, 46 mph). An alternative candidate is the Soviet *Alpha* class, estimated in the West to reach 42 knots (77.8 km/h, 48.5 mph).

Hydrofoils

Hydrofoils are sea wings, attached to a displacement vessel in order that, above a certain speed, the hull may be lifted completely out of the water. This eliminates the previous speed problem caused by water drag rising as the cube of the speed, and as a by-product can be made to give smooth running through choppy seas. The idea is well over a century old and has been realised in several forms. The oldest practical foil boats used ladder foils, with essentially vertical arrays of foils like rungs of a ladder so that, as speed increased, the foils progressively emerged from the water. There were earlier examples, but the first high-speed ladder-foil boat was made by Enrico Forlanini (Italian

builder of airships and helicopters) and attained 38 knots (70.4 km/h, 43.75 mph) in 1905. Today there are few ladder-foil boats, the most common system being the surface-piercing foil, which looks like a flat V in front view, the tips of the foils projecting from the water. As speed increases, more foil emerges until the vessel is riding on the central tip of the V. Count von Schertel patented this simple scheme, which in modified forms is seen on hundreds of passenger ferries today, with speeds up to 39 knots (72.3 km/h, 44.9 mph). For smooth rivers the shallow-draft submerged foil—the nearest to a true sea wing—is common, especially in the Soviet Union, with speeds up to about 47 knots (87 km/h, 54 mph). The fastest hydrofoils of all are the large ocean-going warships with deeply submerged foils driven at different angles by an autopilot, rather like the elevators of an aeroplane. Fastest of this category was USS *Plainview*, a 320 ton ship with a design speed of 80 knots but in practice limited to just over 50, and the Canadian HMCS *Bras d'Or* which achieved a sustained 63 knots (116.7 km/h, 72.5 mph) on calm water but was dropped in

For slow manoeuvring some hydrofoil boats can retract their foils and behave as ordinary displacement vessels. Here USS *Tucumcari* shows its three foil systems—one at the bow and one on each side near the stern—as it crosses Puget Sound, Washington. Such deeply submerged foils are usually faster than the fixed surface-piercing pattern. (Boeing)

1972 through lack of funds. So far as is known the fastest hydrofoil vessel of all was Boeing's *FRESH-1* (Foil Research Supercavitating Hydrofoil 1), which was driven by an aircraft turbofan engine to 105 knots (194.6 km/h, 120.9 mph).

Smaller than Boeing's FRESH-1, but similar in purpose, the HTS (Hydrodynamic Test System) investigated the behaviour of foils at speeds around 185 km/h (115 mph). Use of a turbojet eliminated water disturbance except by the foils. (Boeing)

Air-cushion vehicles

Air-cushion vehicles (ACVs) are also commonly called Hovercraft (a British registered name), ground-effect machines (GEMs) and, in large marine forms, surface-effect ships (SES, in US Navy parlance). All are supported entirely by a large 'cushion' of air at slightly above atmospheric pressure, maintained beneath the craft by continuously pumping in fresh air. Probably the first such scheme to survive in literature was proposed by Swedenborg in 1716; the first actually to be built was tested in model form by John (later Lord) Thorneycroft in 1874. Modern ACVs broadly stemmed from the SR.N1, built by Saunders-Roe to the design of Sir Christopher Cockerell in 1959. This was later fitted with a small booster turbojet and reached 68 knots (126 km/h, 78.3 mph) in 1961.

Since then there have been several distinct classes of ACV. The largest are the oceangoing ships, some of which have flexible skirts, while others have rigid sidewalls which consume no air-pumping power but cause water drag. The majority of sidewall craft are relatively slow (30–35 knots), but two research craft for the US Navy, SES–100A and –100B, have since 1971 set ACV speed records. SES–100A has waterjet propulsion, while her rival has two semi-submerged supercavitating water screws. So far the latter has proved more effective, and on 25

The pioneer air-cushion vehicle, popularly known as a hovercraft, was the SR.N1 of 1959. It is shown after it had been equipped with a booster turbojet, visible along with its bulky air inlet duct on the rear deck, which gave speeds near 129 km/h (80 mph). (Beken of Cowes)

January 1980 SES–100B reached 91.9 knots (170.3 km/h, 105.8 mph) on calm water, a record for a seagoing ACV.

A second ACV class is the skirted type, in which a deep flexible skirt encloses the cushion yet can deflect over waves or solid obstructions. This enables such craft to be amphibious, though for practical reasons the largest ACVs do not operate over land other than to climb up concrete ramps at hoverports. In-service speeds seldom exceed 65 knots, though the Soviet Navy's powerful *Aist* class regularly cruise at 70 knots (130 km/h, 80.6 mph). Small amphibious sporting ACVs exist in hundreds of forms, but 96.5 km/h (60 mph) is seldom attained.

A totally different class of ACV are those guided by tracks; these are discussed as TACVs (tracked ACVs) under 'guided land transport'

Largest amphibious ACVs ever built, the British Hovercraft Corporation Super 4s used on cross-Channel services can cruise at 65 knots (120.5 km/h, 75 mph) on a calm day. (BHC)

Looking down on the fastest marine hovercraft, the US Navy's SES-100B, built by Bell Aerosystems. Unlike water-jet-propelled SES-100A, she is driven by supercavitating water propellers. (Bell via *Jane's Surface Skimmers*)

AIR

Mach numbers, which appear in this chapter, are speeds expressed as a decimal fraction of the speed of sound in the surrounding air, thus Mach 1.5 means 1.5 times the local speed of sound. Many details of record flights, for example between particular cities or countries, are given in *The Guinness Book of Air Facts and Feats*, uniform with this volume.

The differences between lighter-than-air aerostats (balloons and airships) and heavier-than-air aerodynes (aeroplanes, sailplanes and rotorcraft, for example) are so fundamental that these groups are dealt with separately within this section. Winged cruise missiles appear with other military projectiles in the 'Weapons' chapter, while the 'Cosmology' section covers speeds in spaceflight.

The first navigable aerial vehicle was Giffard's airship of 1852, though it could not fight against the lightest of breezes. (Huard, *Le Monde Industriel*, Mary Evans Picture Library)

Lighter than air

In general a balloon cannot have an airspeed (speed relative to the atmosphere around it), though it may have a considerable groundspeed because of wind. Balloons therefore are not included in this book at all. The numerous 'balloon races' of yesteryear—notably the Gordon Bennett trophy, held from 1906 until 1938—were concerned with distance rather than with speed. Several early balloons did attempt to navigate within the air; indeed a long-lasting misconception was that a balloon could 'sail' like a ship. One of the earliest known proposals for a flying machine, ascribed to Francisco da Lana Terzi in 1670, was for an aerial chariot lifted by four evacuated copper spheres giving buoyancy and driven along by a sail. Both the lifting and propulsion methods of this concept were inherently unsound.

Use of mechanical propulsion for a balloon is, of course, possible; but speeds reached so far have not been worth recording. Most persistent of the early aeronauts who tried to navigate a balloon was Jean-Pierre Blanchard, born in 1753. In 1784 he made many ascents, mainly in France, on one of which he tried the best available system (though still ineffectual), a hand-cranked propeller. Later he used oars and a rudder, as in a boat, and had them on the first cross-Channel balloon which just managed to reach the French coast after setting off from Dover on 7 January 1785.

Navigable aerostats are called dirigibles (French for steerable), or airships. The first airships had puny engines (steam, electric or gas) and could make no progress against even a light breeze; the accepted average speed for Henri Giffard's airship on 24 September 1852 is 8 km/h (5 mph), though its builder claimed 3 m/s (11 km/h, 6.8 mph). Speed gradually rose in subsequent airships to over 100 km/h (62 mph) in the Zeppelins of 1917–18. Fastest of all the giant airships was the British R.100, measured at 131.2 km/h (81.5 mph) on 16 January 1930.

Today almost all existing or planned airships are slower than this. The exception is the Airship Industries (of Britain) Model 4060, which is designed to have a maximum speed (not normally used) of 192 km/h (119 mph), though construction had not begun as this book went to press.

Heavier than air

The following is a comprehensive chronology of significant speeds achieved by aeroplanes (fixed-wing powered aerodynes). Those prefaced by letter F are officially accepted world speed records homologated by the FAI (Fédération Aéronautique Internationale), the governing body of international aerial sporting achievements. It will be noted that several of the later FAI records are 'class' records. Other FAI class records are listed later in sections dealing with rotorcraft (helicopters and autogyros) and sailplanes.

17 December 1903 First sustained, controlled aeroplane flights. First take-off, by Orville Wright, covered 36.6 m (120 ft) in 12 s, into wind estimated at 35.4 km/h (22 mph). Longest flight was No 4, by Wilbur Wright, covering 260 m (852 ft) in 59 s. In each case the airspeed was estimated at 48 km/h (30 mph).

5 October 1905 Generally regarded as the first practical aeroplane, the Wrights' *Flyer III* made many good flights, including circuits, in 1905. The speed was slightly higher than the best for the 1903 machine, averaging 62.8 km/h (39 mph). On the longest 1905 flight, on 5 October, just over 24 miles were covered in 38 min 3 s, equivalent to 60.99 km/h (37.89 mph).

12 November 1906 Accepted speed of the tail-first *No 14bis* of Alberto Santos-Dumont, a wealthy Brazilian living in Paris, is 41.27 km/h (25.64 mph). No European aircraft is known to have flown faster than the 1905 *Flyer III* until the first aeroplane meeting, held at Rheims in August 1909.

August 1909 The Grand Prix at the Rheims meeting was won on 27 August by Englishman Henri Farman with a flight of 180 km (118.8 miles) in 3 h 4 min 56.4 s. The Prix de la Vitesse (speed prize) was won by American Glenn H. Curtiss with an average of 75 km/h (46.6 mph) over three laps of a 10-km course on 29 August. The highest speed of the meeting was the Prix de la Tour du Piste (one-lap prize), won on 28 August by Frenchman Louis Blériot at 76.95 km/h (47.8 mph).

23 April 1910 F77.57 km/h (48.2 mph) by Hubert Latham on Antoinette monoplane at Nice.

10 July 1910 F106.5 km/h (66.18 mph) by Léon Morane on Blériot XI at Rheims.

29 October 1910 F109.73 km/h (68.18 mph) by Alfred Leblanc on Blériot.

12 April 1911 F111.79 km/h (69.46 mph) by Alfred Leblanc on Blériot.

11 May 1911 F119.74 km/h (74.40 mph) by Edouard Niéport (Nieuport) on Nieuport monoplane.

12 June 1911 F124.99 km/h (77.67 mph) by Alfred Leblanc on Blériot.

16 June 1911 F130.04 km/h (80.80 mph) by Edouard Nieuport on Nieuport.

21 June 1911 F133.11 km/h (82.71 mph) by Edouard Nieuport on Nieuport.

13 January 1912 F145.13 km/h (90.18 mph) by Jules Vedrines on Deperdussin monoplane with veneer-skinned semi-monocoque fuselage of streamline form. First of seven successive records, culminating in:

9 September 1912 F174.06 km/h (108.16 mph).

The Blériot XI, conqueror of the English Channel in July 1909, set several speed records of up to 125 km/h (almost 78 mph) in 1910–11. This is a modern replica. (James Gilbert)

This modern replica shows the streamline form of the Deperdussin monoplanes which took every world speed record in 1912. (James Gilbert)

17 June 1913 F179.79 km/h (111.72 mph) by Maurice Prévost on Deperdussin, raised on 27 September to F191.87 km/h (119.22 mph) and finally to:

29 September 1913 F203.81 km/h (126.64 mph).

October 1914 During testing by N. Spratt and Maj (later Marshal of the RAF) J.M. Salmond of the S.E.4 built at the Royal Aircraft Factory, Farnborough, level speeds routinely exceeded 217.3 km/h (135 mph). This military scout was intended to have a Celluloid cockpit cover, increasing the speed to an estimated 244.6 km/h (152 mph) but pilots refused to fly with this.

1918 In the final year of war many aircraft, including the Austin-Ball, Packard/Le Père LUSAC-11, Martinsyde F.4 Buzzard, Hanriot H.D.6 and Spad XIII, all exceeded 220 km/h (136.7 mph) in level flight. The fastest regular service types were probably the Italian Ansaldo SVA series, first flown as a prototype on 3 March 1917 and capable of 230 km/h (143 mph) in single-seat form, and the French Nieuport-Delage NiD 29 of September 1918, which reached about the same speed but was subsequently modified as a racer (see below).

7 February 1920 F275.22 km/h (171.01 mph) by Sadi Lecointe on NiD 29 racer.

28 February 1920 F283.43 km/h

(176.12 mph) by Jean Casale on Blériot-Spad XX (S.20).

9 October 1920 F292.63 km/h (181.83 mph) by Baron de Romanet on Blériot-Spad S.20*bis*.

10 October 1920 F296.94 km/h (184.50 mph) by Sadi Lecointe on NiD 29.

20 October 1920 F302.48 km/h (187.95 mph) by Sadi Lecointe on NiD 29.

3 November 1920 F309.01 km/h (192.0 mph) by Baron de Romanet on Blériot-Spad S.20*bis*.

12 December 1920 F313.00 km/h (194.49 mph) by Sadi Lecointe on NiD 29.

3 November 1921 F318.33 km/h (197.80 mph) by Curtiss test-pilot Bert Acosta on Curtiss CR-2.

20 September 1922 F330.23 km/h (205.20 mph) by Sadi Lecointe on NiD 29.

21 September 1922 F341.00 km/h (211.89 mph) by Sadi Lecointe on NiD 29.

13 October 1922 F358.77 km/h (222.93 mph) by Brig-Gen W.A. 'Billy' Mitchell, US Air Service, on Curtiss R-6.

15 February 1923 F374.95 km/h (232.98 mph) by Sadi Lecointe on NiD 29.

29 March 1923 F380.75 km/h

(236.59 mph) by Lt Russell Maughan, USAS, on Curtiss R-6.

2 November 1923 F411.04 km/h (255.41 mph) by Lt A. Brown on Curtiss R2C-1.

4 November 1923 F429.96 km/h (267.16 mph) by Lt Alford (Al) Williams, US Marine Corps, on R2C-1.

11 December 1924 F448.15 km/h (278.47 mph) by Adj-Chef A. Bonnet on SIMB (Ferbois) V-12.

4 November 1927 F479.21 km/h (297.77 mph) by Maj Mario de Bernardi on Macchi M.C.52; first of the seaplane records resulting from the series of contests for the Schneider Trophy[1] which was competed for only by water-based aircraft.

30 March 1928 F512.69 km/h (318.57 mph) by Maj Mario de Bernardi on Macchi M.C.52*bis*.

29 September 1931 F654.90 km/h (406.94 mph) by Flt Lt G.H. Stainforth RAF on Supermarine S.6B.

23 September 1932 F473.5 km/h (294.22 mph) by James H. Doolittle on Granville Gee Bee Super Sportster (landplane record).

4 September 1933 F490.08 km/h (304.52 mph) by Jimmy Wedell on Wedell-Williams 44 racer (landplane class record).

10 April 1934 F681.97 km/h (423.76 mph) by Warrant Officer Francesco Agello on Macchi M.C.72.

23 October 1934 F709.07 km/h (440.60 mph) by Lt Francesco Agello on M.C.72. Last of the Schneider seaplane records.

25 December 1934 F505.85 km/h (314.32 mph) by Raymond Delmotte on Caudron C.450 Rafale (landplane record, notable for Renault 12RoI engine of only 450 hp, compared with 3100 hp for M.C.72).

[1] There were many other Schneider Trophy speed records which were not ratified by the FAI and are not listed here.

This Curtiss R3C-2 won the 1925 Schneider Trophy race for the USA and typified racing aircraft of the early 1920s; a predecessor set speed records in 1923. (Curtiss-Wright)

Dangerously difficult to fly, the 1932 Gee Bee Super Sportster set a landplane record at a time when Schneider seaplanes were faster. As it was almost all engine it was difficult to see how aircraft could be made much faster. (Pratt & Whitney Aircraft, via James Gilbert)

13 September 1935   F567.11 km/h (352.39 mph) by Howard R. Hughes on Hughes Racer (landplane record, and the last absolute speed record gained by the self-funded efforts of a single individual).

6 June 1938   F634.73 km/h (394.4 mph) by Ernst Udet on Heinkel He 100 V2 (closed-circuit record over two laps of 50-km course, preparatory to attack on absolute speed record, never in fact made with this aircraft).

30 March 1939   F746.61 km/h (463.92 mph) by Hans Dieterle on Heinkel He 100 V8. Return of world absolute speed records to landplanes.

26 April 1939   F755.14 km/h (469.22 mph) by Fritz Wendel on Messerschmitt Me 209 V1 (described at the time for political reasons as an 'Me 109R'). Ernst Heinkel planned a further attack on the record with the He 100 V8, confident of attaining 770 km/h (478.5 mph), but was officially requested to desist as the world believed the record-holder to be a version of the Luftwaffe's standard fighter, the Bf 109. In fact the Me 209 was one of the most unpleasant and dangerous racers ever built, but its record stood officially for more than 30 years as far as piston-engined aircraft are concerned.

18 April 1941   780.5 km/h (485.0 mph) by Fritz Schäfer on Heinkel He 280 V1 twin-jet fighter; first occasion on which the official world speed record was exceeded by jet-propelled aircraft, though the event was not announced. Later the He 280 V6 (sixth prototype) reached 819 km/h (509 mph).

July 1941   Exact date not recorded, first of many powered flights by Me 163A V1 tail-less rocket aircraft reaching level speeds of 800/885 km/h (497/550 mph).

2 October 1941   1004 km/h

Professor Willy Messerschmitt congratulates Fritz Wendel on not only getting the world speed record but also managing to land the dangerous blue-painted racer in one piece. This record was to stand for over 30 years! (Messerschmitt-Bölkow-Blohm)

(623.86 mph) by Heini Dittmar on Me 163A V1; first run with rocket propellant tanks completely filled, Mach number about 0.84 at height of 4 km (13 120 ft).

6 July 1944   High-speed test of Messerschmitt Me 262 V12, specially prepared version of a twin-jet fighter/bomber then in mass production; some reports state 1005 km/h (624.5 mph) was reached, while others give best level speed as about 917 km/h (570 mph). Either way, a record for air-breathing (ie, not rocket) propulsion.

4 August 1944   816 km/h (507 mph) by Republic XP-47J Thunderbolt, believed to have been the highest (unconfirmed) level speed by any piston-engined

fighter. The next-generation Republic XP-72 was potentially faster and should have reached nearly 837 km/h (520 mph) with the fully developed R-4360 engine, but this fighter was cancelled after VJ-Day.

7 November 1945   F975.67 km/h (606.25 mph) by Gp Capt H.J. Wilson, RAF, on Gloster Meteor IV. First officially homologated record since 1939, this was also the first gained by a jet aircraft and the first by a regular production fighter (the only modification being to fair over the gun ports with smooth skin).

7 September 1946   F990.79 km/h (615.65 mph) by Gp Capt E.M. Donaldson on a different Gloster Meteor F.4 (by 1946 mark

The tube-like Douglas D-558-I Skystreak, which was painted bright red. (Douglas Aircraft)

numbers were written in Arabic numerals), with a special metal cockpit hood.

19 June 1947 F1003.58 km/h (623.61 mph) by Col Albert M. Boyd, USAF, on a Lockheed P-80R Shooting Star; standard jet fighter modified for record purposes with drag-reducing features including a cockpit canopy of greatly reduced dimensions.

20 August 1947 F1030.92 km/h (640.60 mph) by Cdr Turner F. Caldwell, USN, on a Douglas D-558-I Skystreak.

25 August 1947 F1047.30 km/h (650.78 mph) by Maj Marion E. Carl, US Marine Corps, on same D-558-I.

14 October 1947 1127.6 km/h (700.66 mph) by Capt Charles E. Yeager, USAF, on Bell XS-1 (later redesignated X-1). First supersonic flight in history; Mach number about 1.06. Air-launched, so disqualified from FAI homologation as a record.

26 March 1948 1544.65 km/h (959.8 mph), Mach 1.45, by Capt Yeager on X-1.

15 September 1948 F1079.58 km/h (670.84 mph) by Maj Richard L. Johnson, USAF, on North American F-86A Sabre; first record by swept-wing aircraft and first by absolutely unmodified squadron fighter.

Summer 1951 Progressive speed increases by US Navy Douglas D-558-II Skyrocket research aircraft (various pilots): 5 April, Mach 1.36; 18 May, Mach 1.72; 11 June, Mach 1.79; 23 June, Mach 1.85; 7 August, Mach 1.88. The last figure in speed terms is 1999.9 km/h (1242.68 mph). Air-launched, so not qualifying for FAI homologation.

19 November 1952 F1123.85 km/h (698.35 mph) by Capt J. Slade Nash, USAF, on North American F-86D Sabre (heavier radar-equipped interceptor version, with engine thrust boosted by afterburner as in all subsequent air-breathing records).

16 July 1953 F1151.62 km/h (715.60 mph) by Lt-Col William F. Barnes, USAF, on another F-86D. Part of the reason for the higher speed, compared with Capt Nash's figure, was the fact that this record was established in summer, with local air temperature 40.55°C (105°F). Until fully supersonic aircraft were created, the maximum speed was limited by air temperature. On a cold winter day the speed of sound might be 1143 km/h (710 mph), whereas on 16 July 1953 in California it was 1283 km/h (797 mph), in each case at the low altitude then mandatory for all speed-record attempts. Speed records thus involved a search for hot air.

7 September 1953 F1170.73 km/h (727.48 mph) by Sqn Ldr Neville F. Duke, RAF, on the original prototype Hawker Hunter, specially modified for high speed (as the Hunter F.3) with an afterburning engine and addi-

As a USAF captain, Charles 'Chuck' Yeager was the first human to fly faster than sound. He is pictured, as a major, with the later X-1A, first flown in February 1953 and in which he reached 2655 km/h (1650 mph) in December 1953 (far above the official world speed record at that time). (Bell Aerospace)

Takeoff of the Douglas D-558-II Skyrocket, boosted by rockets. At this time (1948) a turbojet was installed, as shown by the dark air inlet visible under the fuselage. (Douglas Aircraft)

tional smooth windshield ahead of the cockpit.

25 September 1953 F1183.70 km/h (735.54 mph) by Lt-Cdr Michael J. Lithgow, RNVR, on Supermarine Swift F.4 prototype; in hot air at El Aziziyah, near Tripoli.

3 October 1953 F1211.45 km/h (752.78 mph) by Lt-Cdr James B. Verdin, USN, on prototype Douglas F4D-1 Skyray; air was cooler than ideal, though course was laid out below sea level at Salton Sea, California.

29 October 1953 F1215.02 km/h (755.0 mph) by Lt-Col Frank K. Everest, USAF, on prototype North American YF-100A Super Sabre. This record was the first gained by a supersonic aircraft (apart from air-launched research aircraft which could not qualify for official records), but it was achieved on a cool day in low-level conditions that precluded the fighter's full performance being attained. In 1954 the FAI changed the rules for absolute speed-record attempts, permitting runs to be made at high altitude, over a course 15 or 25 km in length instead of the previous measured course of 3 km. This was possible because of the development of extremely accurate radar, cameras, theodolites, timing gear and other instrumentation which henceforth enabled speeds to be calculated with greater accuracy than before, despite the runs being made at about 11 km (36 000 ft) above the ground. As before, the speed had to be the average of two (previously four) runs made in opposite directions, with no loss in altitude between the start gate and finish gate. Setting a record thus demanded very accurate flying—in effect 'threading an invisible needle' at the start and end of each run.

20 November 1953 2137.3 km/h (1328.1 mph) by National Advisory Committee for Aeronautics test pilot Scott Crossfield on Navy Douglas D-558-II; Mach 2.01, all-rocket power, air-launched and inadmissible as record.

12 December 1953 2655.3 km/h (1650.0 mph) by Maj Charles E. Yeager on Bell X-1A; Mach 2.44, air-launched and inadmissible as record.

20 August 1955 F1322.99 km/h (822.09 mph) by Col Horace A. Haines, USAF, on North American F-100C Super Sabre. First record ratified under the new FAI rules allowing high-altitude flight, and the first at supersonic speed (Mach 1.244).

10 March 1956 F1821.39 km/h (1131.79 mph) by company test pilot L. Peter Twiss on Fairey F.D.2 research aircraft. Gained in the teeth of opposition by the UK Ministry of Supply and even the makers of the engine, this record itself set a record in beating the previous figure by almost 500 km/h! This is despite the fact that limited fuel supply forced each run to be started at well under the maximum speed. Speed rose steadily through each run, the finish gate being crossed at just over Mach 2 (2127 km/h, 1323 mph). The average Mach number was 1.73.

23 July 1956 3058.31 km/h (1900.4 mph) by Col Frank K. Everest, USAF, on Bell X-2; air-launched, not eligible for record.

27 September 1956 3370.2 km/h (2094.2 mph) by Capt Milburn G. Apt on Bell X-2; air-launched, not eligible for record, but the first-ever flight at over Mach 3 (3.196). Apt was on his first flight in the X-2 and hit precisely the correct trajectory, but lost control later in the mission and was killed.

12 December 1957 F1942.97 km/h (1207.34 mph) by Maj Adrian Drew, USAF, on McDonnell F-101A Voodoo.

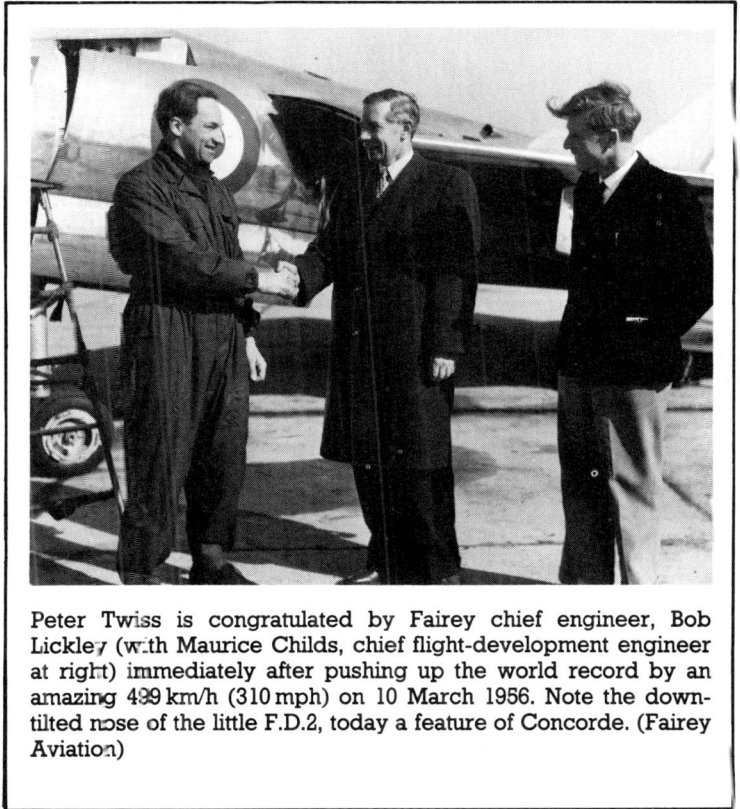

Peter Twiss is congratulated by Fairey chief engineer, Bob Lickley (with Maurice Childs, chief flight-development engineer at right) immediately after pushing up the world record by an amazing 499 km/h (310 mph) on 10 March 1956. Note the down-tilted nose of the little F.D.2, today a feature of Concorde. (Fairey Aviation)

16 May 1958 F2259.18 km/h (1403.83 mph) by Capt Walter Wayne Irwin, USAF, on Lockheed F-104A Starfighter. First FAI record at over Mach 2 (2.124).

31 October 1959 F2387.48 km/h (1483.55 mph) by Col Georgii Mosolov, Soviet VVS, on MiG Ye-66 (slightly modified MiG-21).

15 December 1959 F2455.68 km/h (1525.93 mph) by Maj J.W. Rogers, USAF, on Convair F-106A Delta Dart.

9 April 1960 F877.212 km/h (545.089 mph) by Ivan Sukhomlin and crew in Tupolev Tu-114; this record by what was then the world's largest airliner was homologated as the record speed round a 5000-km (3107-mile) closed circuit whilst carrying a payload of 25 tonnes, but it remains the highest ratified speed for any non-jet aircraft, over any distance or with any load.

12 May 1960 3397 km/h (2111 mph, Mach 3.19) by Joe A. Walker on North American X-15 hypersonic research aircraft; like subsequent X-15 flights (which explored a wholly new realm of aeroplane flight performance, winning the pilots official Astronaut wings!), it was air-launched and thus not eligible for homologation as a record.

4 August 1960 3534 km/h (2196 mph, Mach 3.31) by Joe Walker on X-15.

7 February 1961 3661 km/h (2275 mph, Mach 3.50) by Capt Robert M. White on X-15.

7 March 1961 4675 km/h (2905 mph, Mach 4.43) by Capt White on X-15.

21 April 1961 4947 km/h (3074 mph, Mach 4.62) by Maj White on X-15.

25 May 1961 5311 km/h (3300 mph, Mach 4.90) by Joe Walker on X-15.

23 June 1961 5798 km/h (3603 mph, Mach 5.27) by Maj White on X-15.

7 August 1961 F912 km/h (566.69 mph) by Nikolai Andriyevskii and crew in Beriev M-10; highest ratified speed by any

marine aircraft, in this case a large jet flying boat (see under the later subheading Seaplane).

12 September 1961 5816 km/h (3614 mph, Mach 5.25) by Joe Walker on X-15. (Note: Mach numbers on this and following flights were reduced by varying air temperature, speeds nevertheless increasing.)

28 September 1961 5826 km/h (3620 mph, Mach 5.25) by Cdr Forrest S. Petersen on X-15.

11 October 1961 5869 km/h (3647 mph, Mach 5.21) by Maj White on X-15.

17 October 1961 6276 km/h (3900 mph, Mach 5.74) by Joe Walker on X-15.

9 November 1961 6587 km/h (4093 mph, Mach 6.04) by Maj White on X-15.

22 November 1961 F2585.36 km/h (1606.51 mph) by Lt-Col Robert B. Robinson, US Marine Corps, on McDonnell F4H-1 Phantom II

1 May 1965 F3331.41 km/h (2070.1 mph) by Col Robert L. Stephens and Lt-Col Daniel Andre, USAF, in Lockheed YF-12A interceptor.

18 November 1966 6840 km/h (4250 mph, Mach 6.33) by NASA civilian pilot William J. Knight on X-15A-2.

3 October 1967 7297 km/h (4534 mph, Mach 6.72) by Knight on X-15A-2; limit of X-15 programme and unlikely to be exceeded by any other aeroplane apart from Shuttle Orbiter.

14 August 1969 F776.426 km/h (482.462 mph) by Darryl F. Greenamyer in his greatly modified Grumman F8F Bearcat World War II fighter, thus at last breaking the piston-engined record set more than 30 years previously.

28 July 1976 F3529.47 km/h (2193.17 mph, Mach 3.32) by Capt Eldon W. Joersz and Maj George T. Morgan Jr, USAF, in Lockheed SR-71A; this record by a standard reconnaissance aircraft remains the World Absolute Speed Record as this book goes to press.

14 August 1979 F803.116 km/h (499.047 mph) by Steve Hinton in the *Red Baron*, a much modified North American P-51 Mustang World War II fighter, thus setting a new piston-engined record.

Left:
The first official record at supersonic speed was gained in 1955 by a USAF F-100C identical to these. Air speed records are gained not by the aircraft but by the pilot, in this case Col H.A. Haines. (North American Aviation Inc)

Below:
No other aeroplane has ever approached the speeds and heights reached by the X-15s, though as all were air-launched they could not set an official record. This example is shown after being turned into the X-15A-2, with giant external tanks and a different cockpit windshield. (North American Aviation Inc)

second prototype, well-worn standard fighter except for water/alcohol coolant sprays in inlet ducts.

27 June 1962 6605 km/h (4104 mph, Mach 5.92) by Joe Walker on X-15.

7 July 1962 F2681.0 km/h (1665.9 mph) by Col Georgii Mosolov on MiG Ye-166 high-speed research aircraft (his second run ended at over 3000 km/h (1864 mph)).

Col Robinson, USMC, with the early prototype Phantom II which in 1961 set a record at over 2575 km/h (1600 mph), faster than practically all fighters of today. (McDonnell Aircraft)

Aircraft categories

The following are the currently accepted record figures for particular classes or categories of aircraft. In many cases some elaboration is needed on the bare figure(s).

Airliner, see Commercial transport, SST.

Autogyro
An autogyro is thrust forward by a propeller, ducted fan or other propulsive device, whilst being lifted by a free windmilling rotor. The FAI record is F179.00 km/h (111.23 mph) by the ultralight Wallis WA-116/Mc on 12 May 1969. Later Wallis autogyros, notably the WA-121/ Mc, have easily exceeded this and 240 km/h (150 mph) is being approached, but no record attempt has been made.

Biplane
It is unsatisfactory that two claimants recorded similar speeds of 520 km/h (323 mph). The two aircraft were the Canadian CCF Gregor FDB-1 of December 1938 and the Italian Fiat C.R.42DB of March 1941 (according to some reports the FDB never exceeded 420 km/h, 261 mph, but this is unreasonably low for so small, powerful and well-streamlined an aircraft). The later Nikitin-Shevchyenko prototypes in the Soviet Union could exceed 520 km/h but only after retracting their lower wing, turning themselves into monoplanes!

Bomber
One of the largest, heaviest and most powerful aircraft in history, the fastest bomber was the North American XB-70 Valkyrie, which never went into production. On 19 May 1966 the No 2 XB-70 reached Mach 3.08 (3277 km/h, 2036 mph) on its 39th flight, and cruised at over Mach 3 for 33 min whilst orbiting the Western United States. Of bombers in service, the USAF General Dynamics FB-111A can reach about Mach 2.5 (2655 km/h, 1650 mph) in the clean condition, but with bombs or missiles on its wing pylons seldom exceeds Mach 1. Thus the fastest in operational trim is the French Dassault Mirage IV-A, carrying a single nuclear bomb recessed into its belly, at about Mach 1.9 (2018 km/h, 1254 mph).

Commercial transport
It so happened that a Douglas DC-8-40, one of the first generation of jetliners, exceeded Mach 1 (about 1126 km/h, 700 mph, at the height and air temperature on that occasion) in a shallow dive; but this is immaterial. All aircraft speeds considered in this book, unless otherwise qualified, are for level flight. Thus the DC-8-40 ceases to become a contender. In its day the fastest airliner was the Convair 990 Coronado, of 1961, which reached 1001 km/h (622 mph) and could cruise at 990 km/h (615 mph). The fastest of the subsonic transports is the Boeing 727 (the best-selling jetliner, with sales of 1832) which in standard 727-200 form, at an initial weight of 83.82 tonnes (184 800 lb) has a maximum speed of 1017 km/h (632 mph) at 6585 m (21 600 ft). Like most jetliners the 727 can cruise easily at 950 km/h (590 mph), but

Above:
Official holder of the world speed record as this book went to press, the Lockheed SR-71A reconnaissance aircraft has also made many other notable flights including crossing the North Atlantic in 1 h 55 min! (Lockheed-California Co)

Right:
Fastest autogyros in the world are those produced by Wing Commander Ken Wallis. This one was fitted out for a James Bond film! (James Gilbert)

since the 1973 'fuel crisis' almost all airlines have flown for economy rather than speed.

Convertiplane

This is the name given to aircraft which can operate in an aeroplane mode in cruising flight but in a helicopter mode for VTOL (vertical take-off and landing). The official record is F356.3 km/h (221.4 mph) by the Soviet Kamov Ka-22, flown at Bykovo on 24 November 1961 by D. Yefremov and crew of two. The fastest convertiplane, however, is the Bell XV-15, with maximum speed of 615 km/h (382 mph), but this has not yet gone for a record.

Executive jet

No clear winner; plans for supersonic business jets withered with increasing price of fuel, when speed became less important than low cost of operation. The Dassault Falcon 10 can cruise at Mach 0.87 and has a published maximum cruising speed of 912 km/h (566 mph), the same as the first executive jet of all, the Lockheed JetStar. Over long distances it would be hard to beat a Gulfstream III cruising at Mach 0.85, which exceeds the maximum cruising speed of the Falcon 10 and JetStar at heights below 10.36 km (34 000 ft), rising to over 966 km/h (600 mph) at 20 000 ft.

Fighter

In clean condition, without missiles in place, the MiG-25 (so-called 'Foxbat-B') can reach Mach 3.2, equivalent to 3400 km/h (2115 mph) at high altitudes and to higher speeds lower down (though Mach number is restricted at lower levels). At this speed the MiG-25 has little power of manoeuvre. Except for the French Dassault company most fighter manufacturers regard extremely high speeds as of very limited interest. In several million hours of combat flying in Vietnam Mach 2 was never even approached, and Mach 1 rarely exceeded. In the past, however, much higher speeds were aimed at. The Republic XF-103 of the late 1950s, cancelled before first flight, was designed to reach Mach 3.7 or 3936 km/h (2446 mph) at all heights over 12 km (40 000 ft).

Fastest bomber in history, the XB-70 Valkyrie was also the most powerful aircraft of any kind ever built. For combined distance and speed nothing flying in the atmosphere can equal it, but each flight was said to cost $800 000. (North American Aviation Inc)

Though it set no speed records, other than for flights between particular cities, the de Havilland Comet 1 of 1949 effectively halved journey times wherever it flew—as Concorde did over 25 years later. (DH Aircraft)

Flying boat, see Seaplane.

Formula One racer

Formula One is an international class of small racers powered by piston engines of not more than 100 hp and with many other design restrictions. The fastest is generally believed to be the Vin-Del/Owl *Lil Quickie*, in the early 1980s often timed at speeds above 410 km/h (255 mph). But there are many other small American sporting aircraft that achieve remarkable speed on even less power. The Condor Shoestring flies at about 370 km/h (230 mph) on 85 hp; the Monnett Monex, designed for fuel economy, reaches 338 km/h (210 mph) on 80 hp; the Quickie Aircraft Corporation's Q2 can attain 290 km/h (180 mph) with an adult passenger aboard on 64 hp, while the Super Quickie Q2 manages 322 km/h (200 mph) on only 22 hp, with fuel economy of 32 km/litre (90 miles/Imp gallon); and the Rand Robinson KR-1 has an economical cruising speed at 5485 m (18 000 ft) of 402 km/h (250 mph) on a 90 hp engine.

Glider, see Sailplane.

Helicopter

The FAI official record is F368.4 km/h (228.9 mph) gained on 21 September 1978 by a Soviet Mil A-10 (Mi-24 modified) flown by Gourgen Karapetyan near Moscow. The fastest regular production helicopter today is the American Sikorsky S-76A executive transport; an unmodified example was flown round a 500 km (311 mile) closed circuit at 345.74 km/h (214.83 mph) by Thomas Doyle at West Palm Beach on 8 February 1982. In the past several faster research helicopters were built, including the Lockheed XH-51A (487 km/h, 302.6 mph, in June 1967 with a J60 booster turbojet) and the Bell 533 (509 km/h, 316 mph, in May 1969 with two J60 turbojets).

Light aircraft

Discounting the vast and relatively recent categories of hang gliders and microlights, where meaningful 'fastest' figures cannot be given, this category is intended to cover aircraft

Probably the fastest conventional helicopter is the Sikorsky S-76 Mk II, a British-registered example being pictured. The same manufacturer's XH-59A has flown at 487 km/h (303 mph), but it uses an unconventional form of rotor. (Sikorsky Aircraft)

for the private buyer. Some figures are given for types with piston engines, turboprops and turbojets, but the boundaries are blurred; one rich American bought a Lockheed F-104, capable of Mach 2, and modified it to go even faster! He appears in the turbojet section below.

Piston Among aircraft currently available, the fastest is the Colemill Panther Navajo, a conversion of the familiar six-/eight-seat Piper Navajo, which reaches 498 km/h (309 mph) and can cruise at 459 km/h (285 mph).

Turboprop The American Smith Lightning 400, a small pusher, was supposed to fly at 741 km/h (460 mph), but it was abandoned after a forced landing with a supporting research machine. The record thus goes to the beautiful Learfan 2100, whose two PT6A Canadian Pratt & Whitney engines are geared to a single propeller at the tail. The maximum speed is 684 km/h (425 mph).

Turbojet As long ago as January 1954, the small French Payen Pa 49 delta attained 500 km/h (311 mph) in level flight on a Turboméca Palas engine so small that the pilot could lift it out of the aircraft. Today the Microjet 200 flies two adults seated side-by-side at a cruising speed of 463 km/h (287 mph) on two engines smaller than a TV set and weighing 32 kg (70 lb). At the other end of the scale, the FAI-ratified absolute speed record under the old rules, for flight at very low altitude over a 3-km course, is held by Darryl F. Greenamyer (once the piston-engine record holder) in the modified *Red Baron* Lockheed F-104RB Starfighter, strictly a private

Fastest piston-engined private-owner aircraft, the Colemill Panther is seen here taking off with Surefire low-noise booster rockets, hence the white smoke. (Colemill Enterprises)

aircraft; the record was set on 24 October 1977 at F1590.45 km/h (988.26 mph).

Man-powered aircraft
No official speed records exist, and speeds vary too much through each short flight for meaningful comparisons to be made. By far the longest flight on pedal power alone was the Channel crossing by Bryan Allen in the Gossamer Albatross on 12 June 1979; his airspeed varied up to about 24 km/h (15 mph).

Microlights
The international definition of these simple aeroplanes is that their empty weight (W) must not exceed 150 kg (330.7 lb) and their wing area must not be less than 0.1W m². There are now recognised microlight speed records. Class 1A/0 records were set by Zane Eldo Myers at Momar, California, on 3 January 1982, in a Wizard with 38 hp Kawasaki engine: 89.94 km/h (55.89 mph) over the 3-km course and 83.18 km/h (51.69 mph) over the 15-/25-km course. In fact the Monnett Experimental No 1, one of a series of streamlined lightplanes (see 'Formula One' section) built by John T. Monnett's company in Wisconsin, qualifies as a Microlight but is of a different and much more powerful character, with a 70 hp Monnett Aero Vee (modified Volkswagen) engine. On 3 August 1982, at Fond du Lac, Wisconsin, Charles T. 'Chuck' Andrews set the following records round closed circuits: 100 km (62.1 miles), 297.72 km/h (185.0 mph); 500 km (311 miles), 293.5 km/h (182.3 mph).

Model aircraft
The official free-flight speed record is 343.92 km/h (213.70 mph) set by a radio-controlled speed model by V. Goukoune and V. Myakinin, both of the Soviet Union, at Klementyeva on 21 September 1971.

Piston-engined aircraft
The FAI-homologated record is F803.116 km/h (499.047 mph) set on 14 August 1979 by Steve Hinton in the *Red Baron* P-51 Mustang. In 1944 an XP-47J was allegedly measured at 816 km/h (507 mph) as listed earlier, and in the same year unmodified Spitfire IX fighters were dived by Sqn Ldr Martindale to fractionally beyond Mach 0.9, about 1030 km/h (640 mph). Speeds

just exceeding 800 km/h (497 mph) were achieved by two 1945 Soviet fighters whose piston engines were boosted by a compressor and fuel-burning jet, the fastest being the MiG Type N, or I-250, at 825 km/h (513 mph). A speed of 836 km/h (520 mph) was unofficially suggested for a modified Hawker Sea Fury raced privately in 1966.

Rocket aircraft
As listed earlier, 7297 km/h (4534 mph, Mach 6.72) by North American X-15A-2 research aircraft. The Shuttle Orbiter reaches speeds of around 28 325 km/h (17 600 mph) on each mission.

Sailplane
Fastest competition type currently available, the Akaflieg München Mü 28, in its short-span (12-m, 39 ft 4½-in) version, is cleared to be flown at 380 km/h (236 mph) in smooth air, and to 310 km/h (193 mph) in turbulent conditions.

Seaplane
The FAI-ratified figure, gained by a Soviet Beriev M-10 flying boat on 7 August 1961, is F912.0 km/h (566.69 mph). The hydroski-equipped Convair YF2Y-1 Sea Dart fighter of the US Navy exceeded Mach 1 in a shallow dive on 3 August 1954, reaching 1127 km/h (700 mph); its design speed on the level was 1328 km/h (825 mph). A much larger aircraft to exceed Mach 1 in a shallow dive was a Martin P6M-2 SeaMaster four-jet flying boat of the US Navy, in early 1959; speed exceeded 1127 km/h (700 mph) but was not published, the maximum level speed being 1040 km/h (646 mph).

Solar-powered aircraft
Though it is structurally unable to exceed 56.5 km/h (35 mph) at low altitudes, the Gossamer Solar Challenger cruises ten miles above the Earth at 113 km/h (70 mph), in perpetual sunlight (until sunset).

SST
The fastest supersonic transport was the Soviet Tupolev Tu-144—now no longer in service—with a maximum cruising speed of Mach 2.35, or 2500 km/h (1550 mph). The Concorde was designed for Mach 2.2 (2333 km/h, 1450 mph), but normally is cruised at Mach 2.05 to conserve fuel and prolong airframe life.

Trainer
The first supersonic trainer was the Northrop T-38A Talon, still the advanced pilot trainer of the USAF, which reaches Mach 1.23 (1305 km/h, 812 mph). Today this is exceeded by the Japanese Mitsubishi T-2 which has a maximum speed of Mach 1.6 (1702 km/h, 1058 mph). Of course, trainer versions of some combat aircraft are much faster, both the MiG-25U and Lockheed SR-71B being able to exceed Mach 3.

Turbojet aircraft
The FAI figure is the Lockheed SR-71A record gained on 28 July 1976 of F3529.47 km/h (2193.17 mph).

Turboprop aircraft
The FAI figure for speed in a straight line is F806.10 km/h (500.89 mph) set by Cdr D.H. Lilienthal and crew in a US Navy Lockheed P-3C Orion anti-submarine patrol aircraft on 27 July 1971. It is odd that no straight-line record was ever sought by the much faster Soviet Tu-114 series which only hold the record over a 5000-km closed circuit, with payload of 25 tonnes, as far back as 9 April 1960; as listed earlier this record stands at 877.212 km/h (545.089 mph).

V/STOL aircraft
Vertical/short take-off and landing aircraft (other than rotorcraft and convertiplanes) fall into many classes, of which the fastest are jet aeroplanes in cruising flight. The fastest in history was the Dassault Mirage III-V, a much larger aircraft than the Mirage III fighter, which on 12 September 1966 attained Mach 2.04 (2170 km/h, 1348 mph) in level flight. Today's British Aerospace Harrier reaches 1186 km/h (737 mph) at low level (subsonic, though Mach 1 can be exceeded in a dive); the Soviet Yak-36MP can exceed Mach 1 in level flight at altitude, but the speed is only 1170 km/h (720 mph).

Woman pilot
The highest speed ever achieved by a woman aircraft pilot is 2683.44 km/h (1667.42 mph) by Svetlana Savitskaya, USSR, reported on 22 June 1975. She was flying the Ye-133, a version of the MiG-21.

Circumnavigation

It is obviously not possible to list all the point-to-point air records, but the circumnavigation of the globe is exceptional. The FAI requires that such flights should take off and land at the same place and follow a route not shorter than the Tropic of Cancer, 36 787.6 km (22 858.75 miles). The fastest trip round the world was made from 16 to 18 January 1957 by three Boeing B-52B bombers of USAF Strategic Air Command, which took off from March AFB (Air Force Base), California, and flew non-stop, with four in-flight refuellings. The distance was 39 147 km (24 325 miles) and the elapsed time 45 h 19 min, an average of 845 km/h (525 mph). One tail gunner never left his post and thus circled the globe flying backwards. The best normal flight, refuelling on the ground, was set by Capt Walter H. Mullikin and his PanAm crew flying a Boeing 747SP; on 1 to 3 May 1976 they flew NY–Delhi–Tokyo–NY in 46 h 0 min 50 s to give an overall average, including stops, of 809.24 km/h (502.84 mph). The fastest trip by an ordinary fare-paying passenger is faster, because from 8 to 10 January 1980 David J. Springbett, of Taplow, England—British Salesman of the Year, 1981—used Concorde from London to Singapore. He continued via Bangkok, Manila, Tokyo, Honolulu and Los Angeles to record an elapsed time of 44 h 6 min for 37 124 km (23 068 miles).

Which is faster, the hare or the tortoise? Concorde has yet to make a flight around the world, but the ultra-long-range tortoise, the Boeing 747SP—a special version of the 'Jumbo jet'—did it in just 46 h. (Boeing)

Transatlantic flight

In recent years a novel speed challenge has been taken up by well-heeled businessmen. The idea is to reduce to a minimum the time needed to travel from London to New York and vice versa. The reigning champion is David Springbett, who made the journey from the heart of New York to Battersea Heliport, London, in 3 h 40 min 40 s on 9 Feb 1982. He took a helicopter from Wall Street to Kennedy Airport, thence by Concorde to London Heathrow, and by helicopter again to Battersea. It took him 8 min to clear Customs. His time for the outward trip was also a record for passenger flying—he did the City of London to Wall Street dash in 3 h 59 min 44 s.

This compares with the fastest of all transatlantic (North Atlantic) crossings, by USAF Majors Jim Sullivan and Noel Widdifield on 1 September 1974, whose Lockheed SR-71A took 1 h 55 min 45 s to fly from a radar-measured point opposite New York to another 'gate' 5570.8 km (3461.53 miles) away opposite London, averaging almost 2000 mph despite slowing down for refuellings. They returned on 12 September from Mildenhall to Los Angeles in 3 h 47 min, averaging 2382 km/h (1480 mph). (A greater achievement was over 24 140 km (15 000 miles) by Lt-Cols Thomas B. Estes and Dewain C. Vick in 10 h 30 min in another SR-71 in April 1971.)

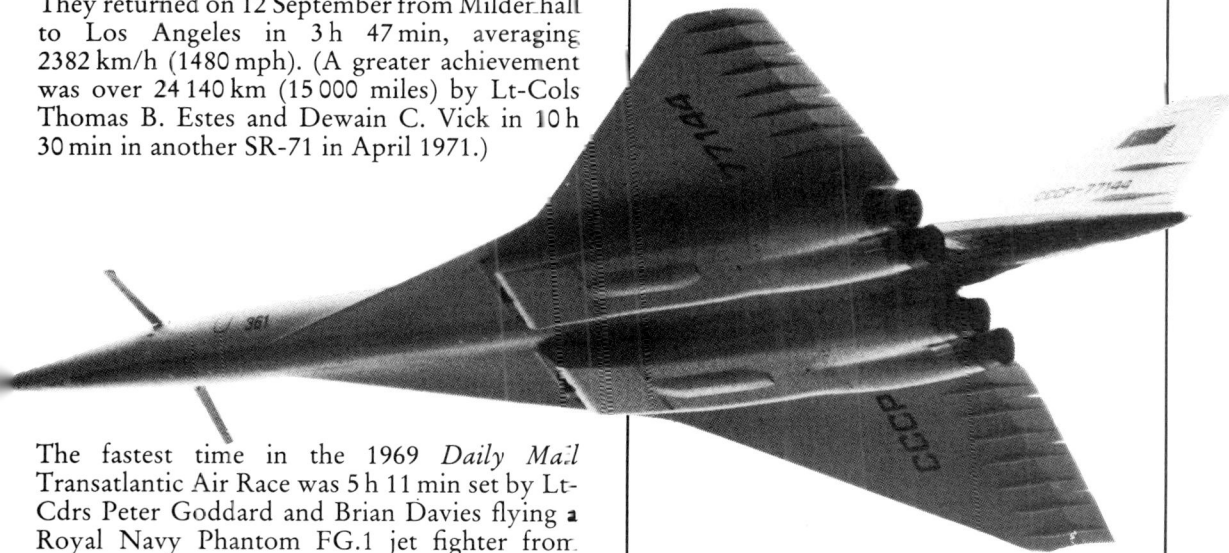

It is amazing that, though all tactical aircraft will one day have to be V/STOLs, the fastest ever built was a French type abandoned in the 1960s! The Mirage III V reached more than twice the speed of sound, but is seen here hovering. (Avions Marcel Dassault)

The fastest time in the 1969 *Daily Mail* Transatlantic Air Race was 5 h 11 min set by Lt-Cdrs Peter Goddard and Brian Davies flying a Royal Navy Phantom FG.1 jet fighter from New York to London Heathrow with air refuelling. An earlier Atlantic pilot—Charles Lindbergh—spent 33 h 29 min in the air to get from New York to Paris, from 20 to 21 May 1927. Previously, on 14 to 15 June 1919, RAF Capt John Alcock and Lt A.W. Brown had crossed from Newfoundland to Ireland in only 16 h 27 min. The 1969 race, however, was timed between the centres of the two cities.

Though it was eventually abandoned, the Soviet Tu-144 SST was the fastest transport aircraft ever built. A production example is seen here in the slow-speed regime, with elevons depressed along the wing and the canard foreplanes extended. (James Gilbert)

WEAPONS

Numerical information on early (say, pre-18th century) weapons is almost non-existent, except in the matter of effective range. One thing that appears indisputable is that velocities, like other aspects of performance, were inferior to the best values attained today. For many weapons there are two significant speed figures: maximum projectile velocity and number of shots per minute.

Hand-thrown projectiles

There is evidence that slings could increase the throwing speed of a stone from 40–60 m/s (from about 89–136 mph), though effective range is generally given as a mere 27.4 m (30 yd). This is less than the 40 m (40–50 yd) variously quoted as an effective limit for javelins and thrown spears, though velocity for the latter cannot have exceeded 28 m/s (62.7 mph).

Stored energy

Because of the superior design of modern archery equipment, and in particular the laminated construction of modern bows using glass and carbon fibre materials unavailable previously, performances with modern flight shooting surpass those of earlier bows used as weapons. Effective ranges of medieval short bows (50.3 m, 55 yd) and longbows (182.9 m,

Here seen in a fanciful representation of the Battle of Crécy in 1346, the English longbow was the dominant weapon of the medieval period. At close ranges it was possible to pierce many suits of armour. (Frassart, Mary Evans Picture Library)

200 yd) give a falsely low picture of initial arrow velocity. Most of the well-chronicled exceptional range achievements were done with large bows supported by the feet and drawn by both hands (today called a footbow). The range was in these cases achieved mainly by using a heavier arrow, and it is doubtful that release velocity was higher than normal. In recent years there has been a great upsurge of interest not only in archery in general but also in archery in antiquity. Many attempts have been made to measure performance of real or, more often, reproduction medieval bows. A typical set of results quoted by actor Robert Hardy (in his book *Longbow*) is: release velocity for a longbow of traditional form with 31.7 kg (70 lb) draw weight, 64.1 m/s (143.5 mph) with a flight arrow (for maximum range), 60.1 m/s with a target arrow, 46.5 m/s with a bodkin point and only 38.7 m/s (87 mph) for a broadhead arrow. In contrast it is common for a modern long-bow to accelerate a flight arrow to 120 m/s and the record is 152m (499ft)/s, 547.5 km/h (340.2 mph).

It is worth noting that, because the acceleration is extremely rapid, a modern flight arrow easily beats the fastest dragster over the standing quarter-mile, even though the dragster's final speed is much higher.

There are numerous forms of weapon that can loosely be called crossbows (though most have other more precise names) in which, at a penalty in reduced rate of fire, much higher draw weights are possible by using a windlass to cock the bow. In general these achieve slightly higher maximum velocities than simple bows, though usually the projectile has higher drag and shorter range. One reproduction 15th-century cross-bow with a 113 g (4 oz) quarrel was measured at 84 m/s (188 mph).

Meaningful figures for catapults, ballistae, onagers and similar large siege engines are almost non-existent. A typical figure for launch velocity is thought to be 32 m/s (72 mph), which tallies reasonably for the effective range of a trebuchet with a 45 kg (100 lb) rock hurled to 366 m (400 yd).

Guns

Early artillery achieved muzzle velocities which depended on the mass of shot, how well it fitted

A selection of medieval siege engines, all of which relied upon kinetic energy. Nos 1 and 2 are both catapults, though with very different action and projectile(s); 3 is one form of ballista, essentially a very large crossbow; 4 is a form of onager the energy source in this example being two heavy weights; 5 is a scorpion, a large crossbow with pivoted mount; 6 and 7 are battering rams, relying on large mass moved at low V (under 3 m/s, 10 ft/s). (Mary Evans Picture Library)

the bore and how much powder the gunner poured in, and on many other imponderable variables. There are abundant data on ranges achieved—a typical figure for a 14th-century bombard of 32-pounder size being 183 m (200 yd), and for 16th-century cannon maximum ranges were as much as 500 yd for a 6-pounder and 1829 m (2000 yd) for a 32-pounder. In the 19th century the development of more accurately machined bores and shot, the invention of rifling, the introduction of breech-loading (which at first led to reduced chamber pressures and thus to lower muzzle velocity) and, in 1891, the introduction of cordite and other high-power smokeless propellants, all had profound effects on gun performance.

From 1800 onwards there are a wealth of numerical data which not only show occasional very high velocities but also, as proved by recent testing, commendable accuracy. Velocity used to be measured by firing shot through rapidly spinning pairs of discs or sideways through a spinning cylinder and measuring the angular movement between the first and second holes. Today more accurate measures are obtained with radar, lidar—laser radar—and other methods involving electromagnetic waves.

Typical muzzle loaders of the first half of the 19th century achieved 366 m/s (1200 ft/s), but the spread was large. British naval muzzle loaders of 1863 were measured at 1423 ft/s for the 68-pounder but only 780 ft/s for a 200-pounder, while no breech-loader of the same year exceeded 1190 ft/s. The largest-calibre gun in history, the *Tsar Pushka* (which had a bore of 914 mm (36 in) but was more like a mortar than a cannon), did not hurl its 2400 lb stone or iron ball with greater velocity than 76.2 m/s (250 ft/s). In sharp contrast an Armstrong 6-in long-barrel rifled gun of 1885 achieved the muzzle velocity of 975 m/s (3200 ft/s), while a giant 17.72-in gun of the same era reached 1700 ft/s with a 2000 lb shell.

With cordite propellants projectile acceleration could be much greater still, coupled with new methods of fabricating the gun chamber and barrel to prevent it bursting (for example by shrinking on outer layers, and by winding on great lengths of high-tensile steel wire). In special tests the British Ordnance Committee in 1904 achieved 1219 m/s (4000 ft/s), but at the cost of unacceptable barrel wear. It was agreed in most countries that it would be better to prolong gun life by firing heavier shells at reduced muzzle velocity. Thus, while the 12-in guns of HMS *Dreadnought* (1906) had m.v. of 861 m/s (2825 ft/s), the 13.5-in main armament of the chief battleship classes of World War I did not exceed 2400 ft/s, and m.v. rose only to 2450 ft/s in the 15-in guns of the battleships and battle-cruisers of the 1918–39 period. Today naval guns are smaller but generally have m.v. in the bracket 750–1000 m/s, a typical example being current British 4.5-in guns with published m.v. of 850 m/s (2789 ft/s).

Land artillery diversified into guns, howitzers (lower m.v., lobbing shells on to the target from above) and mortars (an extreme case in which low-velocity bombs are lobbed from near-vertical tubes which can be manhandled by infantry). Field guns in both World Wars have typical m.v. in the range 535 m/s (1700–1800 ft/s), while howitzers lie in the range 183–335 m/s (600–1100 ft/s) depending on propellant charge.

It was the advent of the tank that prompted the development of guns with much higher m.v., because the armour-piercing capability of plain shot depends—among other factors—on its kinetic energy, which is proportional to the square of the projectile speed. As a very rough guide the thickness of plain steel armour that can be pierced by an AP (armour-piercing) solid shot is 1.3 times the gun calibre at 2000 ft/s, 1.8 times at 2600 ft/s and 2.8 times at 3500 ft/s.

At the start of World War II some tanks had guns of quite low m.v., the US Army M3 75-mm gun having a value of only 2030 ft/s and the 75-mm gun of the German PzKpfw IV tank having an even lower m.v. In contrast, the British 17-pounder gun attained 2950 ft/s and the outstanding German '88' (this was its calibre in mm) reaching 3340 ft/s (1018 m/s). The development of AP shot took a leap forward with APDS (armour-piercing discarding sabot) ammunition, in which the outer layers of the projectile comprise light packing pieces that fit the bore of the gun but fly off as the projectile leaves the muzzle. The extremely dense but slender core is thus accelerated to much higher velocity than can be attained by simple ammunition, one of the earliest APDS shells, fitted to Churchill tanks in 1944, reaching 3950 ft/s, just 1000 ft/s faster than the regular 17-pounder ammunition from the same gun.

Back in the 1930s Guerlich and others discovered that projectile m.v. can be increased by making the gun barrel tapered, from a large chamber to a slightly constricted muzzle; the Guerlich anti-tank gun which accompanied the Panzer armies in 1940 had a bore tapering from 28 mm to 21 mm and achieved an average m.v. of 1265 m/s (4150 ft/s), with peak values around 1506 m/s (4590 ft/s). Even the big 88-mm gun in Pak 43 form with a taper-bore reached 1217 m/s (3993 ft/s). But by the 1950s APDS ammunition and the later development of sub-calibre fin-stabilised projectiles driven by an integral piston had led to much higher m.v. still.

Today typical tank or anti-tank guns have m.v. of about 1463 m/s (4800 ft/s) with APDS ammunition and 1676 m/s (5000–5500 ft/s) with fin-stabilised projectiles. These values are well above the limit of 4500 ft/s attained by a specially constructed British gun of 1942 which had an 8-in tube fitted inside a 13.5-in former naval gun and achieved a range of 92 km (57 miles) at the cost of fierce barrel wear. In Germany, at Peenemünde, in 1943, an arrow-shell with a dart shape and four fins was fired at an estimated 1590 m/s (5200 ft/s) from a 12-cm tube in a 31-cm gun, reaching a range of 151 km (93.8 miles).

Some of the most impressive research into high-velocity guns was performed in 1955–70 at the Canadian Armament Research and Development Establishment at Valcartier, Quebec. Part of it was in connection with the use of guns for

The most famous tank of World War II was probably the German Tiger, which set a new standard in both firepower and armour. Its superb 88-mm gun, originally an anti-aircraft weapon, combined tremendous hitting power with a muzzle velocity exceeding 1 km/s. (RAC Tank Museum, Bovington)

Right:
Virtually the standard gun of American fighter aircraft since the mid-1950s, the M61A-1 Vulcan is popularly called a 'Gatling' because of its basic similarity to the 19th-century gun of that name in having many barrels. The M61 has six barrels of 20-mm calibre, and fires up to 100 shots per second with the high muzzle velocity of 1036 m/s (3400 ft/s). (General Electric)

An Israeli APFSDS penetrator shown in the hole made by a similar penetrator in hostile tank armour during Middle East warfare (the armour, of course, has been cut through in line with the hole). (Ian V. Hogg)

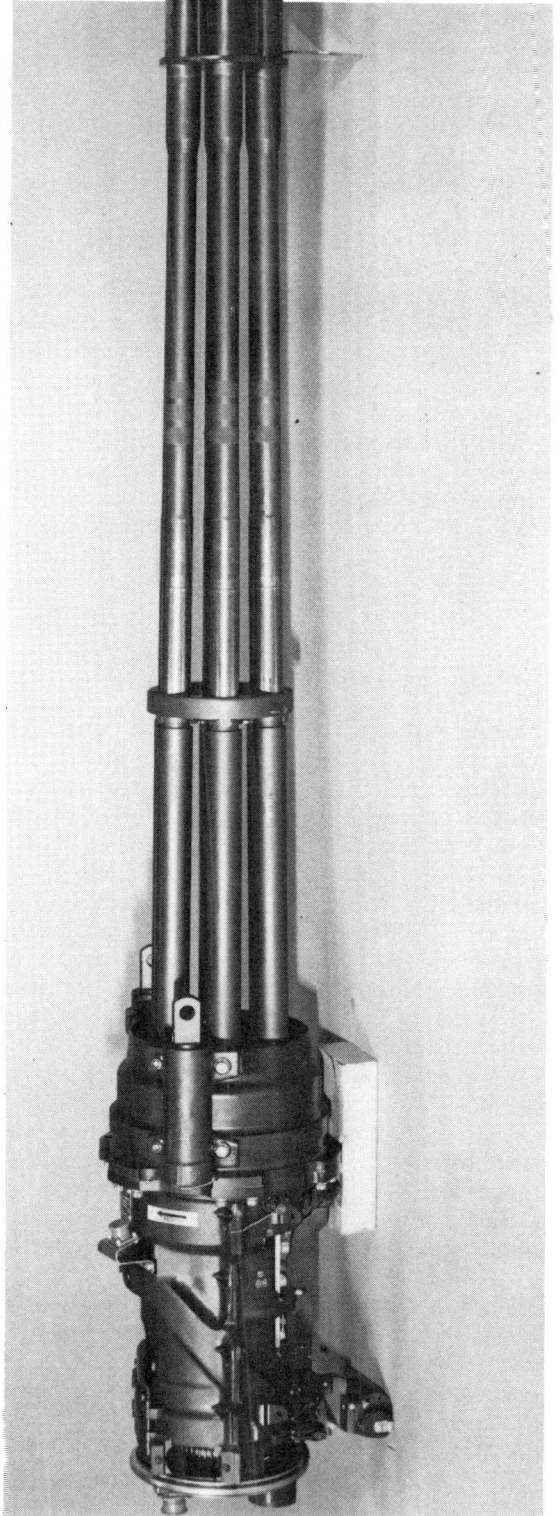

launching space probes and even artificial satellites, using a test site in Barbados. Much of the work was done with the largest available naval gun, of 406.4 mm (16 in) calibre and normally firing a 3000-lb rifled shell with m.v. of 2800 ft/s. Fitted with a new smooth-bore liner of 16.5-in calibre it fired fin-stabilised sub-calibre projectiles weighing 400 lb at an average m.v. of 1829 m/s (6000 ft/s). Further trials with a 17-pounder (as already stated, this had m.v. of 2950 ft/s with solid shot and 3950 ft/s with APDS shot) achieved m.v. just in excess of 2134 m/s (7000 ft/s) firing 1 lb fin-stabilised projectiles along an enlarged smooth bore. In further tests two barrels were placed in tandem, giving an effective length of 100 calibres; with similar 1 lb sub-calibre projectiles the m.v. then reached 2789 m/s (9150 ft/s), possibly the highest ever attained with a conventional gun.

Small arms

Throughout this century, most hand guns and infantry small arms have used either rifle ammunition or pistol ammunition. The latter, as well as rimmed-case ammunition for revolvers, fires solid jacketed bullets with m.v. of only 274–305 m/s (900–1000 ft/s). Rifle bullets, from a rifle or machine gun, had a typical m.v. of 732 m/s (2400 ft/s) in both World Wars. In the post-1945 period Britain pioneered the use of smaller calibre with higher m.v., but was thwarted by the political power of the USA. When a similar style of rifle was developed in the USA in 1955 it achieved success, entering service as the M16 Armalite, with m.v. of 991 m/s (3250 ft/s), giving it great power even at the small calibre of 5.56 mm. This m.v. is as high as that of anti-tank rifles of World War II (now an extinct species), but by no means the limit for small arms. Sporting Magnum rifles reach m.v. of 1052 m/s (up to 3200–3450 ft/s), and the highest m.v. published was reached by a special FN rifle with 7-mm barrel fitted with a sub-calibre tube of 4.5 mm, giving m.v. of 1410 m/s (4625 ft/s). Shot guns, which fire pellets, have m.v. typically at the speed of sound, about 335 m/s (1100 ft/s).

The rate at which guns can fire varies from two shots an hour, typical of medieval bombards, up to 167 shots per second. Today the limiting factors are ammunition supply and barrel life and cooling. In general, the fastest-firing guns are fitted to aircraft, where lethal damage may have to be caused in brief moments of time. The US General Electric Co pioneered the rebirth of the famed 19th-century 'Gatling' in 1952 by developing a series of aircraft guns with multiple barrels. The whole barrel section rotates, each barrel firing in turn. Almost all US fighter aircraft use the M61A-1 gun, with six barrels of 20 mm calibre, which normally fires at 6000 shots/min, or 100 shots per second. The noise is that of a continuous explosion! In a much smaller calibre, 5.56 mm, basically the same gun fires at 10 000 shots/min.

Bombs

Almost all bombs prior to 1950 fell at below the speed of sound.

Typical velocities of impact after release from 6 km (20 000 ft) were:
100 lb GP (general-purpose) US-type M30, 860 ft/s; 1000 lb GP British, 1050 ft/s; 1600 lb armour-piercing US, 1070 ft/s; 100 lb cluster fragmentation US, 650 ft/s; incendiary 4 lb British, 605 ft/s; 4000 lb light-case 'blockbuster' British, 660 ft/s; and (the supersonic exception) 22 000 lb Earthquake British, designed by Sir Barnes Wallis, about 1300 ft/s. Another exception, but not a free-fall bomb, was the so-called Disney bomb for piercing the roof of U-boat shelters. The latter were reinforced concrete 6.1 m (20 ft) thick. The Disney fell normally until it was 5000 ft above the ground, when rocket motors in the tail ignited and drove it down to hit the target at 732 m/s (2400 ft/s).

Missiles

As the earliest mass-produced self-propelled (and in recent decades guided) missiles, torpedoes soon became much faster than surface ships, and with compressed-air propulsion often ran at 45 knots (83.4 km/h, 51.8 mph). Since World War II torpedoes have been driven by various means, notably electric motor, monopropellant (fuel-burning but without air) and thermal/pneumatic (compressed air) power. Many do not exceed 25 knots, but the American Mk 48 runs at twice this speed (93 km/h, 57.8 mph). The first widely used aerial

Painted black and white to assist cameras and theodolite trackers, one of the first A 4 (V-2) rockets thunders skyward from the Peenemünde test station in 1943. (Ian V. Hogg)

bombardment missile, the so-called V-1 flying bomb of 1944 (actual designation, Fi 103), cruised at just under 644 km/h (400 mph), fast enough to make interception by fighter aircraft no easy matter.

Only a few weeks behind the V-1 followed the great ballistic rocket commonly called V-2 (actual designation A 4), which set a totally new level of missile speed with a maximum of 5800 km/h (3600 mph, or a mile a second). As the monster rocket plunged down through the atmosphere the friction heated its nose red-hot, so that despite careful glass-wool thermal insulation the Germans had to use a relatively weak explosive warhead to avoid premature detonation (which in fact did often occur).

V-2 was the first of the large wingless ballistic missiles whose speed is limited only by the allowable acceleration and the time for which their engine(s) can continue to be supplied with fuel. In the 1950s the development of missile airframes, rocket engines and guidance systems, and of re-entry vehicles able to protect the warhead from the searing white heat of even faster travel down through the atmosphere on to the target, led the way to today's terrifying population of ICBMs (intercontinental ballistic missiles). Only a step away from space launchers, the big Soviet ICBMs can accurately lob heavy payloads (which in modern weapons comprise numerous separately guided warheads, each for a different target) on to exact locations on the far side of the globe, up to 18 500 km (11 500 miles) distant. To do this their engines must accelerate them—in some designs quite gently, with motors burning for up to three minutes—to about 27 400 km/h (17 000 mph), or 26 times the speed of sound. The re-entry vehicles separate from the main propulsion stages and, after being trimmed to the exact final commanded velocity, arch up to an apogee (highest point) some 966 km (600 miles) above the Earth. They then plunge down again, in prolonged free fall, like bright meteors until they hit the target.

No missiles are known to fly faster than ICBMs, though some accelerate many times more violently and one may even reach a higher final velocity. Intercepting an ICBM warhead is complicated both by the fantastic speed

Special ultra-fast cameras were needed to record the launch of a Sprint, the last-ditch missile in the defunct American ABM (anti-ballistic missile) defence system. In just 8 s it had to rise from its deep silo, ignite its main engine and travel at least 40 km (25 miles) through dense atmosphere. The spots are fragments blown out of the silo. (R.T. Pretty)

necessary and by the fact that modern ICBMs can throw out clouds of decoys and make it difficult for the defence to decide which is/are the real warhead(s). The only certain way to tell warheads from decoys is to wait until the atmosphere has filtered out the low-density decoys—by which time the true warheads, each able to destroy a city, are about eight seconds from impact. In the US ABM (Anti-Ballistic Missile) system, a long-range missile called Spartan was partnered by a last-ditch missile called Sprint which was fired in these last eight seconds. In that time it had to rise out of a vertical silo, ignite its motors and cover a distance of not less than 40 km (25 miles). Starting from rest this called for sustained acceleration not far short of the level in a howitzer, to reach a final velocity of more than six miles a second, despite the drag of the atmosphere. This amazing task was fully met by the ABM system, which was built over a ten-year period, put into active service to defend Washington on 1 October 1975, and then deactivated by order of Congress on 2 October 1975!

A contrast in modern weapons. The American DD-963-class destroyer *Merrill* is launching a Tomahawk cruise missile. This climbs away quite slowly, and flies at only 885 km/h (550 mph), but has a devastating warhead. On deck can be seen the ship's 5-in (127 mm) Mk 45 gun, which fires up to 20 (specially reduced from 40) shots/min with m.v. of 815 m/s (2675 ft/s). (General Dynamics, Hughes Aircraft)

Explosive charges

Notwithstanding the great speeds attained with rocket propulsion, rockets operate by steady combustion, just as does the flame in a domestic gas cooker. In contrast, the combustion in an explosive is much swifter, once the explosive has been properly detonated. There are relatively slow-burning explosives, such as gunpowder and cordite, which are used as propellants to drive bullets and shells along the barrels of guns. So-called high explosives are capable of much faster decomposition, called detonation, which causes a shockwave of intense pressure and heat to spread out like a bubble from the explosion. Initially this moves at a speed of from 2–6 km/s (7200–21 600 km/h, 4475–13 420 mph). More recently it has been found that fuel/air explosives (FAE) can, weight for weight, give more powerful blast effects even though in this case the shockwave moves more slowly, typically 2.2 km/s (7920 km/h, 4920 mph).

A special kind of explosion is generated by a device called a shaped charge. If an explosive is made with a large hemispherical or conical cavity, its effect is focussed into a narrow jet (made up of hot gas plus the metal casing of the cavity) which is projected in a straight line with great speed. Tests showed that this jet could be made to travel fast enough to pierce any known armour, so today almost all anti-tank missiles have warheads with a basically conical forward-facing cavity which is detonated at the optimum distance away from the armour. Penetration does not depend on the velocity of impact of the missile, which can be quite low, and not even on the speed of the jet (though this must be at least 2438 m/s (8000 ft/s) to pierce the best steel armour) but only on the length of the jet and its density relative to that of the material of the armour. With a well designed shaped charge the jet velocity invariably exceeds 5 km/s and the highest published velocity for a shaped-charge warhead appears to be 30 570 km/h (27 970 ft/s, 19 000 mph). At such fantastic speeds the

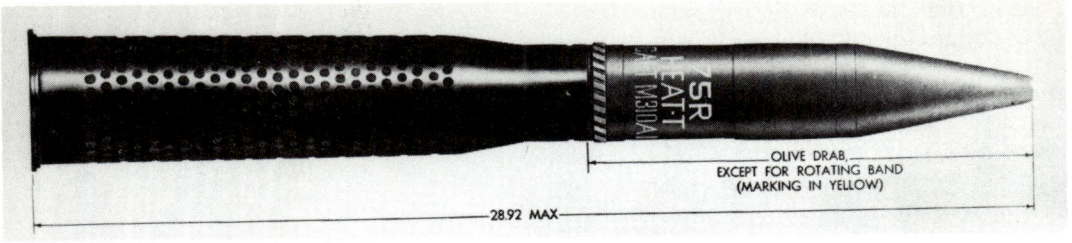

A typical round for a recoil-less anti-tank gun, the projectile of which relies not on its own speed but on the fantastic velocity of the jet projected forwards from its hollow charge. The distance from the tip of the empty ogive nose to the apex of the cone is arranged to give maximum penetration. (Ian V. Hogg)

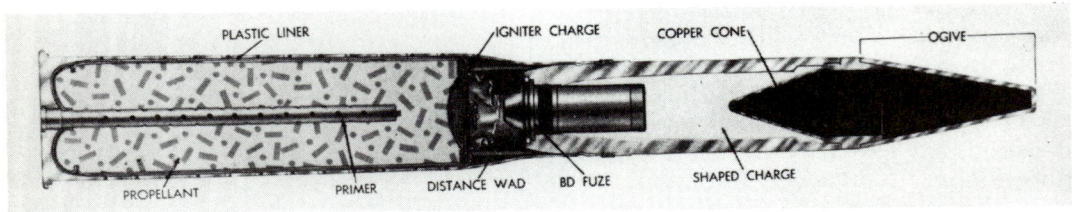

The entrance hole made in a block of tank armour 250 mm (9.84 in) thick by a hollow-charge shell similar to that illustrated on this page. To give scale, the block is 300 mm (about 12 in) wide. (Ian V. Hogg)

pressure exerted on the armour is about 2000 tons/in², far greater than the yield point (breaking stress) of the armour, which thus ceases to behave like solid metal but instead behaves as a perfect fluid to be accelerated out of the way. Modern anti-tank warheads generate jets that punch in a split second through armour four or more times as thick as the diameter of the warhead; thus, a 5-in calibre warhead can pierce 20-in armour. One of the earliest weapons to make use of a shaped charge was the US Bazooka anti-tank rocket of World War II. With an ordinary warhead it would have had little effect, because its maximum flight speed was a mere 82.3 m/s (270 ft/s, 184 mph).

COSMOLOGY & SPACE FLIGHT

Once we look beyond our immediate surroundings we realise that notions of speed are all relative. If a passenger in a car asks the driver: 'How fast are we going?' the driver expects to satisfy the questioner by giving the speed of the car. He is unlikely to take into account the speed of the road, even though the road is built on the surface of a planet that is rotating on its axis and moving bodily in an orbit around a star. In turn, though we think of most stars as being 'fixed', our Sun is itself moving through space in one of the spiral arms of our Milky Way galaxy, taking its solar system along with it. And, as the reader may have guessed, having got in the habit of thinking of speed as a relative measure, the galaxy itself is moving at high speed as part of what we believe to be an expanding universe. So the passenger in the car might be very surprised if the driver tried to give him a complete answer.

We usually credit Copernicus with realising, at great personal risk to himself, that the planets of our (or any) solar system revolve around the Sun and not the Earth. Like the Greeks, Copernicus assumed the planets moved in perfect circles, but in the early 17th century Johannes Kepler not only showed that the orbits are ellipses but

stated the rule that their speed in orbit varies inversely with distance from the Sun (one of the two foci of each orbit), such that the imaginary line joining each planet to the centre of the Sun sweeps through equal areas of space in any given period. Put another way, when planets are nearest the Sun they are moving fastest, and when they are at their furthest from the Sun they move slowest. In practice most of the orbits are almost circular, so the differences between maximum and minimum orbital speed are small; only the outermost planet, Pluto, has a highly eccentric orbit which actually takes it from time to time inside the orbit of Neptune. Of course, the innermost planets must have the greatest orbital velocity, as the following list shows:

	AVERAGE DISTANCE FROM SUN	SIDEREAL PERIOD[1]	MEAN ORBITAL VELOCITY			ROTATION PERIOD[2]	ROTATION PERIPHERAL VELOCITY AT EQUATOR		
	million km	*days*	*km/s*	*mile/s*	*mph*		*km/s*	*mile/s*	*mph*
MERCURY	58.3	87.9686	47.9	30	107 030	88 days	0.002	0.0012	4.32
VENUS	108.2	224.7	35.0	21.8	78 480	247 days	0.0018	0.0011	4
EARTH	149.6	365.26	29.8	18.5	66 600	23 h 56.07 min	0.47	0.29	1044[3]
MARS	228	687	24.1	15	54 000	24 h 37.4 min	0.26	0.16	576
THE ASTEROIDS	Between the orbits of Mars and Jupiter there are well over 35 000 bodies called asteroids, ranging in scale from specks of grit, via rocks of all sizes, up to minor planets as large as many countries on Earth. Their periods vary from about 3 to 7 years, with correspondingly variable orbital speeds. One, Hidalgo, has a very eccentric orbit reaching out as far as the orbit of Saturn; another, Icarus, has a highly eccentric inner orbit crossing that of Earth and passing very close to the Sun (closer than Mercury), where it has to travel at over 60 km/s (134 000 mph).								
	years								
JUPITER[4]	778	11.86	13.1	8.12	29 232	9 h 55 min[5]	12	7.3	26 280
SATURN	1426	29.46	9.65	6.0	21 600	10 h 30 min	9.5	5.8	20 880
URANUS	2870	84.02	6.85	4.25	15 300	10 h 50 min	3.8	2.5	9 000
NEPTUNE	4496	164.8	5.47	3.4	12 240	16 h	2.5	1.5	5 400
PLUTO[6]	5900	248.4	4.84	3.0	10 830	6.4 days	0.03	0.02	72

[1] Apparent time to make one complete orbit, which in all measures made from Earth has to be adjusted to correct for the Earth's own movement.
[2] Planetary rotation varies enormously. Mercury always presents the same face to the Sun, while Venus spins very slowly indeed in a retrograde (reverse) direction. Jupiter, in contrast, spins so rapidly that it is visibly distorted into an ellipsoidal shape; indeed different latitude layers rotate at different speeds, and the figure in the list is apparently exceeded by points at other latitudes.
[3] The point where the peripheral velocity is highest is the summit of Cayambe (5790 m, 18 996 ft) in the Andes. Kilimanjaro is higher, but further from the Equator.
[4] By far the largest planet.
[5] At Equator.
[6] Furthest of the planets, Pluto also has a much more eccentric orbit than the others and its plane of rotation is inclined at more than 17 ° compared with the other planets, which all rotate in almost exactly the same plane.

Comets are relatively short-lived bodies, moving in orbits which usually are highly eccentric. Contrary to the popular impression, their orbital velocities in the outer reaches of the solar system are low, but if they come close to the Sun they can move faster even than the inner planets, and the solar wind causes a bombardment with charged particles which blows part of the coma (a gas cloud around the comet) away from the Sun to form a bright tail. The relative sideways motion between the comet and its tail makes the latter appear curved.

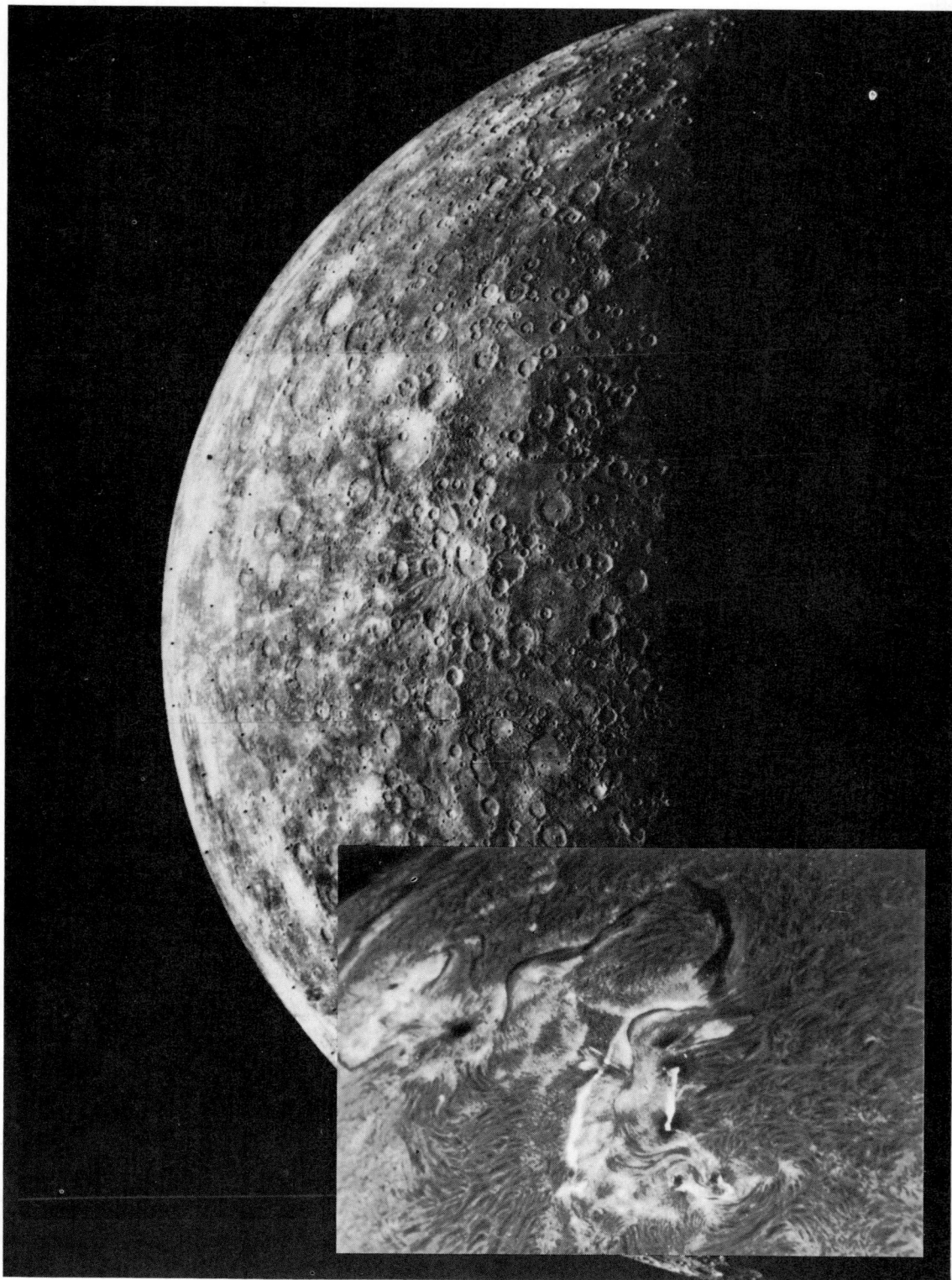

Left:
Left:
Newton completely calculated the dynamics of planets or comets moving in elliptical orbits. The closer the body is to the Sun, the faster it moves, so Mercury is the fastest of all planets of the solar system with a mean velocity of 172 000 km/h (107 000 mph). (Space Frontiers)

Inset:
A small portion of the photosphere, the visible surface of the Sun, taken on 28 April 1978, showing a major flare developing. Relative speeds between the small spicules, each 800–1600 km (500–1000 miles) across, is in the order of 1.6 km/s (1 mile/s). (Holloman AFB Solar Observatory, Space Frontiers)

The Moon, a very large satellite compared with its partner, follows a nearly circular orbit around Earth with a mean radius of 384 400 km (238 860 miles). The lunar month is about 29.53 days, but (measured relative to fixed stars) the sidereal period is 27.322 days; and the Moon's orbital velocity (relative to Earth) ranges from 0.945 km/s at apogee (furthest from Earth) to 1.11 km/s at perigee (nearest), the mean being 1.022 km/s (0.635 mile/s, 2286 mph). The Moon rotates on its axis once every 27.322 days; thus, it always presents the same face to Earth.

Meteors are bright streaks of light, also called shooting stars, caused by the incandescent heating of solid bodies in free fall from outer space through the Earth's atmosphere. The actual solid particle is called a meteoroid, and one that survives its passage through the atmosphere and strikes the Earth is called a meteorite. Vast numbers fall to the Earth, and doubtless to the other planets, every day, often in showers all coming from the same part of the sky. It is clear that at least some orbit the Sun as a cloud or even a continuous ring through which Earth passes at intervals. Others appear to come from outside the solar system, but their maximum observed velocity strongly suggests that this is not the case. As measured (by radar and other methods) from Earth, the velocities of meteoroids range from 12 to 72 km/s with more than 98 per cent in the range 16 to 50 km/s (10–31 miles/s, 36 000–111 600 mph). This range must be adjusted by the orbital velocity of Earth of about 29.8 km/s. As the fastest meteoroids are those meeting Earth head-on it follows that their actual (heliocentric) velocity must be about 20 km/s rather than 50 km/s. Thus, typical meteoroids accelerate towards planets to reach speeds up to anything between 20 and 42 km/s, the latter figure being very rare. The smallest known solid particles in space, called micrometeoroids, have similar velocities. A special class of glassy debris found on the Earth's surface, called tektites, have never been found with characteristics suggestive of an atmosphere entry speed exceeding about 11 km/s, and this is thought to indicate lunar origin.

The Sun is a fairly average star, situated in one of the spiral arms of our own galaxy which we call the Milky Way. As the galaxy itself is rotating, the Sun is rotating with it, giving a speed of some 220 km/s (135 miles/s, 486 000 mph) to the entire solar system. In fact, the billions of stars in the galaxy's spiral arms do not move together, but differ greatly in speed and direction. Each has what is called its own peculiar velocity, that of our solar system being about 20 km/s in the direction of the constellation Hercules. The Sun is also rotating on its own axis (which differs by some 7° from that of our Earth, so that sunspots appear to cross the Sun in a slightly slanting direction). As the Sun is not a solid body, no precise rotational measure applies. The rotational period varies from 25.4 Earth days at the solar equator to 33 days at 75° N or S latitude. At the solar equator the speed due to rotation alone is 1.98 km/s (1.23 miles/s, 4428 mph).

The Sun's surface is intensely active; indeed there is no 'surface' in the sense found on Earth, and the visible photosphere merges at its outer layers into the intensely hot but optically transparent chromosphere, beyond which again an irregular region called the corona extends for vast distances. Knowledge of all solar regions remains imperfect, but it is evident that, no matter what electromagnetic wavelength is chosen for observation, there are rapidly moving phenomena all over the Sun. A normal and continuous feature is the projection of about 100 000 spikes, like pointed mountains or hedgehog spines, called spicules. These rise above the general level of the chromosphere at speeds in the region of 30 km/s (18.6 miles/s, 67 000 mph) to heights of some 16 000 km (10 000 miles). Much rarer are flares, sudden bright features which project to heights of some 10 000 km (6200 miles) and emit powerful radiations of various kinds. Even larger are giant disturbances resembling flames, called prominences, which arch up from the Sun following the lines of force of the local magnetic field. They travel at speeds up to 2000 km/s (1200 miles/s, 4.32 million mph) as far as 150 000 km (90 000 miles) from the Sun.

Flares and other solar disturbances release gigantic amounts of energy in the form of electromagnetic radiation (such as heat and light), charged particles (such as solar protons) forming a plasma cloud travelling along magnetic lines of force, and other particles which with the protons form the gentle rain from space we call cosmic rays. (Not all cosmic radiation emanates from the Sun; much is of galactic origin.) Speeds of many of these particles approach that of light. While many proton clouds do not move faster than 500–800 km/s, some high-energy particles, including the nuclei of heavy elements, leave the Sun at speeds exceeding 100 000 km/s (62 000 miles/s, 223 million mph). Vast tongues of charged plasma, shot from the Sun, carry before them a hydromagnetic shock front which moves along the magnetic lines of force at a speed according to a formula derived by the Swedish astrophysicist Hannes Alfvén. Alfvén waves travel through space at speeds in the region of 280 km/s (175 miles/s, 630 000 mph) in the vicinity of Earth. Interactions between the solar emissions and the Earth's environment cause disturbances in the ionosphere (affecting radio reception), radiation in the upper atmosphere that is dangerous to human life, and also the bright aerial display called the Aurora Borealis.

Because of the constant gravitational attraction of all masses, energy must be expended in accelerating matter away from a planet's surface. Moreover, such matter will fall back again unless it is accelerated tangentially to more than a certain critical speed called the circular orbit speed. This has its maximum value at the planet's surface; as height above the surface is increased, the orbital velocity falls (the same feature is seen in the orbital velocities of the planets round the Sun). At the same time, bodies on the surface of a planet must be accelerated, not to a lower speed to reach a high orbit but to a higher one, in order to overcome the parent body's gravitational pull. The limiting case is the speed needed to reach an infinitely high orbit,

which allows the body to escape from the planet's gravitational field entirely. This is called the escape velocity.

The following are the escape velocities for the Sun and its planets:

BODY	km/s	miles/s	mph
Sun	617.5	383.7	1 381 320
Mercury	4.2	2.5	9 000
Venus	10.0	6.2	22 320
Earth	11.2	6.95	25 020
Moon	2.4	1.49	5 370
Mars	5.0	3.1	11 160
Jupiter	61	38	136 800
Saturn	37	23	82 800
Uranus	22	13.7	49 320
Neptune	25	15.5	55 800
Pluto	not precisely known		

The escape velocity for Earth is the limiting value of the characteristic velocity, the measure of the kinetic energy that must be imparted to a body if it is to reach a particular orbital height (*not* the actual satellite speed relative to Earth). The following are the characteristic velocities required for satellites in circular orbits at various selected heights above the Earth's surface:

HEIGHT ABOVE SURFACE

km	miles	km/s	miles/s	mph
0	0	7.91	4.92	17 712
161	100	8.00	4.97	17 892
322	200	8.10	5.03	18 108
644	400	8.26	5.13	18 468
1 609	1 000	8.66	5.38	19 368
8 045	5 000	9.85	6.13	22 068
35 880	22 295	10.8	6.68	24 048
infinite		11.2	6.95	25 020

The peculiar property of the 35 880-km (22 295-mile) orbit is that it has a period of precisely 24 h, and thus an artificial Earth satellite launched in an easterly direction into a circular orbit at this height will co-rotate with the Earth. Another adjective for such an orbit is synchronous. Synchronous satellites remain always over the same spot (in practice they usually describe very small figure-8 patterns over one spot) and so can relay TV, radio and telephone communications day and night all year round.

Earlier it was pointed out that the actual speed of a satellite varies inversely with its distance from the primary body, being fastest just above the parent body's surface. In the case of Earth it is impossible to have a satellite just above the surface, not only because of mountains but also because it would burn up due to atmospheric friction. Even at a height of 100 miles (the nominal low Earth orbit, below which no satellite is practicable) the small drag of the upper atmosphere causes the orbital speed to fall off quite rapidly, so that the satellite soon spirals back to Earth (it is said to have rapid decay, or a short lifetime). Satellites in high orbit may last for thousands of years, though their on-board systems may soon cease to function.

The following are the speeds at which artificial satellites move in perfectly circular orbits round the Earth:

HEIGHT ABOVE SURFACE

km	miles	km/s	miles/s	mph
0	0	7.91	4.92	17 712
161	100	7.80	4.85	17 460
322	200	7.70	4.79	17 244
644	400	7.53	4.68	16 848
1 609	1 000	7.06	4.39	15 804
8 045	5 000	5.26	3.27	11 772
35 880	22 300	3.07	1.91	6 876

It is possible to put artificial satellites in Earth orbit at much greater distances than 35 880 km, further even than the Moon. The limit is approximately 1.5 million km (930 000 miles), the corresponding speed being only 1070 km/h (665 mph). Any satellite trying to orbit at a greater distance would be captured by the Sun.

An artist's impression of one of the 12 Intelsat V communications satellites, each over 15 m (50 ft) long, in synchronous orbit at a height of 35 880 km (22 295 miles). At this great height a satellite orbits exactly in phase with the rotation of Earth. (Ford Aerospace & Communications)

On the largest cosmological scale, Man's very limited knowledge taints numerical data with the suspicion of being mere speculation. Einstein showed the apparent impossibility of anything moving with a velocity (relative to whatever fixed frame might be chosen) greater than that of light. This velocity, symbol c, is discussed in the Technology section under Light.

When in the present century astronomers began to use frequencies other than visible light with which to study the Universe, new knowledge came like an avalanche. In the more distant reaches of the Universe objects were discovered which at optical wavelengths could not be seen at all. Some were detected from their X-ray emission, some from radio emissions, and today other tools (such as gamma radiation and even the elusive particles called neutrinos) fill in fresh detail every hour. Many of the so-called radio galaxies comprise an (often faint) optical object with a powerful radio source on each side of it, typically at a distance of about 100 kpc (a kiloparsec is 3.09×10^{21} cm, or the distance light travels in some 3300 years). Thus, these objects are somewhat larger than our own galaxy. As well as pumping out various kinds of radio energy with intensities that our mind cannot comprehend, many appear to be emitting visible jets of gas or other nebulous material.

These jets appear to be moving away from the central sources at speeds ranging from a few hundred to a few thousand kilometres per second, in other words at velocities that are small fractions of c. Since 1975, however, some of these jets have shown measured velocities which approximate to that of light; and by 1978 certain radio galaxies, as well as some of the much smaller and even more intense quasars (from 'quasi-stellar objects'), which appear to be amongst the most distant objects known, were causing deep concern to cosmologists in apparently sending out jets moving much faster than light. One source, the distant Seyfert-type radio galaxy 3C-120 (No 120 in the third Cambridge catalogue), is ejecting one object measured at 5c and a second travelling away at 8c. Eight times the speed of light is 8 634 000 000 km/h (5 365 000 000 mph). Apart from being unquestionably the highest speed in this book, it is something for which the world scientific community was wholly unprepared.

An explanation is still a matter of opinion and argument. So, too, is the most fundamental series of questions men can ask? How big is the Universe? Where did it begin, and when?

Our chief key to the answers may lie in a 1912 discovery by V.M. Slipher in the United States. He found that the characteristic line spectra of such elements as ionised calcium in the light from distant galaxies are all shifted slightly towards longer wavelengths than in the spectra of sunlight and light from other local stars. This displacement towards the red (long-wave) end of the visible spectrum was found not only to be present in the light from every remote object but to vary with the object's distance. The Red Shift was immediately interpreted as an indication that the object is moving away from us, in the same way that the pitch of a sound (such as a train whistle or car hooter) is high as it comes towards us and falls as it is receding (this is called the Doppler effect). The speeds associated with the Red Shift are very large, and in all cases are a significant fraction of c.

By the 1950s measured Red Shifts giving an object recession-speed of over 0.1c had been published, and most (but not all) workers in this field had rather helplessly, for want of a better answer, come to believe in the concept of the Expanding Universe, in which—one imagines, viewed from any point in it, not just from our own galaxy—the apparent velocity of expansion increases with distance from the observer, equally in all directions. In 1929 E.P. Hubble drew attention to this, and published the Hubble Constant, numerically equal to the velocity of recession of the distant source divided by its distance. No exact value exists, measures varying in the range 50–150 km/s per Mpc distance (a megaparsec is 3.09×10^{24} cm, the distance light travels in about 3.3 million years).

After prolonged study no worker can say with assurance that the Red Shift is exactly to be equated with a velocity of recession, so the Hubble Constant may be an unreliable parameter. If it does exist, and stays constant throughout the Universe, then the speed of recession becomes theoretically equal to c at a distance of about 3000 Mpc. In practice, actual observed spectra indicate a speed of recession of only 0.916 c at the apparent distance of 11 470 m light-years (quasar Pks 2000–330, the remotest object known). This suggests a limit to the observable universe of roughly 4400 Mpc, or 14 500 million light-years or 13 700 000 000 000 000 000 000 km (8 500 000 000 000 000 000 000 miles). This therefore becomes the distance to the edge of the observable Universe, beyond which nothing can be seen, because everything is moving away too fast for light from it to reach us.

Another plausible conclusion is to assume that the Universe started as a Big Bang at one place and time. This time is the reciprocal of the Hubble Constant, if the concept is valid. Hundreds of measured values give a value for this reciprocal as in the order of 3×10^{17} s or about 10 000 million (10 billion) years. The shortest and longest times derived by this method range between 7 and 20 billion years, and in fact several quite independent calculations suggest an age for our own galaxy, and thus by inference, the Universe, of about 10 billion years.

The entire Universe appears to emit a background radiation equivalent to 3° absolute temperature (minus 270°C, minus 454°F), and this appears to be receding at 0.999998 c. It is loosely interpreted as the sound of the Big Bang after 10 billion years.

Of course, other models of the Universe contrast strongly with the notion of a single Big Bang. One of the simpler difficulties of the Big

Bang idea is that, as the light from the most distant objects we can see must have left those objects several thousand million years ago, then several thousand million years ago they were in the places where they now appear to be, and not near some central Big Bang. Another plausible model is a pulsating universe, in which Big Bangs alternate with periods of maximum size followed by inward collapse, the frequency of oscillation being about once every 8×10^{10} years. Another is the steady-state universe in which the continuous creation of matter, which builds into galaxies and the other parts of the Universe, just balances the conversion of matter into energy.

If the steady-state theory is correct the Universe could be infinite in extent. Almost all of it would be beyond our range of vision, where the speed of recession becomes, relative to ourselves, infinite.

This is only the upper part of the thrust chamber of the Rocketdyne F-1 rocket engine, five of which firing together provided 3 451 896 kg (7 610 000 lb) of thrust to launch the Apollo lunar vehicles in 1969. The two turbopumps at the top pumped under high pressure one ton of RP-1 kerosene and two tons of liquid oxygen every second. (North American Aviation)

Space flight

In space no propulsion system is possible other than the rocket. Rockets accelerate to the rear a high-velocity jet composed of material which is entirely carried on board, unlike air-breathing jet engines whose fuel is combined with oxygen from the atmosphere. The performance of the rocket naturally depends on the speed to which the material of the jet is accelerated. This in turn depends on the temperature reached and on the molecular weight of the gases in the jet: for the highest performance one needs the lowest possible jet density but the highest possible temperature. On the other hand, low density means low thrust, because the mass flow rate of propellants will be small.

The following table indicates the maximum jet velocity attainable at sea level with common chemical rocket systems, assuming a well-designed engine and nozzle:

PROPELLANTS	km/s	mph	ft/s
gunpowder	1.74	3 876	5 700
advanced solid fillings	2.44	5 440	8 000
oxygen/RP-1 kerosine	2.95	6 570	9 660
oxygen/alcohol	2.75	6 140	9 016
nitric acid/hydrazine	2.65	5 910	8 695
nitrogen tetroxide/ hydrazine	2.84	6 345	9 330
fluorine/hydrogen	4.02	8 980	13 200

The following are some of the possible space propulsion systems now being studied:

SCHEME	km/s	mph	ft/s
limit for chemical rocket	4.12	9 195	13 500
hydrogen/radioactive heat	5.89	13 160	19 320
hydrogen/nuclear heating	8.99	20 100	29 500
hydrogen/electric grid	9.76	22 165	32 000
hydrogen/arc jet	19.82	44 330	65 000
hydrogen/cavity reactor	34.0	76 390	112 000
fission-bomb pulses	21.5	48 100	70 500
electrostatic colloid	18.66	41 740	61 200
cesium-ion/electrostatic	58.5	131 000	192 000
magnetohydrodynamic plasma	244	545 600	800 000
photon (theoretical value)	speed of light		

By making a spacecraft launch vehicle with

Liftoff of an Apollo spacecraft, *en route* for the Moon. Thrusting upward are the 1st-stage engines burning liquid oxygen and RP-1 (jet velocity 10 573 km/h, 6570 mph); later the 2nd- and 3rd-stage engines burned liquid oxygen and liquid hydrogen (13 744 km/h, 8540 mph), and on return to Earth the Service Module (large dark drum) was stabilised by the small projecting groups of attitude control motors burning hydrazine and nitrogen tetroxide (10 211 km/h, 6345 mph). Highest speed reached by a manned craft is 39 897 km/h (24 791 mph) reached by the Apollo 10 Command Module (large white cone riding on the Service Module) on its entry to Earth's atmosphere. (NASA)

several stages, each with its own propulsion system and jettisoned after use, it is possible to accelerate a payload to velocities much higher than the jet velocity of each individual rocket motor. Moreover, there are today various advanced forms of rocket which can produce jet velocities much higher than the limit for chemical (ordinary combustion) type rockets. (See table on p. 153.)

The speeds achieved by early Earth satellites were in the region of 27 360 km/h (17 000 mph). Flight to the Moon demanded much higher velocity, more than 99 per cent as high as the Earth escape velocity. The speed reached at final motor burnout or cutoff on departure from Earth is similar to the peak speed reached on return to Earth after a long free fall. The highest speed reached on any manned spaceflight was at the start of re-entry to the Earth's atmosphere at the conclusion of the US *Apollo 10* mission as noted below. The greatest velocity so far reached by an unmanned space probe was at the final stage cutoff of propulsion of the *Helios 2 (Helios B)*, developed mainly by West German companies, which left Earth on 15 January 1976 for close orbit of the Sun (where it is hot enough to melt lead). The American Titan-Centaur booster accelerated the 4.2 m (13 ft 8 in) spacecraft to 240 000 km/h (149 129 mph).

The fastest speed at which human beings have travelled is 39 897 km/h (24 791 mph) when the Command Module of *Apollo 10*, carrying Col (now Brig-Gen) Tom Stafford, USAF, Cdr (now Capt) John Young, USN, and Cdr Gene Cernan, USN, passed 121 920 m (400 000 ft) altitude on its trans-Earth return on 26 May 1969.

The highest speed ever attained by a woman is 28 115 km/h (17 470 mph) by Jr Lt (now Lt-Col) Valentina Tereshkova-Nikolayev of the USSR, in *Vostok 6* on 16 June 1963.

The Earth

Various data for the Earth's motion as a planet appear in the preceding section on Cosmology and Space flight. The following are measures related to the Earth itself, ignoring the planet's own motion.

Avalanche

The mechanics of avalanches are complex, and at high speeds the aerodynamics become very important. The first time a high speed was recorded, using accurate measuring equipment, was on 6 March 1898. The speed was 349 km/h (217 mph), and, as this was the average speed over a distance, the peak velocity must have been appreciably higher. The location was near Glärnisch, Switzerland. The avalanche descended a 44° slope, crossed a valley about 1.6 km (1 mile) wide and then ran far up the hillside opposite. The front of the avalanche was timed

Earth, photographed from above the eastern Caribbean. Average velocity of the atmosphere (not just at sea level) is roughly 15 m/s; average velocity of the oceans is believed to be about 2.2 m/s; average velocity of the land is unknown, and though very small, is not zero. (NASA)

The white river of death that killed over 3500 humans, and a far greater number of domestic animals, on 10 January 1962: the avalanche of ice, rock and mud below Nevado de Huascaran, Peru. (Servicio Aero-fotografico Nacional, Lima, Peru, Frank Lane)

to cover 6.9 km (4.3 miles) in 72 s. The avalanche triggered on 18 May 1979 by the eruption of Mt St Helens, Washington State, USA, was measured at roughly 400 km/h (250 mph), the volume involved being estimated at $2.8 \times 10^9 \, m^3$ (96 000 000 000 ft³). A slower, but even larger and more damaging, avalanche occurred on 10 January 1962 when an estimated 4 million tonnes of ice fell from near the peak of Nevado de Huascaran (6768 m, 22 205 ft) in Peru. It plunged along a valley, ricocheting from side to side, maintaining about 98 km/h (61 mph) for 10 min and coming to rest 18 km (11 miles) from the start after 15 min. Over 3500 people, and a much larger number of domestic animals, were killed.

Continental drift

Though several geologists hold contrary views, it is generally accepted that the Earth's crust is made up of enormous plates which essentially float on the magma below. Most evidence suggests that the land above sea level was originally a single super-continent, Pangea, which about 180 million years ago began to break apart. Since then, portions of the land have travelled thousands of kilometres. One section which travelled inwards rather than away from the main mass is India, whose late and relatively fast voyage from the south crumpled the land on which it impacted to form the Himalayas. A typical speed for continental drift today is up to 10 cm (4 in) per year, measured between distant coasts. Accurate position measures taken over many years at astronomical observatories show definite movement; for example, Heidelberg has moved 12 cm (4.72 in) almost due south since 1900, quite a slow speed. Extremely accurate surveys by satellite are continually being made to increase accuracy of ICBMs (intercontinental ballistic missiles), and all show that the continental masses continue to move relative to each other. At the plate edges rock has to move up or down, and vertical speeds are high in some places. The best-known recent upthrust was the appearance in 1963 of a new island, Surtsey, south of Iceland; vertical speeds there reached 30 cm (1 ft)/h.

Crustal heave
Not all vertical movement in the land is due to continental drift. At the local level, mining can cause sudden subsidence, and many buildings—notably the famed tower at Pisa, Italy—have sunk or tilted because of imperfect foundations. On a much larger scale most land masses are slowly rising, falling or tilting. Western Europe as a whole is sinking at the rate of 2.5 mm (0.1 in) a year; thus, it has been pointed out, in the year AD 120 062 the tip of the Eiffel Tower may be expected at last to vanish beneath the waves. Britain has an added tilt: the island is slowly rotating about an axis running roughly from the Severn estuary to The Wash, the north rising and the south falling at a rate of some 30 mm (1.2 in) per year. Thus in 800 years the coasts have gone up or down some 25 m (82 ft), so that the sea gateway of Harlech Castle (for example) is now far above the sea as well as being well inland.

Currents, see Oceans, Rivers.

Erosion
The wind (often laced with abrasive grit and sand), the rain (freezing in winter) and many other influences combine to break up the surface of the land and transport it away, mostly into the oceans. Over all the exposed land surface an approximate average rate of erosion is 1 m every 22 000 years (0.045 mm, about two thousandths of an inch, per year). Thus, if this process continues without change, after 10 to 20 million years all the land will have disappeared and the last land-dwellers will have to become good swimmers! This is despite the fact that, on an average day, the Earth receives around 15 000 tonnes of solid matter, from dust to large meteorites, from space. The equivalent of several freight-train loads every day, this would by now have deposited a layer 20 m (66 ft) deep over the land, had it not been continually eroded into the oceans.

Glaciers
These rivers of ice flow slowly in the same way that a river flows. Some have speeds of no more than 20 m (65 ft 7 in) a year, but 1 km a year is not uncommon. In volume terms the greatest flow is that of the Jakobshavn in Greenland, which at 3.36 km a year deposits 14 km^3 of ice into the ocean at Disko Bay. The fastest sustained speed is the 7.1 km a year (minimum) of another Greenland glacier, Great Quarajaq. But Iceland's Bruarjökull has been known to surge ahead at a remarkable 120 m a day, 43.8 km (27.2 miles) a year.

Oceans
About 71 per cent of our planet is covered by the oceans; the Pacific alone is bigger than all the land surfaces combined. Most ocean water moves very slowly, but there are gigantic permanent surface currents. The most famous of the latter is the Gulf Stream, which runs northeast from the Gulf of Mexico to north of Scotland at up to 5 knots (9.27 km/h, 5.76 mph). But the West Wind Drift, which encircles the globe just north of the Antarctic, is so much larger in cross-section that it moves about 270 million m^3/s (9 500 000 000 ft^3/s), almost three times the volume flow of the Gulf Stream even though its speed is a mere 0.4 knots (0.74 km/h, 0.46 mph). Local currents are much faster than those in the open ocean; the highest measured speeds have been just north of Vancouver Island, British Columbia, a figure of 16 knots (29.65 km/h, 18.42 mph) being recorded in Slingsby Channel. Vertical movement due to tides can reach 2.7 m (9 ft) per hour in narrowing coastal bays and estuaries. Waves are surface movements superimposed on the classically perfect long waves called swell, which originate under wave action far from land and travel vast distances at a speed of about 57 km/h (35.5 mph) in the Pacific and 54 km/h (33.5 mph) in the Atlantic. As waves approach a beach or coast they are radically altered in character once the water depth becomes less than half the wavelength, and in extreme cases the crest can break with a horizontal velocity of 80 km/h (50 mph). Local velocities caused by the water spreading sideways and vertically in confined spaces can reach over 150 km/h (93 mph), causing rapid erosion. The beacon on the lighthouse at Tillamook Rock, Oregon, has to

be protected by heavy steel gratings against flying rocks, even though it is 42.4 m (139 ft) above the waves! But even these speeds are insignificant compared with the terrifying and wildly destructive waves called tsunamis which result from submarine subsidence (undersea earthquakes). At first these waves can scarcely be detected, but they race across the ocean at speeds between 725 and 821 km/h (450–510 mph). As they cross the rising shelf and approach land, the energy is concentrated into progressively less and less water. When they reach the shore they can attain heights of up to 40 m (130 ft), still moving at over 480 km/h (300 mph).

Precipitation

The atmosphere holds some 13 000 000 tonnes of water, in the forms of vapour, liquid and solid (ice crystals). If it all fell suddenly to Earth it would add a 25 mm (1 in) layer over the planet. This is, in fact, about the amount that falls every eleven days, but its distribution is most uneven. Some places never see a trace of precipitation, but Mt War-'ale-'ale, Hawaiian Islands, is rained upon roughly 350 days per year, receiving an average annual rainfall of 11 455 mm (451 in). The rainfall record for 15 days or over is held by Cherrapunji, Meghalaya, India, with an incredible 22 454 mm (884 in, 73 ft 8 in) in the 31 days of July 1861. For periods from 9 h to 8 days the record is held by Réunion Island, east of Malagasy in the Indian Ocean; during four days in March 1952 a total rainfall of 4140 mm (163 in) was measured at one station, while another recording station nearby logged 1092 mm (43 in) in 9 h on 28 February 1964. For still shorter periods records become unreliable, but a definite reading was taken on Guadeloupe Island, West Indies, on 26 November 1970 when 38 mm (1.5 in) fell in one minute. Raindrops seldom exceed 2.54 mm (0.1 in) diameter for more than a few seconds before breaking up; terminal velocity, usually reached far above the Earth, is rarely as high as 9 m/s (30 ft/s) and usually much less. Drizzle (diameter 0.05–0.5 mm, 0.002–0.02 in) falls at 0.7–2 m/s (2.3–6.6 ft/s). Hail, on the other hand, can reach velocities exceeding 25 m/s (82 ft/s, almost 60 mph), though accurate measures have not been taken on the destructive hailstones, reportedly of grapefruit size, which can build up after repeated up/down passage

within cumulo-nimbus and related clouds with swift upcurrents.[1] Snowflakes have been found up to 40 mm (1.6 in) diameter, but they still fall at only 1–1.7 m/s (3–5 ft/s). The record snowfall for a 5-day period is 4455 mm (175.4 in, 14 ft 7.4 in) at Thomson Pass, Alaska, on 26–31 December 1955. The 1–day record is 1870 mm (74 in) at Silver Lake, Colorado, on the night of 14–15 April 1921. In January/February 1978 large areas of New York and other US eastern states had drifts of over 9 m (30 ft).

Vertical air currents over Britain seldom reach speeds great enough for hailstones to get as big as this 127-mm (5-in) specimen, which would have struck the ground at well over 100 km/h (62 mph). (E. Webster)

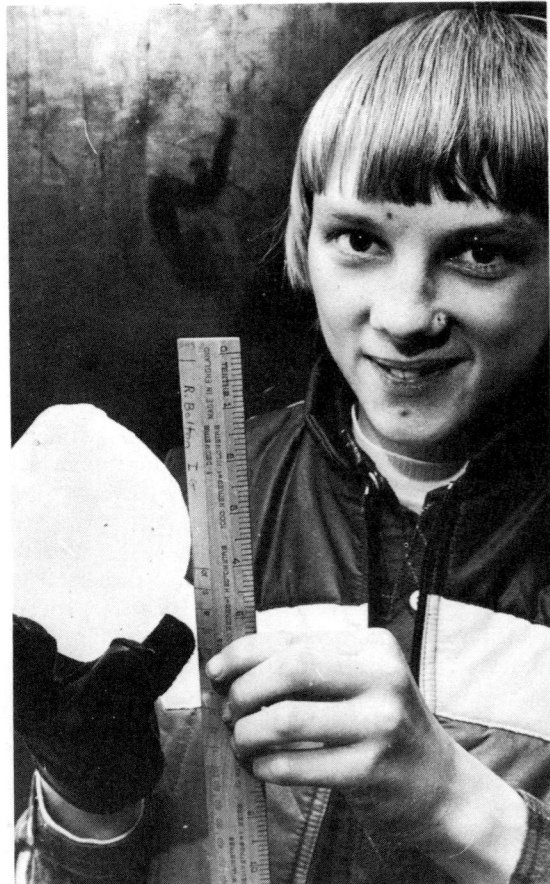

[1] Much information on hail sizes will be found in *The Guinness Book of Weather Facts and Feats* by Ingrid Holford.

Rivers

Velocities of flow vary so widely that no 'fastest river' data can be meaningful. Obviously, the highest speeds are attained near the base of waterfalls! Many young streams in mountainous areas fall steeply (about 1 in 3, a 33 per cent grade, is typical) at average speeds exceeding 50 km/h (31 mph), but their volume flow (rate of delivery of water) is very small. In terms of volume flow the Amazon far exceeds all other rivers; its mean flow of 180 000 m³/s (6.3 million cusecs) is ten times that of the Mississippi and almost 60 times that of the Nile. Waterfalls approximate to the formula $V = \sqrt{2gh}$ where V is velocity, g is the acceleration due to gravity and h the height of the fall. On this basis the speed near the foot of the longest single fall (807 m, 2648 ft on the Angel Falls in Venezuela) is about 126 m/s (413 ft/s, 280 mph). Bores, which are transient (usually annual) floodwaves on certain rivers, travel at speeds of up to about 29 km/h (18 mph), as is the case on the Hugli (Ganges delta), in India.

Seismic waves

Strong shockwaves caused by surface faults (earthquakes) or man-made explosions travel through the crust in two forms, P waves (compression) and S waves (transverse). Their speed varies with depth beneath the surface; it also varies with the stress in the rock. Geophysicists hope to perfect a method of earthquake prediction by measuring the changing velocity as the crustal rock stresses build up at the sites of future epicentres. P waves travel at about 7.6 km/s (17 000 mph) near the surface, rising to 8.05 km/s at 40 km depth; the speed then falls to 7.8 km/s at 80 km and thereafter progressively rises to far beyond the sea-level value in the very hot, dense deep rock of the mantle. S waves travel at about 4.3 km/s (9620 mph) near the surface, rising to 4.6 km/s at 49–55 km depth; then the speed falls to 4.4 km/s at around 100 km, thereafter rising at below 200 km to far above the sea-level value.

Still waters may run deep, but the slow-looking Amazon (here seen at Belem) shifts water faster than the next 36 greatest rivers combined! Indeed the world's longest river, the Nile, has a volume flow only one-sixtieth as large. (Picturepoint)

A lightning strike on the east tower of New York's George Washington bridge, a favourite target, on 10 November 1955. (General Electric Frank Lane)

Subterranean pressures are sometimes greater than the most intense pressures ever devised by man's experiments. Here a relatively modest escape at the newly formed island of Surtsey has all the characteristics of a violent explosion. Maximum velocity might have been 300 m/s (1000 ft/s). (Sigurgeir Jonasson, Frank Lane)

Thunderstorms

Lightning is an electrical discharge between points in the sky and on the Earth at very different potentials, in the range of many millions of volts. The typical 'flash' is in fact a complex series of strokes, beginning with a downward stroke called the leader which at much less than the velocity of light finds its way downwards from an aerial source (usually in cloud) along an ionised path to the ground. Its velocity varies from 150 to 1600 km/s (93–1000 miles/s, 335 000–3.6 million mph). It is almost instantaneously followed by the first return stroke, upwards along almost the same path and carrying a much greater current (and hence far brighter), at around 140 000 km/s (87 000 miles/s), about 47 per cent of the speed of light. Two to five two-way strokes generally follow, the whole sequence appearing as a single flash.

Volcanoes

Volcanic phenomena embrace every kind of velocity from barely moving flows of hot lava to the most cataclysmic explosive eruptions. In the classic Vesuvian form of eruption the quasi-vertical jet of hot gas, pumice, molten lava and other matter typically issues at a speed of some 200 m (650 ft)/s, but in the most violent Krakatoan form velocities certainly can momentarily reach ten times this value. In the Santorini eruption of 1470 BC, which left as a remnant the Greek island of Thira, it is estimated that 62.5 km^3 (15 miles^3) of rock were blown apart at an initial speed higher than a rifle bullet. In the recent (1883) Krakatoa explosion in the Sunda Strait, today in Indonesia, rocks were thrown 55 km (34 miles) into the sky, indicating a peak velocity of some 2 km/s. The pressures necessary to cause such violent eruptions are in the order of 300 GPa (gigapascals) or 20 600 tons/in^2, just double the greatest pressure ever sustained in a laboratory, and exerted over far greater areas.

Waterfalls, see Rivers.

Winds

The fastest winds on Earth are found in the jet streams in the upper atmosphere. They are commonest near the tropopause, the boundary between the troposphere in which temperature falls with height and the stratosphere where temperature is sensibly constant, typically at a height of 11 km (36 000 ft). Each jet stream follows a clearly defined route, usually in mid-latitudes and predominantly in a westerly direction. All exceed 150 km/h (93 mph), and the highest velocity in a jet-stream core so far measured is 560 km/h (350 mph). On the surface, wind speeds are much lower, though on certain exposed peaks the speed has repeatedly exceeded 250 km/h (155 mph). The highest known accurately measured speed is 371 km/h (230.5 mph) at the observation station on Mt Washington, New Hampshire, USA, on 12 April 1934. The highest recorded gust in the UK, measured on standard instruments, was 232 km/h (144 mph) at Coire Cas ski lift, Cairngorms, on 6 March 1967. Giant tropical

revolving storms, variously called hurricanes, typhoons and cyclones, can generate gusts of up to 360 km/h (224 mph) near the calm central eye. The localised spiralling tornadoes leave a much narrower trail of damage but are even more intense; peak measured speed is 450 km/h (280 mph) at Wichita Falls, Texas, on 2 April 1958. Vertical speeds in the atmosphere are usually much lower but, when a giant cumulus or cumulo-nimbus cloud is in the process of building, the vertical updraught in the centre of the cell can typically have a speed of 20 m/s (45 mph), enough to cause injury to any passengers not strapped into their seats in a jet misguided enough to enter the core. The highest recorded updraught velocity is 43 m/s (96 mph); if blundered into by a jet airliner it would almost certainly emerge minus its wings.

The US Government maintains a weather station on top of Mt Washington, New Hampshire, which suffers unusually severe weather. The highest wind speed ever recorded was measured here in April 1934.

FREQUENCIES & RATES

Grouped here are speeds of repetitive or oscillating devices. Some measures, including those for rotating masses normally given in rpm (revolutions per minute), are for uniformity expressed in Hz (Hertz, cycles per second), or in the multiples megahertz (MHz), gigahertz (GHz) or terahertz (THz), which are respectively $\times$ 10^6, 10^9 and 10^{12}.

Atomic resonance

Today the invariant natural resonant frequencies of molecules or atoms are the ultimate standards with which we measure time. The first atomic frequency standard was that of the ammonia molecule (NH_3) containing a nitrogen atom with a periodic oscillation at 23 870 MHz, or 23 870 000 000 Hz. Next came the cesium clock, whose standard was the transition in the precession axis of the outer electron in the cesium atom, at a fixed rate of 9 192 631 770 Hz (about 9.19 GHz). Today's most precise standard is the similar transition frequency of the hydrogen atom, at 1 420 450 751 694 Hz (about 1.42 THz). Accuracy is one part in 2 235 330 000 000, or one second in 1.7 million years.

Communications

Items sent through the post are still the commonest world-wide form of human communication over a distance. The current rate is about 245 billion a year or 8000 per second (8 kHz); of this total the USA accounts for 110 billion (including 76 billion letters) and the UK for 10.3 billion. The Morse buzzer, survivor of the oldest form of telecommunications, operates over a frequency range of 0–100 Hz. The Soviet Union, with a deliberate near-absence of private telephones, leads the world in telegraph services with 500 million messages per year (15.8 Hz), roughly one-thousandth the rate at which messages pass in the USA. The telephone operates over a frequency band of 300–3000 Hz, and in all non-Communist countries is by far the most widely used form of telecommunications.

Though the various changes in form of the telephone are obvious, more significant is the way its numbers have grown. Today the world frequency of telephone calls averages about 17.5 kHz, or 17 500 per second. (British Telecom)

The world total of telephone handsets rose from 20 in 1878 to 120 000 in 1900, 25 million in 1920, 45 million in 1940, 131 million in 1960 and 470 million today. These were used to make 100 billion personal calls in 1958, 250 billion in 1965 and an estimated 555 billion in 1983, of which half were in the USA, a global rate of 1519 million calls per day (17.5 kHz). Radio broadcasting uses a frequency band of 50–15 000 Hz for speech and rather more for music; the number of domestic receivers exceeds 2 billion (half the world population) and about half this number are in daily use. TV requires a transmission bandwidth of 0–5 MHz; each line in the standard 625–line (25–kHz interlaced) system has a transmission time of 64 microseconds, only part of it carrying information for the picture, and the line frequency is 15 625 Hz. The number of domestic receivers is about 404 million—almost as many as the number of telephones—the proportion of colour receivers having grown meteorically from near-zero in 1960 to 75 per cent or more in all advanced countries by 1983. Increasingly, TV signals will be among those sent by fibre-optics and other main transmission links in place of today's broadcasting, microwave links and wires. Today a main transmission link can carry about 4 Gb/s (4000 million 'bits' of information per second). By 1990 this may have to be doubled, but the

Engineers at BAC (now British Aerospace), Bristol, checking the alignment of the horn and dish aerials (antennae) of an Intelsat 4 communications satellite. Such satellites can handle more than 20 000 simultaneous telephone conversations, whilst moving round the Earth at 11 066 km/h (6876 mph), exactly keeping pace with the rotation of the planet. (BAC)

expected boom in viewphones (pioneered by Bell Telephone's Picturephone) has not so far occurred and the growth-rate may be below prediction. A very small proportion of today's traffic is between some 120 000 Telex terminals which use existing transmission lines but give a hard-copy printout on paper. Despite this, electronic communications are still a small part of the whole. In the United States, business communications account for some 70 billion pages a year (a rate of 2.2 kHz). Of this massive total, 69 billion are pages sent through the mail and only 1 billion are electronic pages sent by facsimile, between word processors or on computer networks. But the picture is changing. The fantastic growth of inter-computer traffic is such that by 1990 they will transmit the equivalent of 1050 billion pages of close type per year (33 kHz)—a pile of paper as high as Mt Everest every half-hour! It has been estimated that by 2017 there will be more computer terminals than telephones, a matter of 3.4 billion of each, with the computer terminals growing much faster than telephones. The combined total of 6.8 billion terminals will far exceed today's human population.

Computers

All electronic computers are governed to a fundamental clock rate which determines the speed of the arithmetic processor(s) and memory input/output. Like most things to do with the electronic industry, the speed has risen by orders of magnitude, from a basic 10^{-2} s in 1952 to 10^{-5} s in 1962, 10^{-7} s in 1972 and 10^{-10} s in 1982. In 1983 NASA, the US National Aeronautics and Space Administration, was planning a fantastically fast machine for aerodynamic calculation; it will perform 12 800 million complex calculations per second, a clock speed inside the computer faster than 10^{-11} s. In 1980 a book claimed that the fastest computer was '100 000 times faster than the human brain', but this is already out of date; the brain, though it packs far more cells and quickly available information into a given space than any man-made memory so far, cannot access a single item faster than 80 or 90 bits per second, which is in the order of ten million times slower than the highest computer arithmetic speed. It is hard to grasp what a rate of 10^{10}/s actually means. Most of us could perform basic arithmetic functions—

A Hughes Aircraft engineer fitting standard modules into one of the 12 plates forming the enormously fast and powerful computer used in US Navy Trident-firing submarines. Modern computers are seldom as large as this, but their numbers will probably overtake the total human population in the next century. (Hughes Aircraft Co.)

in the computer they are addition and subtraction of binary digits, but simple sums in the decimal system will do just as well—at the rate of one every 10 s. If we had the dedication and staying power to maintain this speed without a moment's rest during a 12-h day, seven days a week, and kept it up for 6000 years, at the end of that time we would have completed as many operations as the computer performs in one second! Thus, modern computers open up a whole new realm of calculating possibilities. Future machines with novel kinds of memory and perhaps using Josephson junctions in the arithmetic processor, will be much faster; but we must take care not to let them do too many print-outs on paper or they will denude the Earth of its forests. Even on present predictions by 1990 the daily global data traffic will amount to some 2.8 billion pages of printout, which (if actually committed to paper and stacked in a tight pile) would rise higher than an average-size house in 2 s. Fortunately, most of it will never need to be printed. In the 'Communications' section (above) the point is made that by 2017 we expect the number of computer terminals to overtake the number of telephones. By that time the number of bits per second in the computer networks will be so large that we do not have room on this page for all the noughts on the numbers.

Economy

On a gross global scale the world's economy is held to experience boom/slump cycles—known as Kondratyev long waves—with a 50-year period, corresponding to major innovations in economy and resulting growth industry. The last slump bottomed out in 1975 (we all hope), and may now be on the mend; a peak is due in 2000.

Electromagnetic spectrum

EM radiation comprises a succession of perfect sinusoidal electric waves combined with a matching set of magnetic waves oscillating in a plane at 90° to the first. They are able to travel through a vacuum at the speed of light (visible light is one small part of the total EM spectrum) and particular wavelengths can travel through various solids and liquids which may be opaque to other wavelengths. The shortest wavelengths are those of some cosmic rays, at less than 10^{-14} m (about the diameter of an electron); the corresponding frequency is 10^{11} THz or 10^{14} GHz or 10 000 000 000 000 000 000 Hz, so in one second this radiation oscillates through as many complete waves as the wings of the fastest-flapping humming bird perform in about $3\frac{1}{2}$ million years. Moving up to the 10^{-11} m area (still smaller than any atom) we find the gamma rays, which have a frequency of about 10^{11} GHz and will prove dangerous to humans who do not have the benefit of a shield of 2.5 m (8 ft) of special concrete. In the 10^{-9} to 10^{-10} m region, with frequency near 10^9 GHz come the X-rays, stopped by a thin sheet of lead. At around 10^{-7} m is the big UV (ultraviolet) region, with frequency near 10^7 GHz, which in excess is dangerous to humans; fortunately most is filtered out by the atmosphere. In the narrow band from 3.8×10^{-7} to 7.5×10^{-7} m there is

the small part of the EM spectrum which humans can see; the shortest visible wavelength is violet (3.8×10^{-7}), and light progresses through blue (4.5 to 5.0×10^{-7}) and green to yellow (5.7 to 5.9×10^{-7}) and orange and thence to red, (7.0 to 7.5×10^{-7}). Corresponding frequencies range from about 8×10^5 GHz (violet) to 4×10^5 GHz (red). Infra-red, better known as heat, occupies a broad band from the red end of the visible spectrum down to about 5×10^{-3} m, or 5 mm; corresponding frequencies are 10^5–100 GHz, which is becoming manageable. Radars work from the millimetric region along to a few in the region of tens of metres, and here can also be found the ether cluttered with TV and radio, at frequencies in the neighbourhood of 1 GHz (uhf and TV) down to 1 MHz (AM radio). Today special vlf (very low frequency) radios, such as are used for communicating with submerged submarines, operate over wavelengths of tens of kilometres, with frequency of 3–30 kHz.

Energy

Some idea of the penalty of using fossil fuel, which is irreplaceable, instead of nuclear power is given by the fact that an efficient modern 2000-MW (two million kilowatts) power station would run on 10 kg (a bucketful) of fuel for $8\frac{1}{2}$ years if we could convert all the matter in this fuel into energy. Using hydrogen in a fusion reactor it would run on 10 kg for just over two weeks; using a fast reactor it would run for a week, and at the same time make more than 1 kg of fresh fuel; on a traditional natural uranium cycle it would run for about 3 days; but burning oil or coal it would need fresh bucketfuls every one-eighteenth of a second. The Earth's total known reserves of fossil fuel (coal, oil and gas) are roughly equivalent to two weeks' supply of sunshine falling on the Earth, but we use only a tiny fraction of this great flow of energy usefully. Each hour the Sun emits about 3.5×10^{26} kcal (kilogramme-calories) of energy, of which the Earth receives about 1.7×10^{17} kcal. If we could waste only 98 per cent of this influx instead of 99 per cent, our standard of living would be transformed; each member of the human race could consume energy—as food, electric power or whatever we wished—at the rate of 20 of today's Americans, 100 West Europeans or 5000 citizens of Rwanda.

Earth receives solar energy at such a rate that every two weeks we get the equivalent of all the coal, oil and gas left in our planet, but we waste nearly all of it: Solar One, now operating in the Mojave desert, California, focusses sunlight by mirrors to generate 10 MW (ten million watts) of electricity. (McDonnell Douglas)

Flash

The briefest light sources are specially switched lasers, with opaque cells in the output which can be triggered almost instantaneously. Through the 1970s the shortest known pulse length was 0.06 mm (0.0023 in) formed by cutting off a piece of laser beam with a time duration of 0.2 ps (1 picosecond is 10^{-12} s). In April 1982 Charles V. Shank at Bell Telephone Laboratories at Holmdel, NJ, USA, produced a pulse only 30 fs (3×10^{-14} s) long, containing just 14 light waves. The fastest-firing stroboscope, giving a continuous succession of flashes, has a rate of 28 000/s (28 kHz).

Fluidics

The technology of fluids (usually air or other gases, but occasionally liquids) passed through small conducting channels and control devices such as diodes, gates and bistable flip-flops, gives us a useful alternative to electronics in many control functions, with no moving parts and in some cases able to work when almost white-hot. Some pure digital devices, notably of the wall-attachment type, can operate at frequencies of about 2 kHz, and individual gates can switch in a time of 1 ms (0.001 s).

Frequency

The highest frequency generated as an ultrasonic 'note' is 60 GHz, emitted by a sapphire crystal in the beam of a laser at MIT (Massachusetts Institute of Technology) in 1964. The highest measured frequency of any kind is EM radiation at about 520 THz (520 206.528 GHz); as noted earlier, cosmic radiations are known to exist with even higher frequency, but we cannot yet generate them.

Induction heating

This method of heating metals, if necessary to melting point, is done at frequencies ranging

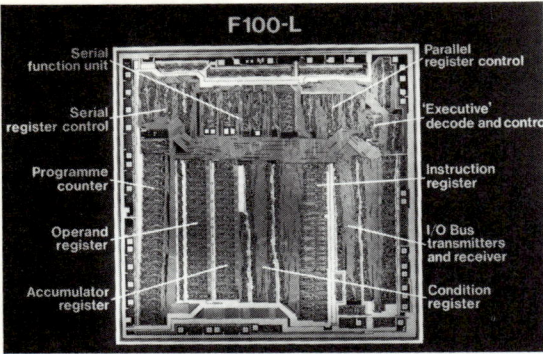

F100-L

Serial function unit
Serial register control
Programme counter
Operand register
Accumulator register

Parallel register control
'Executive' decode and control
Instruction register
I/O Bus transmitters and receiver
Condition register

Above and below:
It needs two photographs to give any idea of what a modern 'silicon chip' is like. This is the Ferranti F100-L, a complete single-chip microprocessor. Not only are such devices fantastically fast, because their dimensions are microscopic, but their growth in sheer numbers is explosive. By the year 2001 there will be about one microprocessor, rather like this, for every two humans. (Ferranti)

from the mains supply (60 Hz in the American-influenced countries and 50 Hz in Britain and many others) up to a maximum of about 5 MHz.

Microelectronics

The speed of small electronic devices such as simple gates and counters is limited by their physical dimensions, which in turn determine how long (at a speed approximating to that of light) the signal takes to travel through the operative subcircuit. Today, operating speeds commonly beat 1 ns (1 nanosecond is 10^{-9} s) to give possible frequencies in the 1 GHz region.

Microwave heating

Microwaves, short radar or telecommunications waves in the EM spectrum, are typically selected at about 10–80 MHz for industrial and domestic applications such as ovens.

Photography

The fastest cameras need special film and for research purposes film is available 3 b times faster than mass-produced colour films; thus a

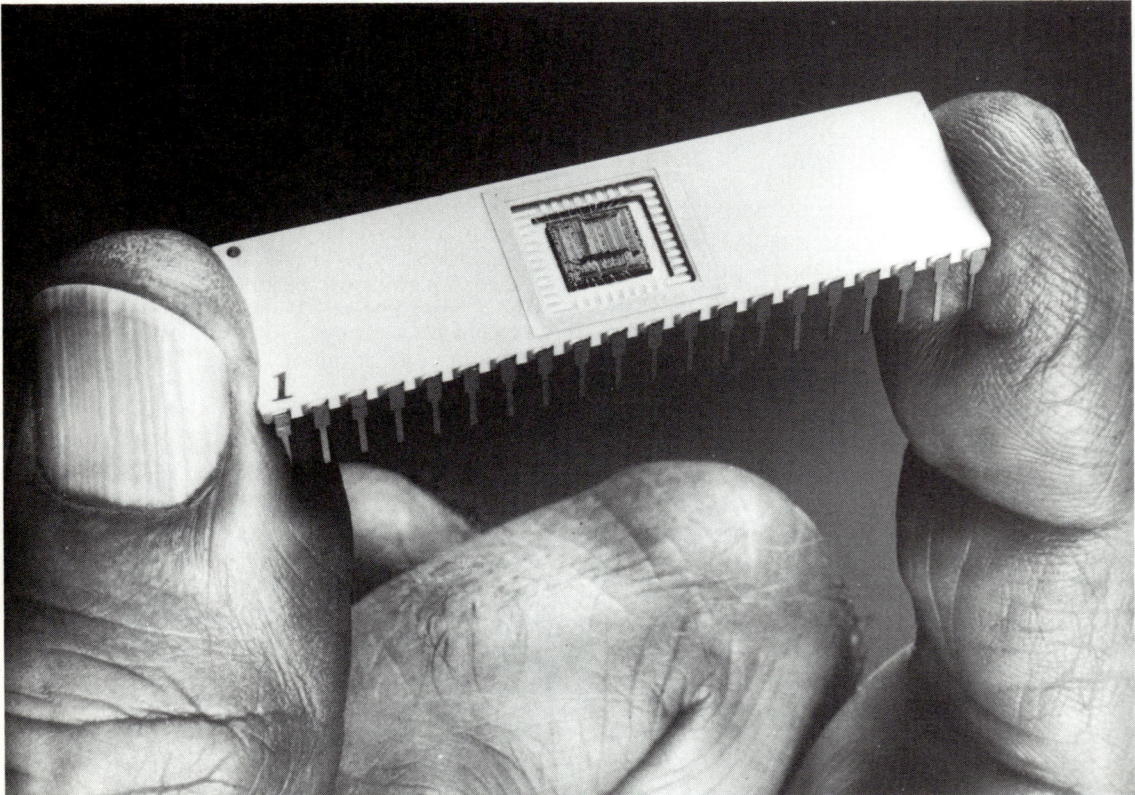

A Pratt & Whitney JT9D turbofan, the engine of many 747 Jumbo Jets and Airbuses, showing its giant fan which rotates at the front. It turns at only 3530 rpm, which is slow for a gas turbine engine, but every second it swallows 769 kg (1695 lb) of air, enough to fill a large theatre. (United Technologies Pratt and Whitney)

0.1-s exposure on this film would give the same effect as a one-year exposure with regular film. Pulsed lasers have enabled successive photographs to be taken precisely 0.06 microsecond apart. Since 1970 Prof Basov in the Soviet Union has taken pictures with a 'shutter speed' of 5×10^{-13} s, and the fastest ciné camera for recording rapid brief events is the Imacon 675 with a rate of 600 million per second (600 MHz). Normal ciné cameras take 30 frames/s, or 20 million times slower.

Printer

The fastest electronic (computer) printout is a machine at Lawrence Radiation Laboratory, of the University of California, with a rate of 30 000 lines/min, each comprising 120 characters (more than double the length of the lines in this book); it could thus print the Bible (773 692 words) in 65 s. Traditional printing of an already established format can be much faster; the largest newspaper presses fed by four or more webs (continuous rolls of newsprint) can deliver 120 000 folded copies of a 32-page newspaper per hour, including four-colour sections if necessary, or 100 copies every 3 s.

Rotating shafts

In medieval times the largest waterwheels often turned under load at a mere 0.0166 Hz (1 rpm), while windmills seldom ran faster than a sail-shaft speed of 0.25 Hz (15 rpm). The earliest steam engines were no faster, until Watt did his condensing outside the cylinder and achieved speeds of up to 0.666 Hz (40 rpm). Internal combustion engines brought a rapid advance in speed. Lenoir's 1852 gas engines could exceed 1 Hz (60 rpm). The engine of the 1885 Benz three-wheel car ran at 3.33 Hz (200 rpm) and the first production motorcycle of 1894 reached 240. Quality cars of 1914 had large engines running at about 12.5 Hz (750 rpm), while subsequent typical maxima for a family car have been 3000 rpm in 1930, 4000 in 1950 and 108 Hz (6500 rpm) today. Racing (Grand Prix) engines reached 7500 rpm in the late 1930s and are not greatly in excess of that value today. Modern road-cruising motorbikes seldom go much above 8500 rpm, but a 50–cc racer can double this (283 Hz, 17 000 rpm). The fastest large steam reciprocating engines were express locomotives at around 500 rpm. Hydraulic motors can run at up to 4000 rpm, though conversely very large and powerful examples can be precisely controlled at 0.000166 Hz (0.01 rpm), which means they would not complete one revolution in 90 min. Gas turbines rotate at speeds determined by the type of compressor (centrifugals and other radial-flow types run faster than axials) and the mean diameter of the blades in the gas path. The largest turbofans in jetliners run quite slowly; at take-off, the giant fans pulling a 747 Jumbo Jet are probably spinning at 3530 rpm. In contrast many small turbojets, turboprops and turboshaft engines run at about 45 000 rpm, and a few very small examples exceed 100 000 rpm. Centrifuges range from monster installations for testing subjects (including humans) under sustained acceleration forces, where rpm is less impressive than the peripheral speed and g, to large ultra-centrifuges in the laboratory, running at 1083 Hz (65 000 rpm). Mechanically

driven dentist's drills turn at some 30 000 rpm, but in advanced countries these have been almost completely supplanted by air-driven turbodrills, spinning at an impressive 8.3 kHz (500 000 rpm) which cut faster and with less heat and discomfort. Among the freest-running spinning objects is a 13.6 kg (30 lb) rotor spun in a vacuum at the University of Virginia at 1 kHz (60 000 rpm); without any input power it would take about three years to slow down and stop. Expansion turbines in helium refrigeration circuits, supported in hydrostatic bearings which remove mechanical friction but do not remove the drag of the gas viscosity, can run at a sustained 12 kHz (720 000 rpm). But experimenters who set out to construct the record-speed rotating object can do much better than this; a team at the University of Birmingham drove a 152 mm (6 in) carbon-fibre rod projecting radially from a hub supported in a vacuum at a rotary speed of 4.2 kHz (252 229 rpm), which, though slower than many smaller objects, achieved the record sustained peripheral speed of 7250 km/h (4500 mph), the highest for any continuously rotating Earth-bound object. The highest rotational speed

The tips of this carbon-fibre rotor travelled faster than any other man-made device on Earth (apart from short-time projectiles). Lifted and centred by the field of an electromagnet, so that it touched no other solid object, the rotor was spun by eddy-current action in a vacuum until the tips were moving at a steady 2.2 km/s (1.37 miles/s). The workers were Prof Philip Moon and research assistant Michael Ralls at the University of Birmingham, England, on 24 January 1975. (University of Birmingham)

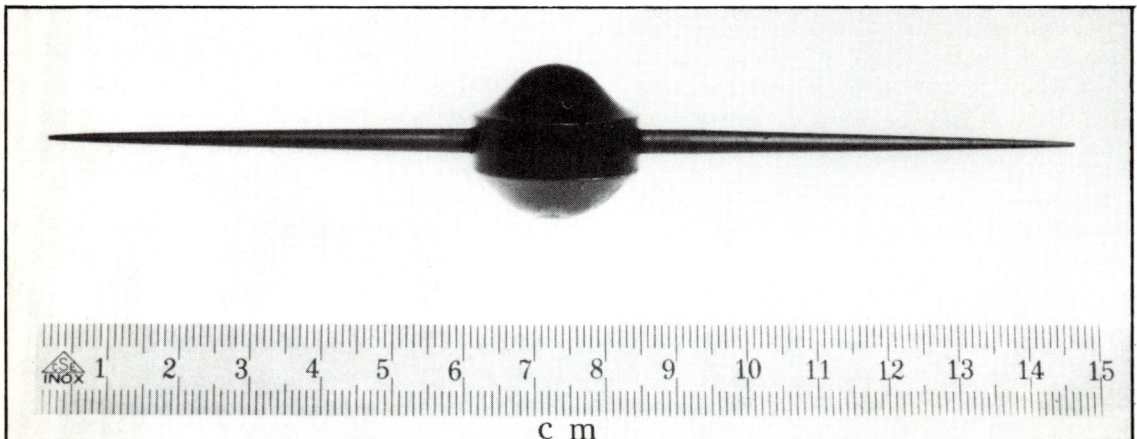

(angular velocity) known for a man-made object is approximately 1.5 MHz (90 million rpm) for a 0.254 mm (0.01 in) diameter steel rotor, resembling a straight fragment of fine wire suspended in a vacuum at the University of Virginia in March 1961. Its peripheral speed was 402 km/h (250 mph).

Sound

The human ear's response to sound varies with age, from limits of about 20 Hz to 20 kHz in youth to perhaps 20 Hz to 5 kHz in the elderly. The range of a concert grand piano is approximately 32 Hz to 4 kHz. Above the threshold of hearing is the ultrasonic region, now very important in undersea warfare (typically around 30 kHz), short-range communications between divers (8–11 kHz), and industrial mixing, cleaning and welding. At the opposite extreme is infrasound, giant low notes often too low for the human ear and yet strong enough to crack walls or cause internal damage in human bodies. The difference in sound power (rate of energy transfer) between quiet sounds and the noisiest sounds is astronomic: the difference between rustling leaves and a pneumatic drill or siren is the ratio $1:2 \times 10^{10}$ (20 000 000 000).

Transport

Almost all transport is growing much faster than the world population. In 1965–72 the world population rose by 20 per cent, UK car registrations by 50 per cent, world air passenger travel by 300 per cent and Japanese road freight traffic by over 500 per cent. Such phenomenal growth in a mere seven years cannot be sustained, but the fact remains that not only do more people exist every day but also a much higher proportion of them become customers for transportation. Few roads can handle more than 3000 people per hour at any one point (10 000 if all cars were full) but one section of the Dan Ryan Expressway, Chicago, USA, has an average flow of 254 700 vehicles, or more than 400 000 people, a day (4.63 Hz). A single rail track can easily handle 60 000 travellers per hour; the busiest self-contained rail network is the Japan National at an average exceeding 18.5 million passengers daily (214 Hz). World airlines now carry more than 500 million passengers a year, or about 1.42 million a day (16.4 Hz).

TECHNOLOGY

In this section are grouped speeds and accelerations concerned with scientific and technological subjects.

Acceleration

Instantaneous values exceeding 10 000 g (g is the acceleration due to Earth gravity at sea level, the international standard value being 9.80665 m/s^2) have been achieved on a gross macroscopic scale in explosions, hollow-charge jets and many other mechanisms. The highest known sustained acceleration is roughly 1 million g for the surface of the slender steel rotor spun at 1.5 million revolutions per second at the University of Virginia (see 'Frequencies and Rates' section). The highest acceleration sustained over a period of several seconds by a large self-propelled vehicle is 650–1100 g by several rocket projectiles in the Boeing-managed HiBEX programme. Records for cars are listed in the dragster subsection of 'Land—Road Vehicles'; for commercially available private cars the record appears to be 0–96.56 km/h (0–60 mph) in 4.2 s and 0–160.934 km/h (0–100 mph) in 9.8 s recorded by various drivers testing the 1965 7-litre AC Cobra.

Brownian movement

The average particulate velocity in water at room temperature is in the order of 2 km/s.

Clock

Until the advent of today's digital clocks and watches nearly all timepieces used the same lever escapement and train of gears, almost always with the same numbers of teeth on each gear, and in small watch sizes with a balance wheel making approximately five oscillations per second. Very large clocks used different drive mechanisms. The tip of the minute hand on the largest clock face (Allen-Bradley Building, Milwaukee) moves about 10.6 mm/s (roughly half an inch per second, 125 ft/h). The frequency standards for 'atomic clocks' are given in the preceding subsection, 'Frequencies and Rates'.

The world's largest four-faced clock (Allen-Bradley Building, Milwaukee) has minute hands whose tips move almost 13 mm (½ in) every minute. (Allen-Bradley Co)

Cracks

In brittle solids, crack propagation can occur with almost explosive rapidity even when the material is not severely stressed. Measured velocities for glasses, metals at low temperatures and various crystalline materials lie in the range of 2 to 5 km/s (up to 11 000 mph). It has been suggested by geologists that if the Earth's crust were to crack, the globe could separate into two in just 6 h. The good news is that the halves would not drift apart.

Electricity

This is the name given for a mass movement of electrons, through a solid conductor, liquid electrolyte or ionised gas. The common belief that such a flow travels at the speed of light is incorrect, though its effect does travel at approximately this speed. If a small current is passed through a large conductor replete with free electrons—such as most metals—each electron need not move very often. In any case, at room temperature the electrons are in continuous very rapid random motion; applying a potential difference across the ends of the conducting medium merely gives all the electrons an extra slow drift (the current). Loosely, electrons flow in a wire of 1 mm² cross-section to carry 1 amp current at a speed equivalent to a human taking 24 h to walk six paces. Electricity gains its effect from the unbelievable number of electrons involved. If a 100-watt bulb is switched on for 1 s, the number of electrons passing through the filament is about 6×10^{12}, or about 1500 times the world's human population. In contrast, the speed of metal parts of electrical machines, such as the conductors moving through the magnetic field in an electric motor, seldom exceed 150 m/s (500 ft/s).

Electromagnetic waves

As explained in the preceding section 'Frequencies and Rates', the perfectly sinusoidal EM wave is a universal phenomenon, extending from the longest radio waves, through microwaves, radar and infra-red (heat) to visible light, and on through ultraviolet, X-rays and gamma rays to the shortest-wavelength cosmic radiations. Loosely, all EM waves travel at the velocity of light (discussed separately in this section) but when such waves are constricted in a tubular waveguide, or solid conductor, this result may need amplification. For example, microwaves in a waveguide invariably travel in a series of zig-zags, with repeated reflections from the wall. Thus they travel further than the straight-line distance down the centre of the guide, so the velocity of propagation, called the phase velocity, can never be less than that of light and is almost always greater. Indeed, for about 20 years physicists have recognised that the popular belief that nothing can travel faster than light is no longer valid. A complete set of non-contradictory mathematical equations can be written for an as yet undiscovered species of particles, given the name tachyons, which at rest have imaginary mass but large energy. As they move faster they lose energy, until all their energy is dissipated by the time they are moving with a velocity which is infinite. Moreover, we know just how to search for tachyons, and the fact we have yet to discover one does not prove they do not exist.

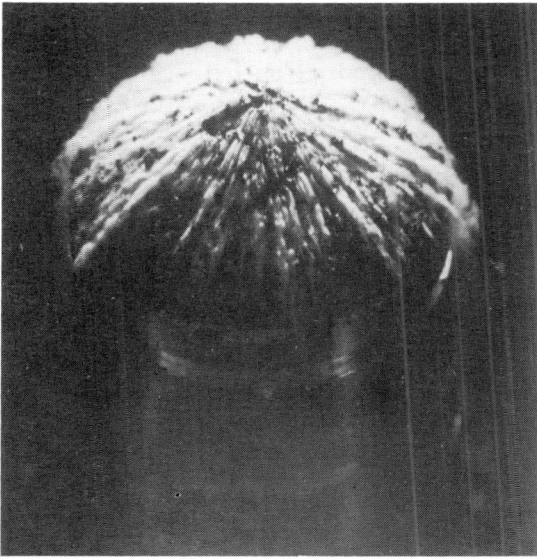

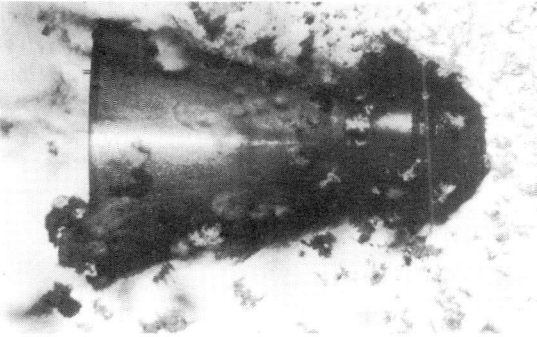

Left:
Three photographs taken at the US Air Force Arnold Engineering Development Center, showing hypersonic research. The upper picture, taken with pulsed laser illumination in two billionths of a second, shows an experiment in water-cooling a missile nose tip at 17 542 km/h (10 900 mph). The middle scene is a projectile flying at 18 910 km/h (11 750 mph) through snow to test erosion resistance. The static scene shows a heat-charred projectile jammed in steel converging rails which caught it undamaged at a speed of 20 100 km/h (12 500 mph). (USAF)

Hypersonics

Hypersonic, meaning several times the speed of sound, is not yet familiar as an adjective for aircraft; but aerodynamicists have been testing bodies at hypersonic speeds for several decades. One of their chief tools is the shock tube, a kind of cross between a gun and a wind-tunnel. The US Naval Ordnance Laboratory at White Oak, Maryland, has regularly exceeded 36 210 km/h (33 000 ft/s, 22 500 mph) with a large shock tube, using air. Boeing Aerospace (the Boeing military and space subsidiary) has demonstrated over Mach 27 (27 times the speed of sound) in air, or about 33 000 km/h (20 500 mph). Cornell Aeronautical Laboratory, New York, has achieved over Mach 30, or 36 735 km/h (22 830 mph), again using air. With other gases, even higher Mach numbers are possible, while for the highest relative velocities small projectiles or pellets are fired at high velocity upstream into a tunnel or shock tube, giving simulated speeds exceeding 48 300 km/h (30 000 mph).

Light

It is a fundamental part of Einstein's General Theory of Relativity that the velocity of light, c, is always the same, no matter what the motion of the observer might be. Thus it makes no difference whether we measure the velocity of light looking east or west; the Earth's rotation does not affect the answer in the slightest degree, and the figure always comes to $2.997924562 \times 10^{10}$ cm/s (186 282.3960 miles/s). Thus, light travels about 18 million km in a minute, or 9.46 million million km in a year. In the shortest-duration laser flash so far achieved in the laboratory the light was able to travel only 0.0009 mm (0.000035 in). This distance contains a mere 14 light waves. Only when the velocity of a light source is itself moving at a speed (relative to the observer) representing a significant fraction of that of light does its apparent emitted wavelength alter, towards the violet end of the visible spectrum if the body is on-coming and towards the red if it is receding. This is the basis for the cosmological Red Shift which is generally interpreted as meaning that the Universe is rapidly expanding, and has a distant boundary moving away from us at the speed of light, thus forever prohibiting observation of objects at greater distances. Einsteinian Relativity also taught us that length, mass and time are precisely and mathematically interdependent. As a body travels faster, its length (the measure taken along the direction of motion) decreases; thus a racing car at speed is shorter than a family car which has the same length when the two are parked, though the difference in this case is too small to measure. Even a jet aircraft contracts by the equivalent of only about one atom, but the apparent diameter of the Earth is distorted by about 60 mm by virtue of its orbital motion round the Sun, discounting the solar system's motion in the Galaxy. At significant fractions of c the distortion becomes grotesquely large. Moreover, the third factor, mass, also becomes significant at very high speeds. The fastest jet aircraft gain mass at full speed roughly equivalent to an extra rivet, and the fastest spacecraft gain nearly 100 kg (220 lb). But at 99.9 per cent c the rest mass of a body would be multiplied about 2000 times; a car at this speed would weigh about 2000 tonnes, despite the fact that the front and rear bumpers would be roughly 25 mm (1 in) apart!

Metalworking

Development of improved materials for the cutting edges of machine tools have multiplied the speeds at which even hard metals can be machined. Free-cutting metals such as brass and aluminium can today be cut at speeds higher than 3 m/s (10 ft/s). High-energy-rate forging can bodily force workpieces into shape in 0.05 s. A typical speed for traditional hand welding is 150 mm (6 in)/min, but EBW (electron-beam welding) speeds exceed 1.25 m (50 in)/min, and foil can be welded ultrasonically at 90 m (295 ft)/min.

MHD

Magnetohydrodynamics is a technology in which intensely hot ionised gas, an electrical conductor, is moved at high speed through apparatus to generate electricity, propel spacecraft or perform other functions. The working fluid is called a plasma, and a typical speed of flow is 2500 m/s (8200 ft/s, 5500 mph).

Particles (energy)

Subatomic physicists believe they are at last nearing the stage where they can describe the whole range of particles of which Earthly matter is composed, and the additional short-lived ones that can briefly be manufactured. Though the velocities of these particles vary over an essentially infinite range, speeds as such are seldom mentioned; instead it is the particle potential, measured in eV (electron-volts) that is of interest. At the core of the atom is the nucleus, composed of neutrons and protons, and the decay of the proton is perhaps the slowest speed in the Universe; its lifetime is not less than 2×10^{30} years. Surrounding the nucleus are the electrons, one of the fundamental building-blocks of the atom, which appear sometimes to be miniature planets orbiting the nucleus at a steady 2200 km/s and at other times to be simultaneously at every point in their orbit, thus forming a cloud or continuous shell. Free electrons forming the beam in a CRT (cathode-ray tube) or TV tube travel at about 0.1 c (c is the velocity of light, given above); at an energy of 0.5 MeV (million eV) they are already moving at 0.85 c, because they are so fantastically light; at 2 MeV they are moving at 97.9 c; and at 70 MeV they are up to 99.99 c. By this time their mass is already 150 times their rest mass, as explained in the note on Relativity under the heading Light (above). Further energisation serves mainly to make the electrons still heavier, rather than faster. Neutrons from the atomic nucleus have no charge, but a rest mass almost 2000 times that of an electron, so for a given potential in eV their velocity is much lower. Thermal neutrons, those in equilibrium with their surroundings, move at some 2200 m/s (7218 ft/s, 4920 mph); accelerated to 10 keV they get up to 1.4×10^8 cm/s and at 1 MeV their speed is 1.4×10^9 cm/s (about 31.4 million mph), but this is still only about one-twentieth of c. In the large research machines built for particle investigations many species can be produced and examined when interacting at high energy. The Bevatron can spew out antiprotons moving at 238 000 km/s (148 000 miles/s), which is about 79 per cent c. A 200-MeV deuteron or a 400-MeV alpha particle, the nucleus of a helium atom, travel at about 140 000 km/s (87 000 miles/s), or 47 per cent c, their mass thus rising to about 1.14 the rest value. Cosmic rays coming to us from space embrace almost all available energies, up to a measured maximum (not necessarily the maximum that exists in the Universe) of 6×10^{19} eV. At such an energy the velocity is to all intents and purposes c, and the mass thousands of times the rest mass. Umbrellas would be useless.

Particles (short-lived)

Nuclear physicists are particularly interested in the most unstable entities imaginable. As this book goes to press the shortest-lived particles are the five baryon resonances N(2220), N(2600), N(3030), Δ(3030) and Δ(3230), all of which have a lifetime of 1.6×10^{-24} s. The mind has no easy way of comprehending such a brief period; if we multiply it by a quadrillion it is still beyond our understanding.

Radioisotopes

Radioactive isotopes, like humans, run down from the moment of their birth, and so do radioactive elements. Among the latter, common uranium (U_{238}) has a half-life of 4.51×10^9 years (the half-life is the time it takes for the radioactivity of a given amount of the substance to decay to half its original value). Thorium$_{232}$ has a half-life of 13 900 million years, and Carbon$_{14}$, widely used for archaeological dating, 5760 years. Cobalt$_{60}$, another common isotope, has a half-life of $5\frac{1}{4}$ years, but countless others have half-lives in the order of thousandths or millionths of a second. The shortest-lived of all known isotopes is Lithium$_5$, with a lifetime of 4.4×10^{-22} s. If each human had the same lifetime, the entire story of mankind would have taken a tenth of a millionth of a millionth of a millionth of a second!

Robot

Not necessarily humanoid in form, robots are independently moving machines programmed to lift, carry or manipulate in some useful way. It happens that virtually all have been seemingly slow moving; for example, the 'cleverest' robot animal built so far is a tortoise, not a hare. Robots include many farm machines, domestic lawnmowers and similar wheeled devices, and could include a Grand Prix car—which, if

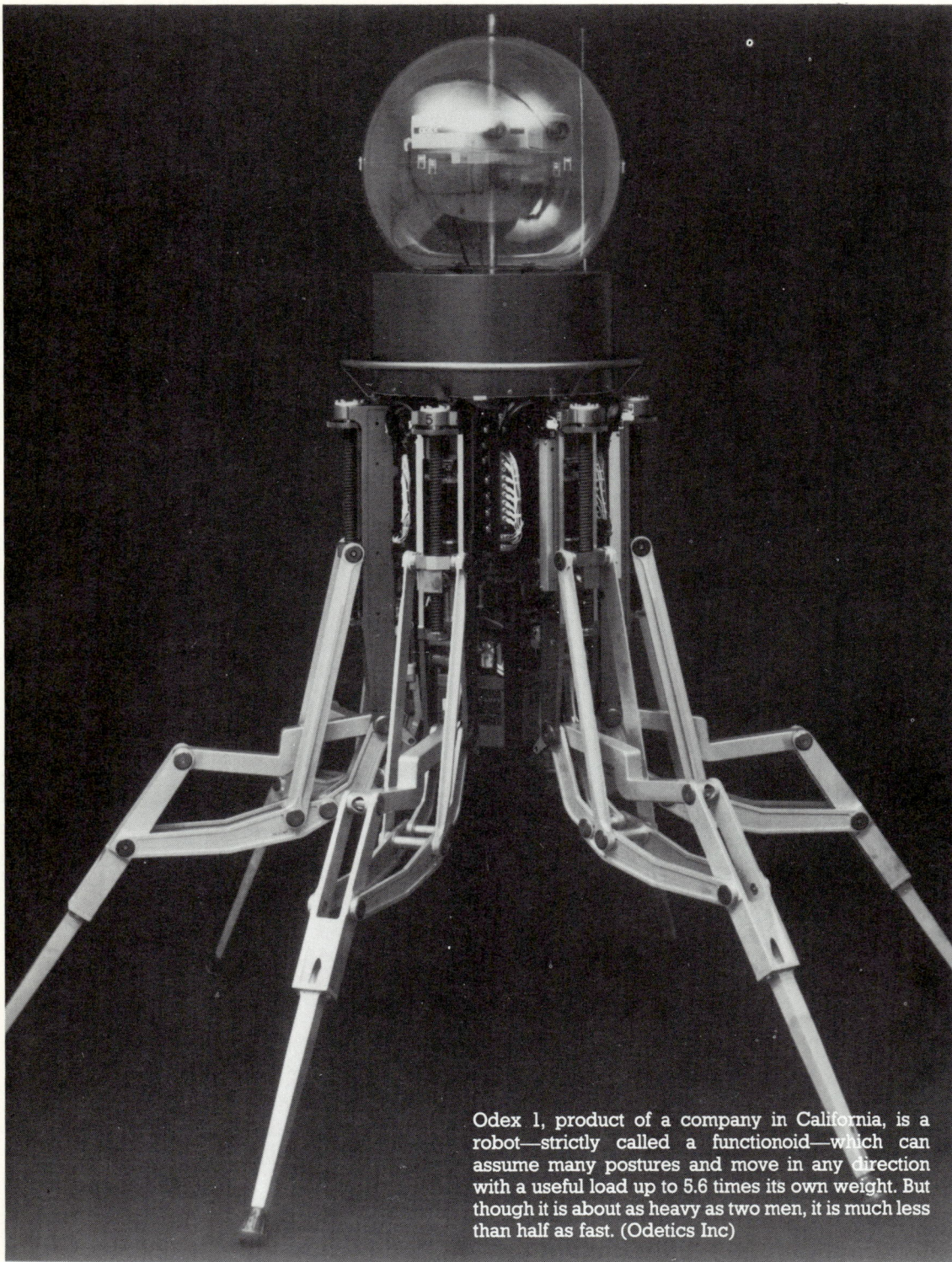

Odex 1, product of a company in California, is a robot—strictly called a functionoid—which can assume many postures and move in any direction with a useful load up to 5.6 times its own weight. But though it is about as heavy as two men, it is much less than half as fast. (Odetics Inc)

carefully programmed, might win many races. But the first production 'functionoid', illustrated, might be caught by a fast snail.

Sound

The speed of sound is commonly given as about 340 m (1100 ft)/s, so that a rule-of-thumb estimate is three seconds per kilometre and five seconds per mile. In fact the speed in air varies according to temperature, and also with the frequency of the sound. On a Standard Day at 15°C the mean speed is 340.294 m/s (1116.45 ft/s, 761.2 mph), but on a hot summer's day it could be over 350 m/s, which explains why in the pre-1955 era, before fully supersonic aircraft were available, speed record flights took place on hot days. To show the variation with frequency, at 0°C a sound of 40 kHz (a high frequency above the limit for human reception) travels at only 332.5 m/s, while one of much higher frequency still, 1.5 MHz, moves at 331.5 m/s. The speed depends upon density; as hydrogen is so very much less dense than air, the speed of sound in this gas is several times greater at 1270 m/s (3871 ft/s, 2639 mph). But the speed is also dependent upon the elasticity of the medium, and in the case of liquids and solids this factor far outweighs the adverse effect of the greater density. Thus the speed of sound in water is about 1.5 km/s (4921 ft/s, 3355 mph), while in brass it is 3500 m/s (11 500 ft/s, 7845 mph). The speed of sound in mild steel is no less than 5050 m/s (16 568 ft/s, 11 296 mph), but lead combines high density with poor elasticity and transmits sound at only 1.2 km/s (3937 ft/s, 2684 mph).

Speed

It may seem strange to have so bald a subheading on the very last page of this book, but the reader by now will appreciate that the word can be interpreted in different ways. This particular entry answers the question: 'What is the highest speed, relative to the Earth's surface, of any tangible object (one that can be seen and touched) made by man?' The answer is 160 km/s (99.4 miles/s; 576 000 km/h (357 910 mph)). This is the speed reached by discs of thin polystyrene foil violently accelerated by an intense pulse of laser light. The pulse, of up to 500 Joules energy, was focussed on a spot on the foil 550 micrometres in diameter, giving an energy intensity of about 5×10^{13} (50 million million) W/cm^2. When the laser pulse hits the foil, part of the polystyrene is explosively vaporised backwards in a sudden bright flash. The rest is accelerated forwards by reaction, in the same way a rocket is driven forwards, and its subsequent behaviour is inferred from its collision with a second foil a short distance away. The experiments were carried out in 1980 by a team at the US Naval Research Laboratory, Washington DC.

Time

The creation of the Universe, if it did happen in a primordial Big Bang, was in the region of 6000 million years ago. Thus, as there are about 100 000 words in this book, if all the words were taken as representing the life of the Universe, man (*Homo sapiens*) has lived during the final 20-odd words only. The last word (60 000 years) contains all of recorded history, and the whole span of human civilisation is summed up in the last of its four letters. And what might loosely be called the modern world, since the time of Christ, is comfortably fitted into the last full stop.

INDEX

References in italic type are to illustrations

Index by Rosie Hunt